MASK OF DEMOCRACY

Mask of Democracy

Labor Suppression in Mexico Today

by

Dan La Botz

An International Labor Rights
Education and Research Fund Book

South End Press **Boston**

Edited, designed, and produced by the International Labor Rights Education and Research Fund and the South End Press collective

Manufactured in the USA on acid-free, recycled paper

Library of Congress Cataloging-in-Publication Data

La Botz, Dan.
   Mask of democracy : labor suppression in Mexico today / by Dan La Botz.
      p.   cm.
   "An International Labor Rights Education and Research Fund Book."
   Includes bibliographical references and index.
   ISBN 0-89608-438-8 : $35.00 -- ISBN 0-89608-437-X (pbk.) : $14.00
   1. Labor--Mexico. 2. Working class--Mexico. 3. Labor laws and legislation--Mexico. 4. Labor policy--Mexico. I. Title.
   HD8116.5.L3   1992
   331'.0972--dc20   92-4821
                                                          CIP

South End Press, 116 Saint Botolph Street, Boston, MA 02115

·99 98 97 96 95 94 93 92   1 2 3 4 5 6 7 8 9

Table of Contents

Author's Acknowledgments

I would like to thank all of the labor union leaders, activists, educators, and officials, the human rights activists, women's rights activists, community leaders, professors, attorneys, managers, and all of the writers, journalists, and editors in both the United States and Mexico who aided me in my research. This study never could have been conducted without their advice, support, and candid and instructive responses to my questions.

Special thanks to Arturo Alcalde for his views on Mexican labor law, Berta Luján of the Frente Auténtico de Trabajo (FAT), Elaine Burns and Mary McGinn of Mujer a Mujer, Matt Witt of the American Labor Education Center, and my friends Ricardo and María Pascoe for their assistance.

My thanks in particular to Pharis Harvey, Executive Director of the International Labor Rights Education and Research Fund, for his guidance throughout the investigation and to Rebekah Greenwald, ILRERF Director of Publications, for her conscientious editing of the manuscript. With appreciation to all parties involved, I am ultimately responsible for the investigation and the opinions expressed in this report.

Finally, very special thanks to my wife Sherry Baron, who, while pursuing her own demanding career as an occupational health physician and epidemiologist, taking care of our three-year-old, Traven, and carrying our new baby, Reed, not only tolerated my absence from our home for two months, but, as always, gave her full support to my endeavors.

Foreword

The International Labor Rights Education and Research Fund was established in 1986 to promote worker rights in conjunction with U.S. foreign trade, investment, and aid policies, and to foster a common vision of worker rights among peoples of all nations. Activities of the ILRERF include: dissemination of information on laws that link respect for labor rights with trade; education and outreach to increase public awareness of labor rights as an international economic concern; investigation and publication of reports on the legal status and effective exercise of internationally recognized worker rights in countries around the world; and pursuit of relationships with counterpart organizations in foreign countries to exchange information and to form a unified approach to ending labor rights abuses.

This study is the fourth in a series of books published by the ILRERF on labor rights in individual nations. Countries included thus far are South Korea, Haiti, Guatemala, and now Mexico. Associates of the ILRERF have also researched and reported on Mauritania, El Salvador, Taiwan, Chile, Sri Lanka, Indonesia, the Philippines, and many other countries in testimony, newspaper articles, newsletters, pamphlets, and various other media.

Mask of Democracy: Labor Suppression in Mexico Today, originally written under the title *A Strangling Embrace: State Suppression of Labor Rights in Mexico*, was made possible by a grant from the North Shore Unitarian Universalist Veatch Program, and the ILRERF extends a hearty thanks for their support of our project on the North American Free Trade Agreement. We would also like to thank Dan La Botz, the author of this study, for all of his hard work and continuing enthusiasm; Steve Beckman, Holly Burkhalter, Bill Goold, and Carlos Heredia for their insightful comments; and Matt Witt for giving us his help when he didn't really have time to give it.

Basic Information on Mexican Workers and Unions

Mexico's population (1)	84,274,992
Size of workforce (2)	24 million
Unionized workers (2)	4 million
CTM membership (2) (largest federation)	1.5 million
Percentage of women in formal economy	30 percent (estimate)
Percentage of women who work for wages	50 percent (estimate)
Unemployment General Manufacturing	25 percent (estimate) 25 percent (estimate)
Maquiladora employment (3) Total employees	459,837 (includes technicians and administrators)
Workers Women Men	371,780 226,483 145,297
Ratio of U.S. wages to Mexican wages (1)	1975 — 4.4 : 1 1985 —10.4 : 1

Sources:

(1) Dirección General de Estadistica, Secretaria de Programación y Presupuesto, Mexico.

(2) Raúl Trejo Delarbre, *Crónica del sindicalismo en México, 1976-1988* (México, D.F.: Universidad Nacional Autónoma de México and Siglo Veintiuno Editores, 1990), pp. 21, 30, 37-8. Francisco Alba, "Logros y limitaciones en la absorción de la fuerza de trabajo en México," gives the figure of 29 million in the economically active population in Sidney Weintraub, *A Marriage of Convenience: Relations Between Mexico and the United States* (New York: Oxford and the Twentieth Century Fund, 1990), p. 34.

(3) Mexican National Institute of Statistics, Geography and Information, 1991 report on *maquiladoras*.

Preface

This report on labor rights in Mexico is based on an investigation conducted in late 1990 and early 1991 for the International Labor Rights Education and Research Fund of Washington, D.C. The project was completed in September 1991 and covers events through the Fall of that year.

Scope of the Investigation

The subject of this report is Mexican wage earners in industry and services, public and private, and primarily those who work in urban areas. While this report focuses on workers' attempts to exert their rights as labor unionists, it is important to recognize that the factors which shape the lives of unionized workers also potentially shape the lives of would-be organized workers who are prevented from organizing a union, or who resist unionization because of bad history or particularly effective anti-union corporate policies. Although unionization may not be the rubric under which agricultural workers and others who labor but are not paid wages unite—farmers, artisans, women who work in their homes, street vendors, aliens employed in marginal work, the unemployed, self-employed, small-business people, and part-time workers—all are affected by and are potentially a part of a broad labor movement which organizes around economic and social issues that affect people in their work lives. Violations of the rights of organized workers have an ancillary effect on unorganized workers, lowering the standards under which they labor as well.

Violations of fundamental labor rights are the basis for this labor movement and also for this report. As they are defined in the conventions of the International Labor Organization (ILO), these rights include: a) the right of workers to free association and to freely form labor unions, b) the right of workers to engage in such union activities as collective bargaining and legal strikes, c) the right of workers to employment and a living wage, d) the right of workers to non-discrimination, and e) the right of workers to a safe and healthy workplace. Mexico is signatory to many important ILO conventions, and can therefore be held accountable to these standards. This investigation does just that. It focuses on these rights and standards as they apply to Mexican workers in general, and in particular to workers in the maquiladoras (or in-bond or twin-plant industries) which are concentrated along the Mexico-U.S. border area.

1

In order to avoid misunderstandings, it must be stated clearly that this book is *not* a comparison study of labor rights in the United States and Mexico. It is, rather, a study on labor rights in Mexico alone. So, while this study is extremely critical of violations of worker rights perpetrated by the Mexican government and by Mexican- and U.S.-owned corporations, it does not imply that these violations are more or less egregious than labor rights violations in other countries. Secondly, as a study of violations of worker rights, it may seem to imply that Mexican workers are solely victims in their struggle to attain liveable standards. This is not the case. Mexican workers have also been the agents of success in their battle for social, political, and economic justice. Had this been a study on the labor movement *per se*, these stories would have been told as well. Lastly, this study is written with profound admiration and respect for the Mexican people, culture, and society. Any criticism of the Mexican government should only be extended as far as the government's embrace can reach.

Sources and Methods

In most cases the activities and events discussed in this book were matters of public knowledge reported in the press and on radio and television. The use of several different kinds of sources, aside from these media, allows for corroboration of these events.

In part, published newspaper reports are the source for accounting of events. In general, two newspapers were used: *Excelsior,* a long-established major Mexico City daily newspaper which generally promotes a point of view close to that of the government, and *La Jornada,* a left-of-center Mexico City daily newspaper which has the most consistent coverage of on-going labor activities. In addition, newspapers such as *El Universal,* another major daily, and *El Financiero,* the daily financial paper, provided important information.

Documentary evidence, such as published pamphlets, books, university theses and dissertations, were also considered, as well as union, business, and government reports. Obviously, the most recently published sources of information were utilized, except in Chapter 3, which cites older books.

Most importantly, however, this report is based on first-hand research and investigation. During the period from December 8, 1990 through February 2, 1991, the author traveled to several major industrial cities and states including: Mexico City, D.F.; Estado de México; Monterrey, Nuevo Leon; Monclova, Coahuila; Chihuahua and Ciudad Juárez, Chihuahua; and Tijuana, Baja California. During that time, he conducted scores of interviews with rank and file workers, labor union officials, labor attorneys, members of women's organizations, employers, officials of employer associations, human rights activists, and academics who are engaged in the study of labor unions. These interviews covered issues of concern to workers employed by publicly owned and privately owned companies, both Mexican and foreign-owned. Some of those interviewed were participants in or victims of the abuses of labor rights discussed in this report. Many, but not all, of these interviews were tape recorded and transcribed and are available for review by interested parties.

A human rights investigation, in this case a labor rights investigation, is not a courtroom trial, and the standards of evidence appropriate to a trial are not appropriate here and do not apply. A human rights investigation, while looking at facts and attempting to verify them, is also looking for an analytical model that makes sense of a particular society, and can account for those facts. In the case of Mexico, the analytical model is well recognized by many scholars in a variety of fields: Mexico is a one-party state which is in the process of privatizing its vast nationalized industry. Mexican society is currently in the midst of economic and political crisis, and in a period of transition—though it is not at all clear what the outcome of this transition will be.

Using this model, the conclusion substantiated in this book is that labor rights have been and continue to be systematically suppressed in Mexico. If anything, the transitional character of the current state of affairs has exacerbated the predicament of workers in this party-dominated state. Suppression of labor rights does not consist of individual aberrant acts which violate workers' rights, nor is it policy decisions which, over time, impede workers' rights; it is, rather, the systematic infringement of constitutionally granted workers' rights by the everyday practice of labor relations as exercised by the state, the judicial system, law enforcement agencies, employers, and official unions.

Clearly, Mexico is not a country like Guatemala where to accept the leadership of a labor union is virtually to sign one's own death warrant. Nor is Mexico, despite some obvious similarities, a totalitarian state like many of the countries in Eastern Europe before 1980, where all opposition labor unions were outlawed and workers were denied any opportunity to speak out, organize, or act in their own defense. Nevertheless, Mexico is a land where labor is straightjacketed and hobbled. While a certain amount of mobility is possible, it can hardly be called freedom.

Any study of workers' rights must necessarily look at the historical, political, legal, and economic issues involved, whether it is a comprehensive exploration of a movement, or an in-depth study of one facet of that movement, as this study is. Mexico is a large country with many large industrial centers, millions of workers, and thousands of labor organizations. The relationship between the workers and their movement is, no doubt, more complex and contradictory than as presented in these pages. It is not the purpose of this report to capture the Mexican labor movement in all its complexity and diversity. Rather, the purpose is to denounce violations of workers' rights, to call them to the attention of the international public, to bring the pressure of public opinion to bear on the institutions, organizations, and individuals which perpetrate such violations, and hopefully, to abate and end them.

Introduction:
Trade-Linked Labor Standards

by Ray Marshall

The opening of negotiations between the United States and Mexico for a free trade agreement has given an old debate a new urgency: why and in what way should international trade be based on rules governing the conditions of production, including labor standards and rights? With the great disparity between labor costs in the United States and Mexico, many opponents of unregulated free trade argue, with great persuasiveness, that greater trade based on low-wage competition will drive down wages and standards in the United States without bringing up those standards in Mexico.

This study by the International Labor Rights Education and Research Fund examines the state of labor rights in Mexico, not as an argument against more trade between our countries, but as an indication of conditions that must be improved to prevent a trade agreement from having a further deleterious effect on Mexican labor as well as exerting a general downward pull on labor rights and standards in the United States and Canada. The *maquiladora* experience, as described in these pages, already provides a good indication of what can happen with increased trade and industrialization. Standards will tend to find a common level. It will either be upwards or downwards, depending on how that trade is structured, and how it is regulated.

This introduction examines in some detail why it is important, not just in the case of Mexico, but in international trade in general, to develop some strong trade-linked standards relating to labor and other social factors.*

The arguments put forth here are based on three major assumptions:

> 1. Trade that will benefit ordinary people in all countries requires rules, including generally accepted labor standards, that meet the usual criteria for good rules: they should be transparent, fair, and enforceable.

* The bulk of this introduction is reprinted from the article by the same title in: Frank J. Macchiarola, ed., *International Trade: The Changing Role of the United States* (New York: Academy of Political Science, 1990). Professor Marshall is president of the International Labor Rights Education and Research Fund and former U.S. Secretary of Labor.

2. International labor standards are necessary to promote equity, efficiency, and balanced economic
growth.
3. While many details must be worked out, experience
and logic suggest that a workable system of trade-
linked labor standards could be established.

Such a system could be created with or without the involvement of the International Labor Organization (ILO), though the best
approach probably would be a joint ILO-General Agreement on
Tariffs and Trade (GATT) undertaking, which would set a precedent for future agreements. The U.S. Congress included trade-
linked labor standards in every major trade act of the 1980s. Efforts
to perfect the implementation of these laws, along with the ILO's
experiences, provide insights into how an effective system of trade-
linked labor standards might be implemented as part of the GATT
system.

Labor Standards, Equity, and Economic Efficiency

Labor standards are critical components of more effective global
development policies, just as they were vital elements of the policies
and institutions industrialized democracies developed to produce
the longest period of equitably shared prosperity in history between
1945 and 1973. Labor standards (whether enforced by government
regulations or collective bargaining) improved economic efficiency
by removing worker (or public) subsidies to firms that could not
pay a living wage or provide acceptable minimum working conditions, thus forcing those companies to compete by becoming more
efficient instead of by reducing labor standards. This, in turn, facili-
tated the shift of resources from inefficient to more efficient uses
and made it possible for countries to protect and develop human resources—their most valuable assets. In fact, rules—including labor
standards—were required to cause markets to benefit all parties to
transactions, as classical economic doctrine claims competitive markets should do. In the absence of rules, stronger or more unscrupu-
lous operators gain unfairly at the expense of others.

The system put in place in all democratic industrial societies
during and after World War II not only promoted prosperity and
economic justice, but increased consumer demand by improving
wages and other benefits, thus stimulating global economic growth.
Indeed, these policies—of which labor standards were integral components—made possible growing middle classes in the industrial
market economy countries (IMECs), strengthening democratic institutions.

A major problem facing us now is the fact that during the 1980s,
the organizations, institutions, and policies that led to what eco-

nomic historians probably will regard as the "golden age" for workers in the industrialized countries were weakened by a complex constellation of forces, especially internationalization and technological change. With intensified international competition it became more difficult for countries or labor movements to limit the adverse effects of competitive markets. Multinational corporations now have the ability to shift jobs around the world and thereby avoid collective bargaining agreements and national labor codes.

The internationalization of markets and production has, in addition, changed the viability conditions of economic enterprises. The mass production industries transformed by these trends benefited mainly from economies of scale, made possible by a virtual monopoly of the large internal U.S. market. The mass production system stressed stability of technology and production systems and relatively rigid rules, regulations, prices, and exchange rates. In the more dynamic internationalized information world, the maintenance of relatively high incomes requires much greater attention to flexibility within production systems, productivity, quality, technological innovations, adaptable economies, and much more participative and less bureaucratic management systems. Mass production systems are producer driven; the more competitive systems are market or consumer driven. The maintenance of relatively high incomes under modern conditions requires heavy emphasis on the development and use of leading-edge technologies which, in turn, places a premium on skilled workers and a high level of worker participation in production decisions.

As the center of economic gravity shifts to the global economy, international trade and development policies become much more important. Traditional assumptions about trade (that it is based on natural comparative advantage in a world where national companies and technologies are relatively immobile) are much less appropriate in a dynamic global economy characterized by multinational corporations (MNCs), national export-driven development strategies, the internationalization of markets and production, rapid technology transfer, and diverse levels of economic development. In this environment, the international trade policies, rules, and institutions developed during the 1940s have become much less effective and must therefore be revamped to cover expanding trade in services and technology, much larger and highly volatile financial markets, and national economic policies and strategies that inflict unacceptable damage on other economies. New financial arrangements also are needed to correct, and avoid the repetition of, serious global disorders like the continuing third world debt crisis that stifled the global economy during the 1980s.

The globalization of markets has, in addition, reduced the effectiveness of traditional macroeconomic policies. It is much more difficult, for example, to achieve full employment and growth through national macroeconomic policies alone. Internationalization, technological changes, and global production systems have weakened the connection between demand stimulus in a particular country and consumption, production, investment, and employment in that country. Measures to increase aggregate demand can now merely increase consumption in the country attempting to stimulate its economy, while investment, production, and employment occur in other countries.

Labor Standards in an Internationalized Economy

Does all of this mean that the former goals of full employment, high and rising standards of living, and economic justice are unattainable? I do not believe it does. In fact, modern technology makes it possible to dramatically improve the economic conditions of people everywhere. But the achievement of these goals will require a strong, consensus-based commitment to these objectives and different strategies by labor movements, governments, and international institutions. It is particularly important to gear policies to the realities of this new international economic environment and to develop new institutions to make the global economy more open, expansive, and equitable.

Rather than discussing all that is required to achieve these objectives, I would like to emphasize two points that can guide future negotiations. First, for reasons that I have spelled out at length elsewhere, it is absolutely essential for workers' representatives to be actively involved in the restructuring of global policies and institutions.[1] These matters are too important to be left to economists and financial experts, who overemphasize financial considerations and abstract (even ideological) economic ideas at the expense of such matters of importance to workers and people in general as production, wages, technological development, labor standards, and equity. Financial and market matters are important, but they should not dominate economic policy at the expense of these other considerations. And they will unless workers' representatives are intimately involved in the restructuring and policy-making processes. In fact, a strong case can be made that the countries with superior economic performance are those that have found a way to make labor and human resource development matters integral components of consensus-based economic policies.

Second, while it has become very difficult to stimulate demand within a country, a global expansion of demand is absolutely essential to the restoration of an open, expanding, and just world economy. In U.S. terms, what we need is a global "New Deal." It is highly unlikely though that adequate aggregate demand will come entirely from an expansion of trade or development in or between the developed countries alone.[2] Inadequate global growth will, in addition, permit the continuation of global overproduction and stagnation, with serious political and social implications.

With the right kinds of policies and arrangements, major opportunities for global expansion could come from a restoration of third world growth to the levels these countries achieved in the 1970s. Indeed, the slowdown in the less developed countries' (LDCs) growth during the 1980s has been an important reason for economic stagnation in the more developed countries (MDCs). During the 1970s, trade between the LDCs and the MDCs was generally beneficial. During the 1980s, by contrast, trade with the newly industrializing countries (NICs) has caused job losses for all developing countries except Japan, and the slowdown of LDC imports caused large job losses in the developed countries. It should be emphasized, however, that these job losses have been due mainly to a slowdown in exports to the LDCs, not to a surge in imports from them. The U.S. share of world imports, for example, increased from 13.3 percent to 19.2 percent between 1980 and 1985, but rose at about the same rate as GNP.[3] The trouble, of course, was that the huge unilateral 1981 U.S. tax cut caused a debt-driven expansion in consumption, much of which was satisfied by imports. The U.S. strategy of an overvalued dollar and high interest rates impeded productive investment and increased consumption in the United States and contributed to the third world debt crisis and a stagnant world economy. The U.S. share of world exports therefore fell from 12.9 percent to 9.3 percent between 1980 and 1985; U.S. exports to the developing countries declined by 24.4 percent overall and by 30.9 percent to Latin America. The significance of plummeting U.S. exports is suggested by the fact that at the end of the 1970s, almost 40 percent of U.S. exports went to the developing countries; this had fallen to only about one-third by 1985. During these years, the United States lost 650,000 jobs because of lower exports to the LDCs and 1.1 million jobs because of the LDCs' failure to grow at their 1970s rate. The 50 percent devaluation of the dollar relative to the yen and deutschmark since 1985 has stimulated exports somewhat, but not by as much as most economists predicted. Their error was in thinking that export problems are cyclical, whereas they are in fact also due to serious *structural* problems.

We should note, however, that labor standards are a necessary but not sufficient condition for a healthy global economy. Growth and competitiveness strategies also are required. Trade-linked labor standards should, moreover, meet the usual criteria for good rules: they should be transparent (so they can be understood), fair, and enforceable. Fair ordinarily means negotiated and multilateral rules that treat countries equitably, which ordinarily has included "infant

industry" exceptions for the LDCs. In the absence of rules negotiated multilaterally, the United States and other industrialized countries are justified in taking unilateral actions that protect the
interests of their own workers and those of other countries where
the denial of internationally accepted workers' rights make it impossible for those workers to protect themselves. Fairness also
means giving most favored nation status to those who are willing to
observe those standards. Through membership in the International
Labor Organization (ILO), most countries have accepted the idea of
labor standards. While the ILO, since its inception in 1919, has performed the very valuable function of building support for labor
standards, its enforcement powers are limited to moral condemna-
tion of offenders. Moral power is a very strong force in the long run,
but it is not adequate for rule-making in the more dynamic and
competitive environment we have today. This is why it is so important to have trade-linked labor standards. In the absence of world
government, or worldwide collective bargaining, this is the only
way that labor or any other standards are likely to be enforced.

Some basic international labor rights have been overwhelmingly accepted by the international community; indeed, these rights
have become the hallmarks of progressive, humane societies. There
can be no legitimate objection to freedom of association and collective bargaining, or to restrictions on trade in goods produced by
forced labor, under discriminatory conditions, where young children are exploited, or under unreasonable conditions of employment, especially violations of minimally acceptable health and
safety conditions or wages limited only by "market" forces.

Those of us interested in international labor standards should,
however, avoid any suggestion that we are aiming for an international minimum wage. Wage differentials are far too great to make
that a practical idea. In the short run, low wages are the main competitive advantage many LDCs have, though low wages rarely constitute the only advantage a country has. Indeed, there is no
correlation between international wage rates and levels of economic
growth. While using low wages to initiate development is legitimate, strategies to gain competitive advantage by suppressing
wages and violating basic standards are not. That is why freedom of
association and collective bargaining are such basic standards.
Workers must be able to organize and bargain to improve their conditions on terms compatible with their countries' stages of economic
development.

It is commonly argued that free labor movements are incompatible with balanced economic growth, but this is a highly question-
able assumption. Labor movements in the developing countries are
at least as interested in economic growth as other economic and political interests. Even if they weren't, joblessness (currently 40 to 50

percent) and the realities of international competition limit their ability to increase labor costs faster than their economies' ability to pay those wages. In fact, the evidence supports the contrary position: under modern production and market conditions, free collective bargaining is likely to support rather than impede balanced economic growth. Free collective bargaining helps build balanced economic growth by giving workers a stake in the system, sustaining purchasing power, improving human resource development, and supporting measures to cause part of wages either to be diverted to high-yield health and education investments or to retirement systems that not only relieve inflationary pressures (by limiting present consumption) but also promote development by building up funds that can be used for investment. Indeed, the denial of worker rights in many countries not only contributes to economic stagnation and limits the benefits of growth to the elites, but also sows the seeds of social instability and political rebellion. From a global perspective, collective bargaining helps stimulate global demand by causing the distribution of income to be more equal. "Keynesian" economic policies have lost some of their impact in domestic markets, but they could be more effective in the global economy, provided that rising and more equitably distributed incomes cause workers to have the power to improve global demand.

The moral and economic rationale for trade-linked international labor standards is thus the same as for enforceable labor protections in domestic markets.[4] The moral reason is to limit the exploitation of workers. The efficiency reasons are to prevent workers, through substandard conditions, from subsidizing inefficient companies. The elimination of these subsidies will encourage enterprises to be more efficient and encourage resources to be shifted to more productive uses. A major economic advantage of trade-linked labor standards in an international information world is to make it possible for workers in the developing countries to maintain their families, thus facilitating human capital formation, and to provide purchasing power for higher aggregate global demand. Furthermore, international labor standards facilitate an open and expanding world economy by reducing worker opposition to such a system and gaining their support for MDC policies to promote growth in the LDCs. These standards have long been accepted by the international community, so it is hard to see why there should be serious objections to making them enforceable.[5] Free traders, who usually oppose trade-linked labor standards, certainly ought to be able to see that enforceable labor standards actually promote an open trading system. Curiously, even many economists and international trade experts who see the need for other international rules object to trade-linked labor standards. This tells us more about their *priorities* than the strength of their case. It is hard to see why rules against dumping, the violation of intellectual property rights, the protection of endangered species, or capital subsidies are more important than rules to protect workers' rights.

The Case Against Trade-Linked Labor Standards

From what I have written thus far, it is clear that I consider the usual arguments against trade-linked labor standards to have little real merit, but let me deal with them specifically. Some opponents contend that trade-linked labor standards are "disguised" protectionism, but this certainly is not true of the position I have outlined or of the organizations with which I am affiliated. We are not interested in protecting noncompetitive companies. Our main interest is in preventing enterprises anywhere from acquiring unfair competitive advantages by exploiting their workers.

Critics argue, further, that the movement to link trade and workers' rights is an arrogant attempt by labor movements and inefficient industries in the developed countries to impose their labor standards on other countries. As noted, this is not the case. Almost all countries, including the LDCs and the Eastern bloc countries, accepted the ILO's purposes when they joined that organization. Actually, in a more competitive global economy, failure to adopt enforceable standards makes it possible for countries that permit the exploitation of their workers to impose their standards on others. This is so because a basic principle of highly competitive markets seems to be that bad standards tend to drive out the good. Competitive markets make it difficult for employers who want to have good standards to do so, even though in the long run it is possible to show that good labor standards enhance economic efficiency.

Trade-linked labor standards, critics argue, impede LDC development by removing their low-wage advantage. As noted, however, this is not a legitimate argument because we do not propose an international minimum wage. Significantly, most third world labor movements seem to favor linking trade and workers' rights, which also was recommended by the Brandt Commission, half of whose members were from the LDCs.[6] There is, however, a vast difference between a country having low wages because of an early stage of development and *suppressing* wages to provide unfair competitive advantage to companies in a country.

Critics contend, further, that it is unreasonable to expect developing countries to meet MDC standards. This can be a valid concern, but proponents of linking trade and labor standards believe that where appropriate, standards should be related to the level of development. This is true, for example, of minimum wages. The concern should be about whether or not countries have reasonable wage floors, not that there be a uniform international minimum wage. There is, however, no legitimate reason for relating occupational safety and health protections or the right of freedom of association or collective bargaining to the stage of economic development.

Some critics argue that trade-linked labor standards would be difficult to enforce. This too is a legitimate concern, and we should do more to demonstrate how enforcement could proceed. I believe there is considerable merit in establishing a joint ILO-GATT group to help with this. We need to establish close cooperation between the GATT and the ILO because the GATT, dominated as it is by orthodox free trade ideas, has never had much interest in, or expertise on, labor matters. Such cooperation would also remove the GATT's traditional excuse that it cannot incorporate a social clause because this is an ILO responsibility. I am, in addition, convinced by logic and the U.S. experience (discussed below) that basic labor standards would be no more difficult to enforce than most other trade rules. Nevertheless, the history of most social legislation suggests that, once these standards are adopted, they will have to be carefully monitored to ensure adequate enforcement.

The U.S. Experience

I wish to conclude this discussion by examining the U.S. experience with trade-linked labor standards and some of the arguments advanced against unilateral standards in U.S. trade laws. North American critics argue that the United States has poor standing to propose linking trade and workers' rights because we have not adopted many ILO conventions. Although it is unfortunate and embarrassing that the United States has not adopted more of these standards, this is nevertheless a weak argument. The United States accepted the ILO's basic purposes when we joined that organization, and all of the basic standards are guaranteed by the U.S. Constitution or by U.S. law. Moreover, we participate in the GATT system, even though the GATT agreement has never been ratified by the U.S. government.

Some critics, apparently ignorant of the ILO and its long history, argue that it would be difficult to define international labor standards. This clearly is a weak argument, especially with respect to the basic standards outlined earlier. North American critics have argued, in addition, that it would be impossible to develop a workable trade-linked labor standard system. While we have a long way to go to develop a really effective system, the limited U.S. experience provides evidence that trade-linked labor standards can work.

Some critics object to enforceable multilateral trade-linked labor standards on the grounds that international labor standards would either damage U.S. sovereignty or be incompatible with U.S. labor laws. A variant of this argument is that the United States actually could be found guilty of violating some international labor standards. I believe all of these are weak arguments. In some sense, of course, all international agreements represent a "surrender" of sovereignty, but the benefits of international cooperation could outweigh the limitations on national sovereignty. I do not believe there is any incompatibility between U.S. law and practice and basic labor standards like those which were included in most trade legislation of the 1980s, including the Omnibus Trade Act of 1988. However, complaints should be filed against the United States or any other country where there is evidence that fundamental international labor standards have been violated. We will not strengthen respect for international law by selectively deciding which laws to obey.

The most active efforts in the United States to link workers' rights and trade came during the 1980s, when the United States took a number of unilateral actions to include labor standards in trade legislation.[7] The Reagan Administration's 1983 Caribbean Basin Initiative (CBI) provided that, as a condition for a Central American or Caribbean country's duty-free admission to the U.S. market, the President take into account the extent to which "workers in such a country are afforded reasonable workplace conditions and enjoy the right to organize and bargain collectively." The 1984 Trade and Tariff Act stipulates that a country's duty-free access to the U.S. market under the Generalized System of Preferences (GSP) depends on its respect for these basic labor rights. Similarly, the 1985 Overseas Private Investment Corporation (OPIC) reauthorization legislation prohibited that organization from insuring business risks by U.S. companies for projects in countries that do not grant their workers these rights. Earlier, in 1991, South Korea was rightfully suspended from the OPIC program. The State Department recognizes these "internationally recognized worker rights" in its Country Reports on Human Rights for purposes of reporting on the enforcement of current U.S. laws. Moreover, the 1988 omnibus U.S. trade act made the violation of basic labor standards an unfair trade practice subject to countervailing action. The 1988 trade act also made the achievement of trade-linked labor standards a U.S. objective in the current round of GATT negotiations. Finally, a 1985 Executive Order established racial employment codes for U.S. companies in South Africa. Among other things, the Executive Order required companies with over 25 employees to pay a minimum wage "based on the appropriate local minimum economic level which takes into account the needs of workers and their families." In 1985, as part of U.S. anti-apartheid sanctions, Congress made this code mandatory for U.S. companies operating in South Africa and Namibia. The application of these sanctions was undoubtedly an important part of the pressure that brought the South African government to seek accommodation with the African National Congress in 1990. While the premature lifting of these sanctions in 1991 may undermine that process, the sanctions did work to support labor and human rights in South Africa.

The mixed success and inconsistent application of these laws make it clear that while access to the U.S. market can be a powerful lever to improve worker rights, the effectiveness of these protections depends heavily on the strength of enforcement. Although the U.S. Customs Service had consistently refused to enforce the 1930 Tariff Act's provision against indentured labor, it was used during the 1970s to force South Africa to change its laws permitting the indenturing of Black miners. South African law had made the violation of miners' employment contracts a criminal as well as a civil offense. South Africa repealed this provision after the United Mine Workers and the state of Alabama petitioned the federal government to use this Act to bar South African coal from American markets.

Partly because labor, religious, and human rights groups have established monitoring mechanisms, the enforcement of the 1984 GSP (Generalized System of Preferences) labor provisions, while spotty and inconsistent, appears more promising. In 1987, after these monitoring groups presented strong evidence that workers' rights had been flagrantly violated, President Reagan denied GSP tariff preferences to Paraguay, Nicaragua, and Romania. Chile was placed in a special category and warned that unless workers' rights improved during 1987, it, too, would be eliminated from the program. In 1988, Chile's failure to correct these violations of workers rights resulted in that country being denied duty-free imports into the United States. In 1990, long-awaited democratic reform resulted in Chile being readmitted to the GSP.

A more legitimate argument against unilateral standards in U.S. trade laws is that the United States (or other countries), instead of acting unilaterally, should make labor standards a part of the GATT. I agree, but think our ability to achieve this objective is strengthened, not weakened, by including basic labor standards in national law as well as in multinational trade agreements. First, the U.S. experience makes it clear that linking trade and labor standards can improve workers' conditions, especially with sincere enforcement efforts. Second, unilateral standards strengthen our bargaining power in getting the GATT to accept these measures. We should not use trade rules to protect noncompetitive industries, but we should not permit governments dominated by those who gain from the denial of basic worker rights to block the adoption of trade-linked labor standards in the GATT. Third, a most-favored-nation approach could make it possible for these national laws and multinational agreements to spread.

The experience of developing trade-linked labor standards in the United States during the past decade is an important precedent for the negotiation of a North American Free Trade Agreement, now underway with Mexico and Canada. There is a solid basis set in U.S. law for insisting on the inclusion of labor rights and standards in the agreement. Furthermore, all three countries are members of the ILO; Canada and Mexico are signatories to most of the important conventions. All three have progressive labor laws, although as this study shows, Mexico's long history of state-dominated trade unionism has made its laws less relevant than they should be. The proximity and diversity of the three countries provides an important crucible to shape rules and enforcement mechanisms that can serve as a model for broader, multilateral trade-linked standards in the framework of GATT and other regional trade agreements.

It should be added that in Europe a similar process is even more advanced, as the European Community nations move towards a common market in 1992. The social charter, buttressed by a European Court, Parliament, and a full panoply of laws, regulations, advisories, and directives, is shaping a consensus in that continent on labor standards that will give a strong impetus to the movement to evolve towards universal rules that link trade and labor standards, perhaps by the next round of GATT talks.

How Trade-Linked Labor Standards Might Work

Experience with the development and enforcement of national and international labor standards suggests some general principles:

- Labor standards should be defined with as much simplicity and precision as possible.

In general, the basic standards outlined earlier should be the ones developed for enforcement purposes. It could be stipulated that countries should strive for a longer list of standards like those adopted by the ILO, but such a list is too general to form the basis for an enforcement program. Enforcement also could specify a relatively small number of criteria to be used to determine whether or not industries or countries were violating basic labor standards.

- Procedures would need to be established for collecting information on the extent to which labor standards are actually being followed in particular situations.

In some cases, violations are easily determined, but, as is true of the enforcement of all rules, in some cases judgments have to be made. The development and dissemination of information on labor conditions is not a well-developed part of U.S. enforcement processes. We therefore should concentrate on a much more effective system.

- Procedures would have to be established for receiving complaints or allegations that companies, industries, or countries were violating labor standards.

An important procedural question is the determination of the parties eligible to file complaints. An effective system would encourage filings by a wide array of well-informed and interested parties, not just those who have a "direct and significant economic interest," as the U.S. trade representative is reportedly contemplating under regulations being developed for the enforcement of the 1988 trade act. It sends the wrong signal to permit complaints only by those who have something to lose materially and economically from trade, rather than knowledgeable people interested in the establishment of an open and expanding trading system within the framework of fair and enforceable rules.

- Decisions also need to be made about the nature and scope of remedies.

It probably makes sense to apply remedies to specific industries and situations, not to whole countries. It would, in addition, probably be wise to give countries willing to make good faith efforts to correct their practices both the time and technical assistance to do so.

As noted, the most effective way to enforce trade-linked labor standards probably would be done through the GATT since this would enable trade-related penalties to be imposed. This could be through amending GATT articles or by providing an interpretive code. The main purpose of GATT rules should be to establish obligations for all member governments to improve general labor standards and to enable a country to restrict or refuse to accept imports produced in violation of the basic specific standards discussed earlier. The process also should provide monitoring of compliance with the decision made by the adjudicating entity. ILO experience suggests the importance of establishing safeguards to screen out frivolous or politically inspired complaints.

Summary and Conclusions

It is time to link workers' rights and trade because international economic matters have become much more important to people all over the world. International trade was significantly less important to the United States and many other countries during the 1940s and 1950s, but it now has much greater impact on all of our lives. In economic terms, we traditionally treated trade as a secondary priority; now it is clearly a top priority. Trade-linked labor standards have therefore become much more essential.

There are no valid arguments against trade and labor standards. The main thrust of such a system should definitely not be to protect inefficient companies or national oligopolies and monopolies. On the contrary, trade-linked labor standards could cause companies to be more efficient. Nor would trade-linked labor standards protect high wages in the developed countries at the expense of lower-wage workers in the LDCs. As noted, we do not contemplate an international minimum wage. We should not, however, let multinational corporations or governments anywhere form alliances to exploit workers behind the screen of export-driven development strategies. There are legitimate reasons for GSPs for the LDCs if they are making good-faith efforts to move toward the time when they can "graduate" and abide by regular international rules. Similarly, some of the labor rights can be geared to stages of economic growth, but there is no legitimate reason to deny workers the freedom of association or the right to organize and bargain collectively.

Finally, we should proceed on an international basis to build support for trade-linked labor standards. A basic objective should be to get a working party to consider amending the GATT to permit governments to introduce selective import restrictions directed at countries that do not respect the basic labor rights outlined earlier. I believe, however, that we also should seize every opportunity to include labor standards in other international economic agreements. With these standards, most-favored-nation extensions could increase the enforcement of labor standards and reduce the resistance to including such measures in the GATT. We should simultaneously work with the ILO and like-minded organizations and individuals everywhere to develop an effective implementation strategy. It is particularly important to address the legitimate concerns of labor, political, and economic leaders in the LDCs. We should stress the positive plus-sum aspects of linking trade and labor rights and overcome the fear that our objective is to protect MDC standards at the expense of third world development. We also should not oversell the importance of labor rights in addressing the problems workers face everywhere. These standards are important and necessary, but, as noted, other policies are also needed for an open, expanding, prosperous, and just world economy.

Chapter One

The General Condition of the Mexican Worker

Mexican workers face long hours, low wages, and dangerous and unhealthy workplaces and communities. Women workers are subject to additional problems in the workplace and in the community, and child labor remains a serious problem. The lack of union democracy has made it difficult for Mexican workers to solve these problems. Moreover, as recent studies show, the Mexican government systematically violates the human rights of workers and other citizens, and it engages in widespread fraud and corruption.

Wages

Most authorities agree that Mexican wages are half, or less than half, of what they were 10 years ago. According to Antonio Tenorio Adame, "The real minimum wage in 1977 was 105.05 pesos [1978 pesos]; in December 1988 it was only 46.06 [1978 pesos] with a loss of 44.4 percent, less than half of what it represented in the year 1978."[1] Rosalbina Garavito, director of the editorial committee of the magazine *El Cotidiano*, published by the Autonomous Metropolitan University-Azcapotzalco, and an authority on Mexican labor, stated in early 1991 that real wages have deteriorated by 60 percent since 1982.[2] Whatever the exact figure is, the message remains the same: Mexico's economic crisis in the 1980s hit workers hard.

Comparing wages in Mexico with those in other countries reveals the tragedy of Mexico's debt crisis. Until 1982, Mexico was one of the wealthiest developing nations. With an abundance of natural resources, Mexico had and still has the potential to become a modern industrialized, prosperous nation. Wages, for those who participated in industrialized sectors, reflected their relative prosperity. Raúl Trejo Delarbre, an important labor historian, writes, "In 1975 the United States had a salary 4.4 times greater than that of Mexico, and ten years later [1985] wages in the United States were 10.4 times greater than those in Mexico."[3] By 1991, the differential had not lessened, despite the fact that wages in the United States were declining as well.

The fall in Mexico of real wages over the last 15 years is one of the most devastating effects of mismanaged development on the material condition of life for the Mexican people as a whole. The causes are multiple, but as this study shows, one significant reason is the state domination and control of the workers' primary instrument for pressing their demands, the trade union movement. Without adequate wages, Mexican workers are trapped in a cycle of deprivation, from which they will be unable to rise to economic parity, even with the rest of the Third World. Without an effective and free labor movement, their hope of achieving adequate wages is minimal.

Unemployment

Another factor acting against the Mexican worker is the rising rate of unemployment. For many reasons, including the national debt crisis, the lack of community-based development, shifts in agricultural production and imports, the retreat of capital out of Mexico, and the reprivatization of vast sectors of the Mexican economy, unemployment skyrocketed in the 1980s. In 1981, the rate of open unemployment in the formal labor market was 3.4 percent of the economically active population; by 1982, it was 7.4 percent, and in 1983 it was 11.7 percent. It did not stop increasing until it arrived at 22.9 percent in 1987.[4] Rosalbina Garavito estimates an even higher rate:

> We have an open unemployment rate calculated at around 25 to 30 percent. Sources of information hide much of their findings, because at an official level the rate is around 7 or 8 percent... In the manufacturing sector I believe, and this is not hard to estimate, we have a rate of unemployment of about 25 percent.[5]

In addition to unemployment, there is a great deal of underemployment, workers who work less than full-time as casual laborers or on a part-time or semi-permanent basis. Many millions of workers also have entered the informal economy in one way or another, including millions of children whose parents cannot find adequate work to support them.

The human meaning of underemployment is miserable and pathetic poverty, millions of *working* people with increasingly inadequate shelter and nutrition. For the millions of workers in the large and growing informal economy, there are no labor union rights or social security. At the extreme, it means living in the streets and begging, which tens of thousands do.

Much of the growing unemployment has resulted from the government's economic program of privatization, industrial reconversion, and modernization. Without any recourse from their "official" unions, workers are fired by the government or their employers (often the same), and left to fend for themselves in a hostile labor environment. The lack of jobs for skilled and unskilled laborers has exacerbated the decline in wages; any job is better than no job, even a low-paying one.

Health and Safety

Occupational health and safety is a complex matter; the issues are not limited to the workers' conditions at work, but include their general standard of living, as well as the effectiveness of labor union action and government intervention. As was already noted, Mexican workers receive low wages which have decreased dramatically, by at least half over the last decade. Consequently, even though women and children have entered the workforce, their standard of living is lower. The result is poorer nutrition, inferior clothing, inadequate housing, and loss of schooling. All of these deprivations factor into the general health and well-being of the worker even before she or he arrives at the office, factory, mine, or other workplace.

Once at work, Mexican laborers face situations which are increasingly dangerous, with few regulations enforced to protect them. Asa Cristina Laurell and Margarita Márquez are two authorities on occupational health, and the authors of a book entitled *El desgaste obrero en México*, which might be translated "The Wearing Out of the Worker " or "The Waste of the Worker." Their book has become a standard work on occupational medicine not only in Mexico but throughout Latin America. An excerpt details the hazards Mexican workers face:

> Mexican industry can in general be characterized as exposing workers in one workplace or another to all the risks enumerated in treatises dealing with occupational health: lead, mercury, arsenic, chromates, vinyl chloride, asbestos, silica, solvents, gases, etc.; the list is too long to write down. Within this general situation, it is necessary to emphasize some particular problems which assume great importance. In the first place, information about the dangers involved in dealing with hazardous materials is not well known in Mexican society, and is accompanied by legislation which is completely lacking in specificity.
>
> In the second place, there is no infrastructure which would make possible a systematic study of the hazards, nor is there a systematic register of the problems caused... In the third place, even if there were samples analyzed for the presence of certain substances, the values established as maximum concentration levels

permitted are calculated in terms of general character-
istics of the environment...which in Mexico are not
usually complied with.

Finally, it is important to see the problem of hazards in light of Mexico's new role in the international
labor market. Now it is Mexico's turn to receive the industries in which workers work with highly toxic substances with proven carcinogenic effects. That is to say,
there is a selective concentration of the most dangerous kinds of production, destined not only for internal
use but for the international market.[6]

The Mexican government's health authorities for all intents and
purposes *do not recognize the existence of occupational illness,* much less
do anything about it. Despite the presence of such known carcino-
gens as asbestos, vinyl chloride, chromates, and petroleum products, the government claims there are no cases of occupational
cancer in Mexico. The problem of occupational cancer and other
diseases related to exposure, however, is fully documented in the
medical press and by the ILO. It is impossible to suppose ignorance
among the union leadership and the experts at the Secretary of
Labor and the Social Security Institute. Rather, their inactivity must
be considered as part of an implicit cover-up. Laurell and Márquez
address this subject as well:

> Given that one can reject the hypothesis that Mexican
> workers have an extraordinary resistance to occupa-
> tional illnesses, we have to infer that in Mexico there
> exists a whole structure which allows the problem to
> be covered up. The corporative [i.e., state controlled]
> union structure, the useless Health and Safety Com-
> missions, the inactivity of the Secretary of Labor and of
> the Mexican Institute of Social Security, together with a
> well worked out employer strategy, are the obstacles
> which prevent the working class from defending its in-
> terests in this field.[7]

Although there is little documentation by the Mexican authorities or by employers as to which chemicals Mexican workers are exposed, or levels of exposure, it is not in question that they are
indeed exposed to hazardous materials on a regular basis. According to Dr. Sherry Baron, an occupational health physician who
worked in Mexico with the Pan American Health Organization, not
only are workers exposed to dangerous levels of hazardous materials, but employers are for the most part not concerned about protecting them. In fact, there is little awareness on the part of the
workers, unions, employers, society at large, or governmental institutions about what materials are hazardous and what can be done

about them.[8] Even basic personal protective equipment, such as masks and gloves, are not supplied to the workers.

Baron asserts that the problem is not only a lack of concern but also a lack of resources. She points out that "even if the government wanted to do something about occupational safety and health, it does not have adequately trained physicians, industrial hygienists and other technicians, nor does it have the equipment it would need."[9] It could be asked, however, whether the pressures for cheap wage competition internationally will keep the budget inadequate even when Mexico's finances allow for improvements.

The government bodies which deal with occupational health and safety are the Department of Labor, which has the authority to enforce safety standards, but neither the resources nor technical expertise to do it; and the Mexican Institute of Social Security, which has whatever resources exist in terms of technicians, but no authority to enforce standards. The Secretary of Labor's office does carry out inspections, but without the proper methods or equipment these inspections are merely visual. Inspectors walk around the plant looking at things:

> ...they do not use the basic equipment of occupational hygiene, which should at the very least include a sound level meter and preferably a dosimeter in order to measure sound; thermometers to measure the effective temperature and radiant heat; a light meter to evaluate the lighting; and some of the apparatuses which are used to measure dust and gases. Neither do they take chemical samples to determine what they are, and what are their injurious effects.[10]

The absence of measurements has immediate implications. Without information, it becomes impossible to determine whether or not an employer is complying with existing standards, whether stronger measures are needed, and difficult to establish a hierarchy of hazards according to their seriousness. Essentially, all action regarding occupational safety becomes stultified.

This lack of information, regulation, or governmental control is extremely convenient for employers who take little initiative to safeguard workers' well-being on their own. Findings reported by Laurell and another colleague, Mariano Noriega, on the state-owned Lázaro-Cárdenas/Las Truchas Steel Mill, indicate that the company was primarily concerned with productivity, and showed little concern for worker health and safety except insofar as it might interrupt production, as in the case of some accidents. Their conclusion is that "it was the firm's policy not to respect the parts of the collective bargaining agreement which referred to workplace health and safety..."[11]

Their study found that the Miners and Metal Workers Union contract, which was the collective bargaining agreement in effect at the mill, was not in and of itself adequate to protect the health and safety of the workers. First, it was most concerned with compensation for accidents after they had occurred, "putting little emphasis on the mechanisms for preventing such hazards."[12] Second, the contract was only concerned with industrial accidents, "but left much to be desired with regard to occupational illnesses."[13] Third, the contract was so poor in specifying working conditions that "there was hardly even a concept of traditional hygiene, much less of the integral relationship between work and workers' health."[14] The contract established no expectations about materials, equipment, or production. "The contract as a whole contained few clauses which permitted the workers to develop a strategy in defense of their health."[15]

The steel industry is not alone in its disregard for workers. Example after example of abuse can be found in the testimony of workers (no official documentation exists) about their working conditions. Foreign-owned and Mexican plants alike are accomplice to these misdeeds. In testimony presented to the U.S. Congress in Spring 1991, Elizabeth Macías of Ciudad Juárez explained her experiences with a subsidiary of Ford Motor Company:

> Monday, October 29, 1990, was the last day I had a good talk with my son Julio Cesar...two days later, on Wednesday, October 31, a revolving belt dragged him to a factory grinder...cutting off his very short existence, when he was just 16 years of age.
>
> My son was hired as a production operator at the rate of US$ .45 an hour for the auto glass plant (*Autovidrio*), which Ford Motor Company has set up in Ciudad Juárez. Even though Cesar was not a sweeper, his immediate supervisor sent him to clean, by himself, an isolated underground tunnel, where, by means of a mechanical belt, the waste from the factory is transported. My son didn't return alive from there. Nobody knows how it was that he died, my small Julio Cesar, since it was only possible to learn that his comrades found him 15 minutes after he had been trapped in the grinder, with his right arm, thorax and head destroyed.
>
> The murderous machine had no mechanism for being stopped in case of emergency. The murderous machine had no barrier or protection to prevent workers from getting near it should they fall accidentally. In fact, the auto glass factory of Ford does not train its workers for cases of emergency in that basement.

> They sent my son to that basement without provid-
> ing him with any safety equipment; he had no glasses,
> no helmet, not even a uniform to protect him from a
> minor accident... He'd been working at the factory just
> five days and it was his first job ever. The factory
> hadn't given him any training in how to operate and
> stop the production belt. My son was hired to carry
> out a job different from the one they sent him to do
> that day.
>
> I have seen that the Ford Company announces its
> safety measures for its cars, such as seat belts, cush-
> ioned panels, special designs, etc., but I've never seen
> them announce the standards that they've designed to
> protect the workers in their plants in Mexico...[16]

What kind of prosecution should this company face for inadver-
tently killing a 16-year-old child? According to the government of
Mexico, none. In the Mexican workplace, no preventive measures
are taken, and there is little or no protection for the workers either
from their employers, the unions, or the state. Moreover, the situation is only likely to get worse, at least for the foreseeable future.

Mexico is in the process of carrying out the modernization of its
industry, which implies changes in both technology and the organization of the workforce. Employers in Mexico, as in advanced capitalist economies such as the United States and Japan, are
demanding greater "flexibility" to utilize workers as they wish. To
attain flexibility, employers are demanding changes in contracts to
get rid of what restrictive clauses exist. Adolfo Gilly writes: "flexibility means weakening or suppressing the work rules which have
been established inside the plant and at each work station as a result
of past struggles and negotiations, and [which are] recognized in
labor contracts, whether national, company or department contracts, [and doing so] all in the name of capitalist efficiency and productivity."[17] State companies and private employers are both
demanding the elimination of these work rules. The result will be
less protection for the workers, with even more detrimental effects
on their health and safety.

Women Workers

It is generally agreed that about 30 percent of Mexican women
work in the formal economy. Many more women work in the informal sector as street vendors, domestic workers, or homeworkers—
sewing or assembling products in their homes. In all, a majority of
Mexican women are wage earners in one form or another. Despite
their contribution to Mexican society, in most cases they do not
enjoy even minimal worker rights or standards, and have even less

access to an adequate standard of living than their male counter-parts. In addition, because they are women, they face unique circumstances which act to repress them even further.[18]

"The majority of women workers in Mexico are not protected by the legal system as established by Federal Labor Law," says Patricia Mercado, a leader of Women in Labor Union Action (Mujeres de Acción Sindical—MAS), an independent association which attempts to improve conditions for working women.[19] This affects them in many different ways. Most women are not labor union members. When they are unionized, the Mexican "official" unions tend to be even less responsive to their needs than they are for men. Mercado explains that women workers are also subject to "protection contracts," contracts previously negotiated between the employer and one of the "official" union organizations without the knowledge of the workers and counter to their interests.

Some women, such as those who work for the federal government, for Teléfonos de México (TELMEX), or in the banking industry, do have unions with negotiated contracts, but these are state-controlled unions. Women union activists face an uphill battle to make their lives easier in the face of systematic sex discrimination.

Women work extremely hard, up to 12 hours a day, and often for wages below subsistence. A few years ago women were struggling for the minimum wage, but now that nobody can even begin to live on a minimum wage, the only people who are paid the minimum wage are women. According to MAS research, most women workers in small shops are earning between the minimum wage, which as of January 1991 was 11,300 pesos ($3.75) per day, and 15,000 pesos ($5.00) per day. A domestic worker in Mexico City probably earns between 20,000 and 25,000 pesos per day.

However, the big issue, as Mercado sees it, is not wages, but benefits. Many women all over Mexico, particularly in small and medium-sized shops, do not receive legally mandated benefits. They do not have access to Social Security, the national health care system. They do not receive their year-end bonus or vacation time. MAS found many women who have worked four or five years without ever having had a day's vacation, paid or unpaid. Both the year-end bonus and paid vacations are mandated under Mexican labor law.

Mexican labor law also calls upon employers to establish day care centers for workers' children. However, says Mercado, "The day care centers that exist in Mexico are not nearly sufficient to meet the needs of the workers." Only 5 to 10 percent of working women are able to take advantage of day care centers. The lack of day care centers has led, she says, to widespread and serious social problems:

> In Mexico City...because there are no day care centers, women leave their little children closed up in the house, without an older person to look after them. You

would think that this wouldn't happen today, but it does. The mothers leave their five- and six-month-old babies on a piece or cloth or a blanket with a bottle so that if they get hungry they can feed themselves until the mother comes back. Or they may leave the older children in charge of the younger, but shut up in the house so that they cannot go outside until the mother returns.

Lilia Reyes, a labor lawyer who works with the Workers' Center (Centro Obrero) in Monterrey, Nuevo Leon, notes that "Child care is a real issue now because now both parents have to work... In addition, there are single women who have families... When they go to a child care center, there are many requirements, and they may have to wait months before they can get a place. There just aren't enough child care centers."[20]

In a changing Mexico, where women are moving into new sectors of society, there is even more need for day care centers than ever. Changing sexual mores, as a result of urbanization and changes in the nature of the workforce, have not been accompanied by the social support which would allow working women to enjoy more freedom. Women have no access to contraception, and single women are denied the right to an abortion. Because of the lack of contraceptives and widespread refusal on the part of men to use condoms, women pay a high price for sexual relationships in the form of dangerous and illegal abortions, or children they cannot support.

There are other devastating costs as well. Sexual harassment in the workplace, bordering on rape, is ubiquitous. Organizations working among women industrial workers report that male supervisors frequently demand sexual favors from female workers, and those who refuse may find that they have been given the most difficult jobs. Among professional or office workers, promotions and salary increases may depend upon meeting the sexual demands of male supervisors. The problem is so widespread that the Mexican government recently made sexual harassment on the job a crime, though it does not yet carry a penalty. Mercado reports that MAS is trying to get a measure against sexual harassment put into the Federal Labor Law that would establish a punishment. This is difficult, she asserts, because sexual harassment is also prevalent in the unions.

Unions have left women out in other ways as well, she notes. The changing character of industrial technology and work organization is eliminating jobs for all workers, but companies fail to give women training to promote them or to assist them in their adjustment to change. Unions frequently ignore the need for training women while they are fighting for the training of men. Jobs are also being lost because of the re-writing of union contracts to give employers more "flexibility." With the loss of contractual protection, real wages stagnate, and women have even less protection as they are considered a second-class and expendable workforce.[21]

Since women are viewed in this way, their role within the labor unions is restricted. In general, men take the leading roles, although particularly assertive women may become members of local union executive boards or even general secretaries. Few women are visible in the labor movement above the local level. Exceptions are unions with predominantly female membership, where some women are elected to leadership.[22] The few predictable unions where women play a highly visible leadership role are the Teachers Union (SNTE) and the flight attendants' union.

Women have a long way to go in the unions and in Mexican society as a whole. If they are to succeed in their new role as providers, they will need a good deal more access to labor rights than they currently have.

Child Labor

Child labor in Mexico is prohibited by the Constitution, the Federal Labor Law, and by other legislation. In addition, Mexico is signatory to several ILO conventions which prohibit children conditionally from participating in night or underground work. In general, children under the age of 16 are not permitted by law to work full-time, although exceptions can be made for children ages 14 to 16 under certain circumstances.

It is widely recognized that these statutes are ignored, and that there is an immense child labor problem in Mexico involving millions of children. The Mexico City Assembly recently estimated the number of children employed illegally to be somewhere between five and 10 million, often in hazardous jobs.[23] The most superficial observation of Mexican society indicates the breadth and depth of the problem. In large cities, children are seen at all hours of the day and night (including during school hours) working on the streets. Some are little more than beggars. Dressed as clowns, or performing as jugglers, boys and girls of 10 or 12 can be seen at the intersections of major streets. Other children between the ages of eight and 18 can be seen singing or playing musical instruments on street corners, in plazas and on public transportation. Some adolescents engage in "fire eating," inhaling and exhaling flammable liquids and gases (gasoline, kerosene, or alcohol), with devastating physical and psychological side effects. Many more young people work as "windshield wipers," cleaning the windows of motorists stopped at intersections.

All of these activities reveal an admirable desire on the part of children to work and be useful, but a terrible failure—on the part of the state—to provide Mexico's children with the education and training that might make them more successful in the future. Worse yet is that in the big cities (Mexico, Guadalajara, Monterrey), the border towns (Tijuana, Ciudad Juárez), and resort cities (Acapulco), children in their teens are brought onto the market of heterosexual and homosexual prostitution with no effort by the authorities to stop it. In cases of extreme poverty or social disorder, it is these same children who learn to steal.

Children are also found working in various industries. One of the most egregious examples is the shoe industry, where children routinely work at tasks where they are exposed to dangerous substances such as adhesives.[24] The garment industry involves much sub-contracting to homeworkers. When women take work home, for example to attach cuffs, collars, zippers, or buttons, they often must involve their children in the work to make ends meet. For these families, home is turned into a sweatshop. Children even find their way into the modern factories. In the *maquiladoras* (border factories owned mostly by U.S. companies), children in their early teens sometimes falsify documents in order to qualify for work in the assembly plants. Employers, social workers, women's groups, and academics all agree that there are significant numbers of underage children working in the *maquiladora* industry though there are no concrete figures. One employer offered the figure 5 percent, though this is simply speculation.

Law professor Héctor Santos Azuela, in an essay titled "Child Labor in Mexico," notes that child labor is widespread. "It is not difficult to find them working with high levels of risk in butcher shops, mills, *tortillerías* (shops which make tortillas), or in other shops of various sorts." While many legal protections exist for children in both Mexican law and ILO conventions, the problem is exacerbated by the authorities' willingness to look the other way:

> Labor inspectors have an important social function which unfortunately they do not fulfill. Their activities are reduced to routinely imposing fines, rather than combating the problem.
>
> Despite the complete suppression of the apprenticeship contract, reminiscent of medieval servitude, the employment of children as labor power, subject to excessively long work days, with low wages and in deplorable and unsanitary working conditions, is frequent.
>
> Nothing has been done in reality to protect the children and prevent this exploitation. Many projects have been designed without any practical results. Frequent modification and reorganization has seriously damaged labor statutes regarding children, carrying the

law ever further away from the extensive protection
that is required.[25]

Federal labor laws give the national government jurisdiction over
only a limited number of industries. In the state of Guanajuato, for example, that jurisdiction comprises only 3 percent of factories. Supervision of the rest, some 22,000 factories, is left to five child labor
inspectors, a number half the level of a decade ago, who would require
two decades just to visit all the factories under their jurisdiction once![26]

Trapped in a poverty they inherit at birth and abandoned by
the government and the official union movement, children have few
advocates. Children work in industry and on the streets to the great
detriment to their bodies and souls, and the adult world does nothing to protect them. Child labor, which is the product of generalized
poverty, cannot be eliminated by the creation of more adult jobs at
below-subsistence wages. Coping with the epidemic of Mexican
child labor requires a combination of improved employment opportunities *and* wage levels for adults and enhanced educational opportunities for children, as well as enforcement by an adequate number
of government officials. Without establishing wage-enhancement
strategies as part of an overall development plan, there is no hope
of lessening the evil of child labor. Cheap labor strategies for adults
mean even cheaper wage strategies for children, leaving Mexico in a
hopeless downward spiral.

Until mothers and fathers do not have to rely on their children's
meager wages, or abandon their children to the streets in despair,
children will never escape from the jaws of premature and crippling
work, and Mexico will never prepare a workforce for an industrially
advanced future.

Workers and Human Rights

Among the many reasons why Mexico's working poor cannot
raise up their voices to protest fiscal austerity measures, the abuse
of their bodies in the workplace, or the sacrifice of their children to
cheap labor strategies, is the likelihood that they will be tortured as
a result of their activities. Trade unionists, peasant activists, and
human rights campaigners, along with criminals, are routinely victims of the brutal methods of torture used throughout Mexico to ex-
tract confessions.[27] The fact that torture is prohibited by the Mexican
Constitution while its perpetrators are rarely brought to justice, is
just one example of the widespread corruption that infests the government.

The National Commission of Human Rights, created in 1989,
has received and acknowledged numerous complaints of human
rights violations. Among those most frequently cited are the use of
torture and extra-judicial murder by various authorities. In addi-

tion, "disappearance" (i.e. kidnapping and murder), continues to be a problem. Human rights investigators charge that Mexican citizens are denied speedy trials, and that convicted prisoners are often incarcerated beyond the terms of their prison sentence.[28]

A 1991 study of torture in Mexico conducted by Amnesty International lists political activity as a primary reason why citizens are tortured, and concludes that "recent years have seen increased attacks on political opponents of the government and trade unionists."[29] Among the many examples of people or groups of people who were arrested and tortured on trumped up charges, or tortured without being charged with a crime, are two teachers, active members of the Teachers' Union (SNTE) section in Tuxtla Gutiérrez, Chiapas, who were arrested in December 1989 and tortured by the Federal Judicial Police. Both Rubicel Einstein Ruiz Gamboa and Oscar de Jesús Peña Esquinca had participated in a demonstration in November of that year at the offices of the state Public Education Ministry, and were held partially responsible for disturbances which occurred during that incident. When they were arrested on December 15, they were hooded, forced into an unmarked vehicle, driven to a precipice over the Grijalba River gorge where they were beaten and threatened with being thrown off the precipice for their political activities. They were then taken to the state prison where they remained for the next five months on charges of damage to federal property, aggression, and theft, all charges they denied.[30] Another case the Amnesty International report cited was that of Martín Sebastian Peña Mejía, a member of the Revolutionary Democratic Party (PRD), who was arrested without a warrant on February 9, 1990 in Jonacatepec, Morelos, and held incommunicado for five days by the state police. During that time he was beaten and tortured by having water forced up his nose and by near-asphyxiation, and he was warned by the police that he would suffer the same fate as many of his comrades, whom they listed by name, who had been killed or "disappeared" in recent years.[31]

Human rights investigators cite the use of the criminal justice system as a means of controlling dissident activity as a primary impediment to an effective justice system. The fact that government officials engage in or permit torture and murder clearly has a chilling effect on political action. The Minnesota Lawyers International Human Rights Committee found in a 1990 investigation into human rights violations in the criminal justice system that respect for human rights within that system is grievously lacking:

> Despite Mexico's constitutional guarantees and its support for improved international human rights norms, chronic and systematic abuses of basic human rights of Mexican citizens by the country's security forces are widespread...

> The abuses include illegal searches, arbitrary deten-
> tion and arrests, extra-judicial killings, and extensive
> use of physical and psychological torture to obtain in-
> formation and confessions. The abuses appear to be
> part of an entrenched system of police abuse. All ele-
> ments of the country's security apparatus are involved
> in the abuses, including the army and the federal, state,
> and municipal police forces. It is the judicial police
> forces, however, who have the worst record.[32]

They also found that illegal detention and torture committed by
the police are so common that they are simply accepted as part of
the system. "Due in good part to their frequency, illegal detention,
mistreatment, humiliation, and even torture of detainees are observed as *normal* procedures. This fact does not, however, prevent
the population from feeling an unexplainable fear at the possibility
of having anything to do with a police officer."[33]

Although overtures have been made by both President Salinas
and his predecessor, Miguel de la Madrid Hurtado to improve
human rights law and the practice thereof, little has been achieved.
Many feel that "seemingly important steps appear to be merely ornamental, designed to boost the image of Mexico in the international community and to provide the *appearance* of action at
home."[34] The 1986 Federal Law to Prevent and Punish Torture, and
the 1991 reforms introduced into the Penal Code for the Federal District to enhance the rights of detainees and limit the role of police in
the interrogation of detainees, are good examples of legal steps that
have been taken but have failed because they are not put into practice. Actions such as these will continue to be ornamental, as long as
confessions extracted through torture are still admissible in court.
According to the Minnesota Lawyers' Committee study, "Even
when there is evidence that the confession was forced, the judge
may still allow it in evidence if there exists corroborating evidence."
Given that the first confession made to the police, whether it was
extracted through torture or not, "has more probative value than
any other statement made by the defendant" in this situation the defendant may well be imprisoned even if he or she is innocent. The
second reason is "the effective immunity from prosecution extended to
law enforcement agents who commit the crime of torture."[35] Even
when a perpetrator of violence can be identified by the victim, and the
victim files a report with the Human Rights Commission or other local
authorities, the victim is more likely to be victimized again for speaking out than the perpetrator is to be punished.

Many labor and human rights activists have been arrested on
false charges, illegally detained, or kidnapped and extra-judicially
murdered. As this study documents, to engage in union organizing
is to put oneself at risk. Countless workers have sacrificed their lives

to the strangling embrace of the state, and if democratic battles are continually forced into the streets and onto company grounds, rather than in voting booths, many more will be stricken with the blows of ineffectual reform.

Workers' Rights and Union Democracy

Among Mexican academics who study unions, as well as among the workers who belong to them, widespread agreement exists that workers' rights are not respected by the state-run unions, which dominate the organization of workers even by force, and that there is little democracy at work in their activities. A multiplicity of citations and quotations, even to the point of redundancy, make it clear that this is not simply the point of view of isolated individuals, fringe groups, or a radical element. It is common knowledge.

Raúl Trejo Delarbre has written several books on the history of the Mexican labor movement. His most recent book, *Crónica del sindicalismo en México, 1976-1988*, is a history, but also a polemic. Trejo Delarbre is not a radical root-and-branch critic of the Mexican labor and political system. On the contrary, he calls for a revamping of the relationship between the ruling party and the unions called neo-corporativism. Because he is supportive of the concept of a corporative set-up, his criticisms of the current system are all the more telling. Trejo Delarbre writes:

> Political bossism as a substitute for the participation of workers, has continued to be the predominant conduct in major Mexican unions. The almost total absence—in many cases the complete absence—of union meetings, union newspapers, workers' commissions, combined with the lack of interest in defending labor union rights, and the infrequent exercise of open protest or strikes, have made the labor movement of our country what it is today: an habitually inactive unionism....[36]
>
> Corruption, which in sectors of public administration has occasionally been a blot and a habit, has been converted in the unions into a source of cohesion between leaders and workers. Authoritarianism, which in the Mexican political system has been one option but not the only option, in many unions has become so prevalent that it is not even questioned.[37]

This is the opinion of a man who thinks the unions are redeemable and their interdependent relationship to the government should be preserved!

Héctor de la Cueva Díaz is the director of the Center for Labor Investigation and Union Consultation (CILAS) and a leader of a left-oriented political party. He was involved with the Ford workers movement in Mexico City from 1987 to 1990 (see Chapter 6) and with other democratic movements within the official unions. He says of Mexican workers' rights:

> Workers have the theoretical right of free association and to form labor unions. In the Constitution and in Federal Labor Law this right exists, but in practice it does not exist. In practice, the workers form legal labor unions under great duress, and can rarely elect their own officials. In recent times there have been many struggles by workers to take over their union executive boards, but these struggles have met with the use of police violence to repress them.
>
> In firms where there are no unions, bosses simply count on firing workers with the complicity of the labor authorities. In some firms there are "protection unions" and "protection contracts" as they are called. Union officials sell these companies a contract and union registration. These are not unions, they have no union officials, but the company has fulfilled the formal requirement that there be a contract. The workers don't know about it, they do not know their leaders, nor do they know the union with which they are supposedly affiliated.
>
> Often even when there is a union the workers still do not have the right of free association, because they cannot form or join another union, or another labor federation. Workers have tried time and again to form more responsive unions and they have been thwarted in various ways to the extent that in a majority of firms the unions are imposed on the workers... It is a frequent occurrence in Mexico that workers who are unhappy with their union leadership or who try to change unions are fired in a clear, cynical complicity between the firm and the labor union bureaucrats, or, as they are called in Mexico, the "charros," and the labor authorities. The union asks the firm to fire the dissident workers, and the labor authorities foster the transaction.[38]

Jesús Sergio Acosta Ortiz is the education director for the Miguel A. Pro Juárez Center for Human Rights A.C. (CDHAC), a group associated with a Roman Catholic order. CDHAC believes that human rights include labor union rights and a decent standard of living for working people. According to Acosta Ortiz, actions by workers to preserve these rights are met with repression even when they enjoy popular support:

Concrete examples of the most important political events of 1990 were three labor strikes, at Ford, the Modelo Brewery, and Tornel. All of them failed, despite the fact that they found an echo in public opinion, and were supported by other organizations both inside and outside of the labor sector. They didn't have to wait long for repression. The government's strategy in all of these confrontations was to drag out the conflict in order to wear them down. They did this using legal measures—rejecting injunctions—and using police methods—direct repression, etc. There is an entire apparatus which exists to stop movements such as these, through direct repression, and the judicial system. The Boards of Conciliation and Arbitration clearly favor companies over workers.[39]

In many if not all cases of labor union strikes, failure is due to the lack of union democracy.

Telésforo Nava Vázquez is an economist, a professor at the Autonomous Metropolitan University, an active member of his university union, and involved in regular discussions with labor union activists in a variety of industries. He finds the lack of union democracy which leads to repression rooted in law:

In Mexico democracy doesn't exist because the law itself makes it impossible. In the Federal Labor Law which regulates Article 123 of the Constitution, it is stated that the workers cannot freely register their unions. Registration of the unions is not at the will of the workers, but rather by decision of government authorities such as the Secretary of Labor and the Federal Board of Conciliation and Arbitration. This allows the government to interfere in company-union relations by deciding to whom they will give registration and to whom they will not. When there is a problem a firm quickly registers a company union, which by decision of the authorities overrides any union which may already exist, and thus negates their actions.[40]

Even employers recognize the lack of democracy for and in unions. José Manuel Loyo Aguirre is the National Director of Labor Relations for COPARMEX, the largest employer association in Mexico. In describing the nature of the Mexican labor unions, he paints a familiar picture:

First, within the unions there is no representation by leaders who represent the members. Second, decisions are made by the executive committee without consul-

tation with the rank and file. Third, the union leaders
enjoy long terms in power, some for 20 or 30 years.
Fourth, there are deals made under the table, and with
representatives of the firm. And there is also charrismo
[corrupt union officials placed in power by the govern-
ment].[41]

Raúl Escobar was a local union official at the Ford Motor Company and was involved in one of the more grotesque violations of
workers' rights in Mexico. His opinion is therefore of some interest.

The Constitution gives employers as well as workers
the right to join together to defend their interests. Nevertheless, for a long time in Mexico the "official" confederations which are the right arm of the government
have been anti-democratic. Workers who lift up their
heads to demand their rights are repressed, threatened,
or assassinated. Or, we might say, these rights exist in
the Constitution—but they are not respected by the
government itself.
    One supposes that the union representatives
should be the negotiators who work out salary and
contract revisions. However, the union representatives
are imposed on the workers, and obviously they must
toe the labor federation line, which adheres to the
government's economic plans. The workers know
nothing more than what they are told—there is going
to be a new contract, or a strike. But they never participate in any preparation.
    These representatives know that it is necessary to
cover the workers' eyes so that they don't appear to be
so shameless. In the end they always sign salary increases behind the backs of the workers. When the
workers are told how much it is, there is no way to
protest, because the contract is already signed. The decision is never put to the workers to accept or reject an
offer. All they get is "This is it, brothers." The union
bureaucracy is trained to always sign behind the
workers' backs, because if there were democratic
unions, obviously there would have to be union meetings.[42]

There are independent or democratic unions in the auto industry,
says Escobar, but they are very few indeed.
    All of these quite different individuals and organizations agree
that workers' rights and union democracy are systematically suppressed in Mexico. The government's ties to the "official" unions
have become a strangling embrace, choking off internal reform as

well as the formation of independent unions. To the most critical eye, this suppression is just another way a corrupt and authoritarian government serves a small corporate elite at the expense of workers and peasants. To those who feel that the labor movement is strong enough to promote change within the emerging political system, this suppression is a mileage marker of how far they have to go. Either way, the fact remains that at present, and as long as the current government holds to a development model dependent on "cheap labor" as its comparative advantage, labor union rights will continue to be compromised.

The Structure of Mexico's "Official" Unions

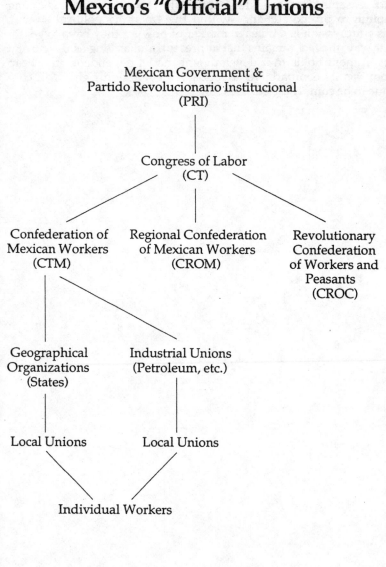

Mexican Government &
Partido Revolucionario Institucional
(PRI)

Congress of Labor
(CT)

Confederation of
Mexican Workers
(CTM)

Regional Confederation
of Mexican Workers
(CROM)

Revolutionary
Confederation
of Workers and
Peasants
(CROC)

Geographical
Organizations
(States)

Industrial Unions
(Petroleum, etc.)

Local Unions

Local Unions

Individual Workers

Chapter Two

Labor Rights and the Law

In order to analyze the status of Mexican workers accurately, it is necessary to lay out some of the fundamental organizational structures and labor laws which workers in Mexico confront, for it is the interaction of these laws and structures which effectively strangles Mexican workers' exercise of internationally recognized labor rights. The relationship between labor unions, the ruling party, and the state is of particular importance to a full understanding of the workers' lot.

Mexico's "Official" Trade Unions and the State

The organized labor movement in Mexico is predominantly a state-controlled movement. Mexico is a one-party state, ruled since the end of the Mexican Revolution in the 1920s by the same political organization. Though it has changed names several times, this organization—the PRI (pronounced "pree"), the ruling Institutional Revolutionary Party—controls the presidency, dominates both the House of Representatives and the Senate, and holds almost all state governorships and most municipalities.

This one-party political system has been called by various names. In Mexico the most commonly used name is *corporativismo* or corporate system. The word is derived from the lexicon of Mussolini's fascism. In fascist Italy, employers and workers were forced to join industrial corporations. Mexico, though obviously not a fascist state, bears some resemblance to this sort of system, with the forced affiliation of whole sectors of the population and organizations to a ruling party-state.

Some authors have described the system as one of "unstable Caesarism" or "Bonapartism" because of the manner in which the Mexican president and ruling party rise above and dominate not only the state, but all social classes and groups. Another name sometimes used is "authoritarian populism," a system which is authoritarian in its political system, but derives its legitimacy from mass or popular organizations which it controls. The most common term used by social scientists, historians, and others is "authoritarian." In any case, virtually no historian, political scientist, or sociologist characterizes the Mexican political system as a democracy, and it is certainly not democratic in terms of its labor unions.[1]

Structurally, the "official" labor unions are integrated into and controlled by the PRI. The relationship between the PRI-state and its unions is hierarchical: the PRI-state dominates and directs union movement, and mandates the support of the "official" union movement to provide a social base of legitimacy for itself as the government. The PRI's "official" trade union movement is organized under the Congress of Labor (CT), which is made up of the various official labor confederations.

The largest and most important of these confederations is the Confederation of Mexican Workers (CTM), headed since the 1940s by Fidel Velázquez, now in his 90s. Other important "official" unions include the Regional Confederation of Mexican Workers (CROM) and the Revolutionary Confederation of Workers and Peasants (CROC). There are several other smaller federations, and a few large industrial unions, such as the Miners and Metal Workers Union (STMMRM), which are affiliated directly with the CT. One major group in the CT is the Federation of Unions of Workers at the Service of the State (FSTSE), the federal public employees union. Peasant organizations do not belong to the CT.[2]

The various confederations—CTM, CROC, CROM, and others— are made up of their various affiliated unions. These include unions organized on a regional, industrial, or company basis. The CTM, for example, includes both state organizations (e.g. the CTM of Puebla state), and some large industrial unions such as the Petroleum Workers Union (STPRM). Many unions, however, simply represent the workers at one firm or even at one plant. Local unions are usually affiliated either with the state labor organizations or belong to industrial unions.

Politically, the "official" labor unions of the CT form the "labor sector" of the PRI, and thus make up part of the official party organization as well as part of its parliamentary delegation. The PRI puts forward labor union officials as candidates for the Senate, for the Chamber of Deputies, for state governorships, for municipal presidents or mayors, and for many other political offices. In most administrations, several senators, many members of Congress, mayors, and even a few governors have been chosen from PRI's labor sector.

Until 1991, workers who were employed in union shops were compelled to join a local union which was affiliated with a federation such as the CTM, CROC, or CROM, which in turn was affiliated with the CT and with the PRI. Thus, to become a union member was simultaneously to become a party member. Consequently, the great majority of all unionized workers were "members" of the PRI by virtue of their union membership. Refusal to join the PRI was grounds for expulsion from many unions, and in many cases expulsion from the union meant termination by the employer. This practice was commonly known as the "forced mass affiliation" of workers to the PRI. It hardly needs to be said that such involuntary membership in the union and in the political party vitiate the principle of voluntary association in both the labor movement and in party politics.

However, in late 1990, the PRI and the CT unions announced that they would no longer engage in the "forced mass affiliation" of workers to the PRI, but that in the future the workers would be individually recruited to join the PRI. On December 11, 1990 Fidel Velázquez, head of the CTM and a principal figure in the CT, and Senator Luis Donaldo Colosio, head of the PRI, signed a document which established voluntary and individual affiliation to the PRI, thus bringing an "end" to forced mass affiliation to the party.[3] Nevertheless, all of the "official" labor organizations retained their affiliation with the PRI, the leaders of the "official" unions pledged to declare their formal membership in the PRI, and an immediate campaign was launched to get the members of the unions to affiliate.[4]

In theory, there should be no objection to a union shop, or to union leaders affiliating with a political party or asking their members to join a political party. However, given the historically authoritarian character of the relationship between the party and the unions, and between the unions and their individual members, there is a good deal of doubt about the "voluntary" character of the individual recruitment of union members to the PRI.

The hierarchical state-party-union system of control means that the official labor unions have as one of their principal tasks the defense and promotion of party and government policy, including economic policy. At the very least, the government and party will expect that its affiliated unions will not act as obstacles to the implementation of government policy. Clearly, this relationship between state, party, and union limits the freedom of action of the labor unions and of the workers who belong to them. At worst, it means that the unions are unwilling and even unable to defend their members against the state, or to advance the interests of the workers when those interests conflict with the interests of the state.

In considering the relationship between the state-party and the union, it should also be noted that the Mexican state has been and remains a principal employer of Mexican workers. The Mexican government controls the petroleum and petrochemical industries, much of the steel industry, and until recently it controlled the commercial aviation and telecommunications industries. The state has historically controlled many other industries as well. This means that in many cases the union leader, plant manager, and local and national political leaders all belonged to the same party organization. Clearly, this has implications for the union's ability to take independent action on behalf of its members, and for the workers who are union members to challenge their employer or their union.

Mexico's Other Unions

In addition to the "official" labor unions, there are two other important kinds of unionism in Mexico. These unions are usually referred to as "white unions" and "independent unions." White unions are employer-dominated labor organizations, usually called "company unions" in the United States. The historic center of the "white unions" is Monterrey, Nuevo Leon, where the employers promoted their own company unions, successfully fighting the inroads of the government's "official" unions.

There are two "white union" federations: 1) The National Federation of Autonomous Union Associations (FNASA), which is made up of company unions in big companies and heavy industry, and 2) The National Federation of Independent Unions (FNSI), which is made up of company unions in medium-sized and light industry. In the state of Nuevo Leon, "white unions" make up about two-thirds of the organized labor movement, while "official" unions make up the other third.[5] The Mexican central government and the PRI have come to accept and tolerate the "white unions" which are not under their control.

The other important kind of union organizations are the "independent unions," which are sometimes also referred to as the "democratic unions." Independent means independent from the CT, from the PRI and thus from the Mexican state. The largest and most important independent unions are the several university unions representing academic staff and workers at the major public universities. In addition to the university unions, there are several small labor federations. Among the most important is the Authentic Labor Front (Frente Auténtico del Trabajo—FAT), which was originally a Christian Democratic union when it was founded in the early 1960s, but is non-sectarian today. While the government has come to accept the existence of the university unions, it has not recognized such independent unions as FAT, which, like other independent unions, has usually been denied labor union registration.

Despite the existence of both the "white unions" and the "independent unions," the "official" labor unions affiliated with the CT and the PRI are by far the largest and most important labor organizations in Mexico. There have also existed at various times sectarian and political unions that were directly tied to the Catholic Church, some other religious organization, or to unofficial political parties such as the Sinarquistas (a Mexican fascist party) or the Communists. However, such sectarian or political unions are virtually non-existent, or ineffectual in the Mexico of today.

Mexican Labor Law

Mexican labor law, like much of contemporary Mexican society, is an outgrowth of the Mexican Revolution which began in 1910. In 1917, a Constituent Congress convened to adopt the Constitution, which included Article 123, a charter of labor rights. Article 123 has been called the most progressive labor law of the time anywhere in the world. It gave workers the right to organize labor unions, an implied right to bargain collective contracts, and the right to strike. It created certain minimum labor standards such as a minimum wage, overtime pay, the eight-hour day, and mandated profit sharing between management and employees. It protected women and children workers, restricted night work, banned pay in scrip and the obligation to purchase goods or services in a specified establishment, and established minimum health and safety standards.

Unfortunately for Mexican workers, Article 123 also established tripartite Boards of Conciliation and Arbitration, made up of equal numbers of employers and labor union representatives, and one government member to break a tie. These Boards were given extraordinary power to resolve industrial disputes, and thus the fate of Mexican workers was delivered into government hands. This would not bode well for democratic ideals.[6]

The underlying motivation for Article 123 was the recognition of a class struggle within society between capital and labor. The role of the Mexican state was to regulate this class struggle and keep it from getting out of hand. The state was to ensure a "balance between the factors of production." Both workers and capitalists were given the right to organize so that they could effectively negotiate to reestablish an equilibrium between the factors of production. In this scheme, the Mexican state was a neutral power, rising above both classes to regulate the struggle between them.

Mexican labor law functioned rather chaotically until 1924 when the Mexican Supreme Court of Justice ruled that the Boards of Conciliation and Arbitration were, in fact, genuine labor courts with the power to resolve individual and collective conflicts and to make binding decisions and awards. Throughout the 1920s, however, it was basically the state legislatures which drafted labor law, and state Boards of Conciliation and Arbitration which enforced it. This was the case until 1929, when reform of the Constitution was undertaken, and Section X of Article 73 and Article 123 were altered so as to deny states the right to enact labor law.

In 1931, the Mexican legislature passed the Federal Labor Law (*Ley Federal de Trabajo* or LFT) which implemented Article 123. The Federal Labor Law is the most important document in the history of Mexican labor, partially because of the rights it granted to workers, and partially for the restrictions it placed on those rights. Throughout the next 60 years, other laws were passed which generally placed even further restrictions on workers' rights.

In 1970, the 1931 LFT was replaced by the New Labor Law, which incorporated most of the Federal Labor Law of 1931 and more. Since then, there have been other alterations in labor law, complicating the situation, and the government of President Salinas de Gortari is said to be contemplating a new fundamental labor law at this time. As one might guess, this state of change in the laws led to confusion, and therefore freedom of interpretation in the courts. This freedom has not worked to the advantage of labor, as the following sections indicate.

The Denial of Legal Recognition *(El Registro)*

The Federal Labor Law of 1931 gave workers the right to form unions without first notifying the authorities, but it also stated that only those unions which had obtained legal registration from the authorities would be legally recognized. As Graciela Bensusan, an attorney and one of the foremost authorities on Mexican labor law, writes:

> In this way, registration was converted into one of the most important forms of state control over labor organization, because it was an essential document in order for the unions to acquire legal standing and, thus, to be able to exercise their collective rights.[7]

Moreover, the law established certain requirements for the formation of a union and gave the authorities the power to decide whether or not these requirements had been met. Unions were also required to inform the government periodically of any changes in their constitutions and by-laws, and of any changes in union officers. The law of 1931 also allowed for the existence of several unions in the same workplace, but granted only the union with the majority of workers the right to negotiate a collective bargaining agreement.

These regulations applied to several different categories of unions recognized by the government: trade unions, unions of particular firms, and industrial unions. Later the government also recognized national industrial unions. If these unions joined together to form federations or confederations, those organizations too were required to obtain registration if they wanted to have legal standing.

It should be pointed out that even the demand that unions be limited in their form and structure to five types is a violation of Convention 87 of the International Labor Organization, since Convention 87 provides that there shall be no government restriction on the form of union organization and no intrusion into the life of the union.[8]

The requirements for obtaining the legal registration document were not burdensome on the surface. The union merely had to give certain very basic information. Nevertheless, granting or denying registration has become one of the most powerful tools for obstructing workers from exercising their right to free association. As Bensusan explains, during the 1940s, "the obligation of communicating changes in the union leadership became much more important, and was transformed into the practice of demanding that the unions obtain the recognition of their officers by the competent authorities."[9] This change in interpretation meant that it was no longer just a question of informing the authorities, but the authorities had to *approve* of the changes in union leadership. Bensusan goes on:

> The importance of this new demand should be analyzed from this double perspective. On the one hand, without this recognition the union officials could not exercise their collective rights. On the other hand, workers whose struggles took place without the support of officials recognized by the authorities were already engaged in unlawful activities. In this way the state could choose the officials to whom it would give recognition, and they would then negotiate with the rank and file the acceptance of themselves as leaders in exchange for helping the rank and file in dealing with capital. So it can be said that this interpretation of labor law favored the consolidation of a strong union bureaucracy.[10]

It should be understood from this that the registration of a union organization is not just a simple matter of some paper work. Particularly when the union in question is an "independent" union—a union independent of the CT and the PRI—gaining recognition becomes a complicated affair. In practice, as Bensusan explains,

> When the requirements contained in the labor law are insufficient to prevent the registration of an independent organization, the authorities can expand the legal requirements at their discretion, and make it harder for the organization to fulfill them. Furthermore, if those mechanisms do not achieve the desired effect sought by the authorities, they can reject registration of the organization without any legal basis.[11]

An American student of Mexican labor law, Amy H. Goldin, wrote recently in the *Comparative Labor Law Journal* about the problem of the government denying recognition to the independent unions: "Today, independent unions are legally permitted to exist, but they are usually not recognized by the Ministry of Labor and are frequently harassed by the state because of their open opposition to party politics."[12]

Once a union is recognized, the situation does not become more open, as the union must periodically report changes in its executive committee to the Board of Conciliation and Arbitration. This process is commonly known as "taking note." This should be a routine matter of merely filing a form with a government agency. But as Bensusan said in a talk she gave in 1990 to labor activists and attorneys: "In practice, as we all know, the taking of notes on new executive committees is usually a real war and a lot of red tape that is not merely notification but rather endorsement..."[13]

For anyone who thinks the situation might have improved since the 1940s, when the consolidation of Board power really solidified, Héctor Sántos Azuela wrote in 1989:

> The union registration operates with greater intensity in the last few years as a mechanism for excluding independent unionism. Its closed and bureaucratic character, having become in these days a serious or even insurmountable obstacle to union freedom and democracy, functions with greater frequency as a highly efficient element for dividing and annihilating democratic activists.[14]

In this way the state is able to prevent independent labor organizations from becoming legal labor unions. If a union is not legal it cannot negotiate contracts or strike.

According to the Secretary of Labor, between 1982 and 1988, only two independent unions were granted registrations, one of which was the 19 of September Garment Workers Union, which only received it because it had become a national *cause celebre*.[15] It can be deduced from this small number that the Mexican labor authorities continue to use the denial of registration to deny Mexican workers their most fundamental labor union right, the right to free association and organization.

Denial of Union Contracts to Worker-Led Unions

According to Mexican labor law today, stemming from the 1931 LFT, the majority union in the workplace is the official holder of the collective contract. However, it happens that other unions may challenge the union which claims to be the holder of the collective contract. Sometimes, for example, if an independent union somehow overcomes the obstacles and is officially recognized, then the employer and the "official" unions will challenge the right of the independent union to hold the contract. In that case, the labor authorities organize an election (*recuento*—literally recount or survey of the workers) so the workers may vote to see which union is the majority and consequently the official holder of the contract.

This election is frequently subject to abuses of various sorts. The most common form of abuse is the practice by "official" unions (CTM, CROC, CROM, and others) of using goon squads, who show up on the day of election to threaten and intimidate the workers. Another form of abuse is employer supervision, which destroys the secrecy of the ballot. In one variation of this, workers are asked to vote with their time cards or company identity cards, depositing their cards in the urn of the union they favor. The "official" unions and the employer can then identify and victimize those who support independent unions or who oppose the official unions. Employers and the official unions may also mobilize management employees, union employees, or others who are not workers in the plant to support the union. The labor authorities are not vigilant in preventing these abuses, and in fact, often show complicity in ensuring the victory of the union preferred by the employer or the official union.

Employer Firing of Union Activists or Dissidents

Article 123 of the Constitution, in an attempt to provide workers with a measure of security in their employment, forbade employers from firing employees without just cause. If a worker was fired, he or she could appeal the dismissal to the Boards of Conciliation and Arbitration. If the firing was found to be unjust, then the worker could choose either to return to work or to give up his or her job and receive three months' pay. According to the law, the choice was completely the worker's.

The Federal Labor Law of 1931 changed this situation, making it the employer's option either to reinstate the worker or to pay the worker three months' wages plus damages for the inconvenience caused by the firing.[16] In practice, this has meant that an employer can at any time fire union organizers, activists, or dissidents, pay them their indemnification and damages, and be rid of them. Employers frequently remove union organizers in this manner, or, with the collusion of the union, they remove dissidents from the workplace.

Union Expulsion of Dissident Members

Also included in the Federal Labor Law of 1931 was the legalization of labor union contract clauses admitting or excluding members. Such clauses provide that when a worker has been expelled from the union, the employer shall also fire that worker. The employer is not automatically obliged to accept exclusion clauses in the contract; rather they must be negotiated by the union and the employer. According to Bensusan, in practice, the employers will only negotiate contracts containing such clauses with unions which are considered reliable, that is, which will use the exclusion clause to eliminate employees who are a problem for management, and perhaps for the union as well. She writes:

> ...exclusion clauses, originally intended to strengthen union organization, have served to guarantee for capital a labor force which is ideologically and politically disciplined. It should be taken into account that many union by-laws establish the obligation of the members of the organization to join the official party [PRI] and that their failure to do so can be considered sufficient reason for their expulsion from the union and so for the loss of their jobs as well.[17]

Jorge Durand, a labor historian and the author of *Los obreros de Río Grande*, studied the history of workers and unions at the Río Grande textile factory in the town of El Salto, Jalisco over a period of 100 years. Durand examined the relationship between the unions and the ruling party, including the use of the exclusion clause. He writes in the conclusion of his book:

> ...it seems that the exclusion clause has a capacity for coercion which goes beyond what is necessary, and on the other hand, confers a power such that it can leave [union members], above all minorities or opposition groups, without the ability to influence or reverse the process... This excessive power granted to the union officials or to the group in power, has led in practice to the implementation of union policies which can border on despotism, to the perpetuation of leaders in power, and to the growing de-politicizing of the Mexican working class.

Durand then speculates on the theoretical possibility that the exclusion clause might be used by opposition groups to take power in the union, though there is little evidence that this could happen. Durand continues:

> Nevertheless, it can be said that the advantages which the exclusion clause grants are not excessive or disproportionate if they are seen from the point of view of the state or of the private company. The power exercised by the unions has been converted into a key piece in the generalized control of the Mexican labor movement and in a mechanism regulating the class struggle.[18]

One example of how exclusion clauses are used is provided by the membership policies of the Miners and Metal Workers Union (STMMRM). Who can be excluded from the miners' union? The statutes of the STMMRM contract provide for obligatory affiliation with the official party, the PRI (Article 146, Section XXII). Those who do not join the PRI can be expelled. In addition, members of the union are forbidden "to propose or to propagate ideas foreign to the union" (Article 211, Section XXII). The union negotiates exclusion clauses in all its contracts "in order to guarantee the life and discipline of the organization" (Article 6, Section VI).[19] With these statutes it is possible to exclude members from the Miners and Metal Workers Union and/or have them fired by the employer not for their actions, but solely for their ideas.

Severance of Whole Groups of Workers

Mexican labor law provides that in the event that a firm must close, the workers who are laid off shall be provided with severance pay equal to a number of days' pay for each year worked, depending on the circumstances. The law provides that the firm may liquidate the workforce when the business has become utterly unprofitable, when there is no more material work (for example in the case of an exhausted mine), or in the event of bankruptcy. The original intent of such indemnification or severance pay seems to have been to protect the worker.

While originally intended to protect the workforce, the law has been used with increasing frequency to allow employers to rid themselves of a labor union, a contract, certain provisions of a contract, "troublemakers" among the workforce, or the entire workforce. By severing the workers and paying them off, employers distort a protection granted to the workers into a convenience for themselves.

Denial of the Right to Strike

Article 123 of the Constitution granted all workers the right to strike, providing that strikes would be considered legal when they had as their goal "establishing an equilibrium between the diverse factors of production, and harmonizing the rights of labor with those of capital." The power to resolve these conflicts was vested in the tripartite Board of Conciliation and Arbitration. When the Federal Labor Law of 1931 was enacted, more than one union often existed in a workplace. It gave the right to strike *not* to the union, but to "the coalition of workers." If a majority of the coalition of workers voted to strike, then they could do so, provided that they struck to bring equilibrium to the factors of production, to harmonize the rights of labor and capital, to win a new contract, to enforce the existing contract, to force the company to comply with the profit sharing provisions of the law, or in solidarity with some other strike that was called for legal reasons.

If the strike was called by a majority for legal reasons, then the Board of Conciliation and Arbitration would declare it "existent," that is to say, legal. If the strike was not called by a majority of the coalition of workers, or if it was not called for a legal reason, then after the strike began, the Board of Conciliation and Arbitration would declare the strike "nonexistent." The power to declare strikes legal or illegal lay with the tripartite Board.

These do not seem like unduly burdensome provisions, but over the years they were modified to put more obstacles in the way of workers. Most of these modifications involved making the strike notification process more complicated. First, beginning at the time of World War II, workers were obliged to file their strike demands with the Board before the strike. Second, before the strike broke out, they were compelled to attend the Board's conciliation sessions. Beginning about 1980, the presidents of the Boards of Conciliation and Arbitration were allowed to judge the legality or illegality of a strike on the basis of the notification process even *before* it broke out, and thus to stop the strike from ever taking place. The Boards also ceased to grant the right to strike to the "coalition of workers," but only to the officially recognized labor union which held the current collective bargaining agreement. As Bensusan writes:

> In this way only an organization which conveniently has dealt with state control by way of the registration proceedings, and with the employers by holding the contract, is able to try to carry out a strike within the framework of the law. The regulation of the collective rights of unionization, of the collective bargaining agreement and of the strike, insures without a doubt the supremacy of official unionism and constitutes a bulwark against labor insurgency.[20]

The system has been extremely effective. The Secretary of Labor reported that between 1982 and 1988 there were 78,801 strike notifications to initiate the process of taking strike action, but only 2.3 percent of those strikes were actually carried out.[21] So the right to strike is extremely limited, and in many cases really does not exist in Mexico.

There is another limitation on the right to strike which should also be noted. Article 123 of the Mexican Constitution and the Federal Labor Law of 1931 granted workers the right to strike against management. Workers legally do *not* have the right to strike against their own unions, federations, or confederations, nor against the labor authorities. There have been some work stoppages, which are in reality strikes, not against the employer but against the union or labor authorities, for example, to win the union's registration or control of the contract. But these strikes have no legal foundation and the workers who engage in them are at risk.

Special Labor Laws

While Article 123 of the Constitution granted *all* workers the right to organize unions and to strike, over the years the Mexican state created special labor laws restricting those rights in certain fields of employment. The first such law was President Lázaro Cárdenas' special order of 1937, called the Regulation of Credit Institutions and Related Organizations. Passed at the urging of the bank employers, this law denied all bank workers the right to organize, bargain collectively, or to strike.

While the law governing bank employees was significant for the limitation it imposed on those employees, it affected a relatively small number of workers. In 1938, a much broader law was enacted, more significant because it affected a larger number of workers. The Statute of Workers at the Service of the Powers of the Union established separate and different labor union rights for federal employees. Their right to strike was even more restricted, and they were required to give advance strike notice to a Court of Arbitration. Most importantly, all federal public employees were confined to one union, the Federation of Unions of Workers at the Service of the State.

In 1960, Article 123 was divided into two different parts, severing the federal employees from the general workforce even further—Part A for private sector employees and Part B for federal employees. Workers in Part B are now denied the right to negotiate a collective bargaining agreement, and can only strike in the most exceptional circumstances. The Mexican government's labor authorities have sometimes used the existence of two separate bodies of law, Parts A and B, as a way of dealing with unions they find troublesome. It has proved possible to have an unruly union previously covered by Part A declared to be in a public service sector, and therefore under the jurisdiction of Part B, eliminating its right to bargain collectively and to strike. Some Mexican jurists have argued that Part B is unconstitutional, though it has not been effectively challenged in the courts.[22] In 1963, Part B was extended to cover other public service employees as well.

The 1937 law on bank employees was revised in 1953 and again in 1972, though it remained substantially the same as the original. However, in 1982, President José López Portillo, in his last State of the Union Address (*Informe del Gobierno*), nationalized the banks and mentioned in passing that bank workers would be allowed to organize unions. Shortly thereafter, however, a constitutional reform of the Federal Labor Law was passed, creating an addition to Article 123, Part B, known as Section XIII Bis, which confined all bank workers to one "official" union, the National Federation of Bank Unions. With the re-privatization of the banks, President Carlos Salinas de Gortari put forward a change in Article 123, modifying Section XXI of Part A and Section XIII Bis of Part B, so that employees of private banks would be covered by Part A and employees of state banks would be covered by Part B. If all of this is not confusing enough, another modification of the status of bank workers occurred with the declaration on July 18, 1990 of the Law of Institutions of Credit, which regulated banks and other lending institutions. It provided that in the event of a strike, bank workers would have to keep some indispensable workplaces open, and that some necessary workers would have to continue to work. In effect, it limited the right to strike again, for percentages of the Part A workers.[23]

It is remarkable that both public bank workers and public employees must belong to the "official" unions. Under the law they may not form other labor unions, or, in the case of the bank workers, if they do, those unions are not covered by the bank workers' labor law. These laws governing public employees are extreme violations of the right to free association, more restrictive by far than the laws governing workers in the private sector.

Other public employee unions may be restricted in their freedom of association by law as well. For example, university employees are governed by a Special Division (Apartado Especial) of Chapter XVII of Title Six, Special Work of the Federal Labor Law, Article 353 N. University workers may only form unions of three types: academic personnel, administrative personnel, or mixed unions of both types. This article then forbids these workers from forming a national university workers union. This is another limitation of the right of free association, since workers are not free to associate with other workers of the same branch of the economy.[24]

Military Seizure of the Workplace

Other restrictions on the right to strike entered the law during World War II. The Law of General Routes of Communication (*Ley de Vias Generales de Comunicación*) gave the government the right to requisition or seize means of transportation, communication, and related services. The process is known as the *requisa* or government seizure of the company and workplace, usually carried out by the military and the police. Originally intended to prevent "possible sabotage provoked by foreign agents," Bensusan writes "the seizure was and continues to be used as a mechanism to avoid or at least to obstruct strikes in the public services, a right constitutionally guaranteed in Section XVIII of Article 123."

Seizure has been repeatedly used against certain groups of workers, in particular against the employees of Teléfonos de México or TELMEX, which was until recently the state-owned telephone company. Throughout the 1970s and 1980s the government used company seizures to put down strikes by telephone workers.[25] Because seizure of the workplace is usually carried out by soldiers and police, it is sometimes accompanied by violence, and always by coercion and intimidation of the workforce and the union. Over the years, various labor unions have protested the use of workplace seizure as unconstitutional and as inhibiting the action of the union and the workers. In 1979, the university workers' unions placed the following advertisement in the Mexico papers to protest the use of seizure against the telephone workers:

> The seizure of the workplace is an illegal and arbitrary act which is contrary to the basic legal arrangements of the country and which is used against the workers. Its frequent use in the last months (against communications workers, and among them, now against the telephone workers) forces us to think about the frequent curtailment of action which workers organizations have encountered in our country. It is said that the use of seizure seeks to preserve the public interest. It is not recognized that it is in even greater interest to defend union rights and to insure that the workers (that is to say, the people of Mexico, in whose name the seizure is applied) have just and appropriate wages.[26]

Protection Contracts:
Behind the Backs of the Workers

As a result of the various limitations put on workers' right to free association and collective action, there has been a loss of control over the process of contract negotiation. In particular, the labor authorities' practice of awarding the registration and official control of the contract only to union officials who are accountable to the government and the employer, means that the workers may have little say in the contract. The workers may not even be informed that there is a contract, which in many cases exists solely to protect the employer from organization by a more representative union. In Mexico, this kind of labor union contract is a veritable institution known as the "protection contract."

Attorney Arturo Alcalde Justiniani, an authority on Mexican labor law, explains this institution:

> The protection contract is that which is arranged behind the backs of the workers between the union and the employer, and then filed with the Board of Conciliation and Arbitration. By virtue of this filing, any other union organization is impeded from attempting to sign a union contract, given that one is already signed and filed.[27]

In a more recent essay, Alcalde writes:

> In facing their employer, workers are habitually beginning their relations in the shadow of a collective contract, or of general conditions of employment with which they never had any involvement. The practice of protection contracts, a very Mexican institution, allows a make believe process by which collective contracts or general conditions of employment are arrived at, without the knowledge or the desire of the workers, either because the contract was already worked out before the plant began operations, or because it was written without the knowledge of the workers...[28]

Another attorney, Manuel Fuentes, said recently:

> We have known many cases in which workers were not even aware that they were affiliated with a union. Nor did they know that they were subject to a collective labor contract, but they are. This happens above all in the small firms and in some medium-sized ones. Workers in plants where there are 30 or 40 people are not aware that they belong to a certain union. These so-called collective contracts are contracts of adherence; those who really choose the unions, and who decide with whom the collective labor contracts ought to be, are the owners.[29]

In January 1991, Ernesto Salcido Villareal, a member of the staff of the CT who acts as a consultant to "official" unions such as the CTM and CROC, and whose specialty is negotiation of labor union contracts, particularly in the auto industry, stated in an interview that "the majority of labor union contracts are protection contracts."[30] Another source estimates that 75 percent of the labor agreements in the Federal District—one of the largest and most important centers of employment and unions in the country—are protection contracts.[31]

Protection contracts are a business. Such contracts are sold by union officials from the "official" unions of the CTM, CROC,

CROM, and other government labor organizations.[32] Most of the officials of these unions never worked in the trade or industry which they represent, and were never elected by the workers they supposedly represent. These unions hold no meetings and engage in no activities other than the selling of such contracts. Salcido Villareal further stated that it is quite common for employers, both Mexican and foreign, to pay off union officials. These practices are partly responsible for what Salcido Villareal describes as the Mafia or gangster character of large parts of the CTM in Mexico. He believes that all of the very large Section 4 of the CTM in Mexico City is a gangster organization.[33]

Pattern Contracts: Over the Heads of the Workers

There is another kind of contract which excludes workers. In Mexico there exists a "law contract" which covers all of the workers in a particular industry. It is a kind of master contract or pattern agreement covering many plants in various parts of the country, and sometimes tens of thousands of workers. At present, Mexico has 19 law contracts in effect, many in the textile industry, others in the sugar industry, the alcohol and related industries, the rubber processing industry, and the radio and television industries.

In order for a "law contract" to be negotiated, it must have the approval of two-thirds of the workers' union representatives and one-half of the employers' representatives. As Manuel Fuentes writes, "it is important to know that the negotiation of the law contracts is a negotiation between the leaders only, in which a few decide what is going to happen to the many that comprise an entire branch of a specific industry."[34] Since Mexican labor unions are not representative of the workers, then obviously the representatives who negotiate these law contracts are even less representative.

How the Boards of Conciliation and Arbitration Actually Function

More important than the laws themselves is the enforcement of those laws by the legal system. To be effective, a legal system must be accessible to those who need it, responsive and responsible to all parties who participate in it, and efficient and speedy in carrying out its business. As the adage has it, "Justice delayed is justice denied." The Mexican labor law system is extremely responsive to the PRI and its official unions, but gives no ear, eye, or hand to the ordinary worker. Workers who have joined together in unofficial unions essentially have no recourse to justice.

At present, the Boards of Conciliation and Arbitration act as part of the repressive machinery which leads to the persecution of workers who stand up for their rights. The government members of the Boards are appointed by the executive branch of government—either the federal government, government of the Federal District, or the state governments—and virtually all are loyal members of the PRI. The employer members are appointed by the employers. The union members are appointed by the unions (i.e. the "official" unions such as the CTM, the CROC, or the CROM). As it stands now, in insignificant cases the members vote in the interest of the group which appointed them. In politically important cases, the PRI-government attempts to make all members vote as the local executive authority wants.

As attorney Ana María Conesa Ruiz writes:

> In fact, the importance of these posts is almost null in matters of political importance, given that in those cases they [the members of the Board] act, by definition, as executors of the presidents of the Boards, or of the Secretary of Labor himself. Otherwise, they are posts which have the potential to bring "economic benefits" by way of negotiations with the parties involved in the dispute, or which serve as steps in one's personal career. Their decisions, in cases where they can make decisions, are in general, for sale to the highest bidder.[35]

Typically, individual workers or independent unions who present cases before the Board of Conciliation which challenge the employer or the official union can expect either that their case will be lost quickly, or that it will be a long, drawn out affair which exhausts their resources, their patience, and their desire to fight for their rights. However, when an "official" union comes to the Board, its affairs are handled as rapidly as its political influence demands.

Manuel Fuentes, a labor lawyer in Mexico City, represented the workers at Ford Motor Company who attempted to organize a democratic movement within a CTM union. With regard to the Board of Conciliation and Arbitration's actions on his case, he said:

> As I see it, the Board of Conciliation and Arbitration is kind of a freezer where labor rights arrive and are frozen. The process is drawn out and rights cannot be exercised. Theoretically this is a court, and when there is violation of the law on the part of the employer, the court should serve to make the employer comply with the law. I say—and I can tell you that I have 14 years experience as a lawyer for workers—the Board of Conciliation and Arbitration has officials who take orders, who do not follow the law, especially when it has to do with cases of this kind. I can say that there are times

when they do what they should, but not in conflicts involving unions and politics. The law is useless in those cases.[36]

Obviously, those cases involving the unions and politics are the most important, for they are the cases where the right to freedom of association is really in question.

Another attorney, Manuel García Espinoza, the general secretary of the Centro Obrero of Monterrey, Nuevo Leon, said of the Board in early 1991:

> With regard to the Board of Conciliation, for example if one is attempting to legally register a union, they speak to the employer, tell him that there are problems, and this is when the employer begins to repress people, when the firing begins, and when they begin to harass and threaten people. In the recent case of the workers at Estructuras Metálicas, just as at other important plants where workers threw themselves into a fight for a democratic and independent union organization, they preferred to fire everybody... So we go to the Collegial Courts to demand an injunction, which is the last resort that we have as workers when the Board of Conciliation declares against us. Whether it is an individual or a collective demand, or the registration of the union, we have to turn to an injunction; perhaps 85 percent of the time, they rule in favor of the workers. The government says "you're right, return to continue the proceedings," and so we go back to the Board, and the company continues firing workers.[37]

It is a significant triumph that the courts are willing to grant injunctions in favor of the workers, against the decisions of the Boards of Conciliation and Arbitration. However, because there is no other recourse but to return to those same Boards, ultimately justice is not served.

Extra-legal State Involvement in the Union

In addition to the state labor authorities who are legally charged with worker and labor union matters—the Secretary of Labor and the Boards of Conciliation and Arbitration—other state organizations frequently become involved as well. Most often the government agencies that become involved in union matters are the office of the President of Mexico, the Secretary of the Interior, and the Secretary of Public Finance. Regents of the Federal District, governors of states, and mayors of cities and towns may all become involved in labor conflicts as well. It is not uncommon for these extra-legal interventions of powerful political figures to take the dispute completely outside the realm of labor law. It would be a mistake to see these interventions as good-will attempts at mediation, as they are sometimes portrayed. In reality, they are politically motivated intrusions. The Modelo strike, discussed in detail in Chapter 4, is a particularly good example of this.

Beyond strike intervention, some of these government agencies, such as Secretary of the Interior, are well known to maintain agents who act as labor spies or *agents provocateurs* within the unions. Various government officials organize and form caucuses or slates within unions and run them in union elections. Sometimes local political leaders simply provide gangsters to threaten and intimidate workers. All of these practices mean that intervention of the state-party in the affairs of the unions is pervasive. Case studies of various disputes, the Ford strike in particular, will show how destructive this kind of intervention can be.

Employers Who Defy the Law

It should at least be stated in passing that many employers simply ignore provisions of the Federal Labor Law. The most commonly ignored provisions are those made for paid vacations, payment of an annual Christmas bonus, and payment of profit sharing dividends. These provisions of the law are most commonly ignored in small companies. Every December and January the newspapers are full of stories of employers who refused to pay a Christmas bonus. Workers who have been cheated out of their vacation, bonus, or profit sharing benefits often file charges at labor courts which, in fact, sometimes assist the workers in satisfactorily settling the matter. In November and December, the Secretary of Labor places advertisements throughout the city, calling upon workers to demand their Christmas bonus. But, given the general nature of labor relations, many workers will not take their just grievances to the labor courts for fear of victimization.

The Underground Economy

Mexico's underground or informal economy, businesses of all sorts which operate outside the law, has grown enormously in the 1980s. These businesses are not licensed, do not pay taxes, and do not pay into the social programs for workers such as IMSS (the national health program) or INFONAVIT (the government's workers' housing program). Neither do these underground businesses or "clandestine" companies, as they are sometimes called, respect labor laws.

While many of those in the underground economy are simply self-employed peddlers, others set up vending stalls or open small shops which actually engage in the assembly or manufacture of a product. Even though most are small operations, they do employ workers. In some branches of the economy, such as the garment industry, there are thousands of workers who, because they work in a legal "twilight zone," have no labor rights whatsoever.[38]

Recent Developments

Because of the government-controlled, bureaucratic, and corrupt character of the "official" labor unions, there have been consistent attempts by workers to find alternatives to them. Sometimes this has taken the form of attempts to overturn the leadership and democratize the "official" unions. At other times, the search for alternatives has taken the form of movements for independent unions. Most recently, the struggle has taken the form of unofficial shop committees which negotiate directly with the employers. As Graciela Bensusan writes, "there is growing recognition in fact, of negotiating committees which exist outside of the [union's] statutes and effectively represent the interests of the workers."[39] Such committees, however, are not yet significant enough to represent an alternative or counterweight to the state-controlled unions.

A second development taking place is the promotion, by employers, of new kinds of worker organizations such as "quality circles," "team concepts," and other "cooperative or joint programs." Since these programs are all employer-promoted, employer-financed, and almost entirely employer-controlled, they amount to a new form of company unionism, even where they appear within a unionized setting. Frequently, the word "cooperation" is used in discussing these programs; however, given the nature of the union, it is cooperation between the employer and government-controlled unions. The rank and file worker has little or nothing to say about such programs. While these programs may in the long run change the nature of Mexican labor relations by giving the employer more control, and reducing the state's control, they have not so far succeeded in doing so. Consequently, despite these new developments, the fundamental form of Mexican labor unionism remains in place: state-controlled unions whose continued existence is ensured by the government's labor boards.

Finally, the government has talked in the last two years about the possibility of carrying out a thorough reform of the nation's labor law. The possibility of labor law reform has led various organizations (unions, lawyers, employers' associations, political parties) to present alternative proposals for a new legal system. For 1991 at least, changes in labor law have been put on hold.

Conclusion

In 1950, Mexico signed Convention 87 of the ILO which provides that workers shall have the right to freely join or form unions of their choice. This ILO Convention calls upon states to respect the rights of all workers without distinction, with or without previous authorization to form or join a labor organization, and at their own discretion. Article III of that Convention specifies that all public authorities should abstain from any intervention in union activity which limits or harms workers' rights. Workers should be legally free to write their own statutes, elect their own representatives, organize their own administrations, and carry out their own activities, including their plan of action. As Alcalde writes:

> Despite the fact that this is the existing law in our country, Convention 87...is not taken into account in practice. Since the Right of Association is limited in various ways, from the registration required for legal standing, to the periodic acceptance of union officials, which is increasingly subject to administrative requirements, there is clear intent towards extra-union political control. With regard to state workers, the failure to comply with this Convention is evident, given that while Part A of Constitutional Article 123 legally guarantees union freedom, Part B and local labor legislation limit this freedom, by not allowing unions in certain branches of the economy, and by legally recognizing a certain federation with its name and surname in the law itself.[40]

The Mexican institutions which deal with labor are organized to ensure control by the official party and its unions, in an embrace that strangles all freedom or initiative. Mexican labor law and the institutions which administer it systematically deny workers their fundamental rights to free association, to labor union organization, to internal union democracy, and to carry out their own programs. Legally speaking, it is a system not for justice, but for the suppression of labor rights.

Chapter Three

The Historical Background of Mexican Labor

Existing limitations on labor unions and worker rights can only be concretely understood as a product of Mexico's particular history. Dating back to the revolution of 1910, workers have played a large and often tragic role in Mexico's political, social, and industrial development. All along the road to modernization, the Mexican government embraced labor with such a controlling grip that it squelched any activities which would allow workers a democratic voice in determining their relations with both their employers and the state.

The Mexican Revolution and the Labor Movement

Mexican workers' organizations first appear in the middle of the 19th century, when a variety of educational societies, mutual aid organizations, labor unions, and political parties were being formed. Many of these organizations were inspired by anarchist and socialist ideas imported from Europe. By the end of the 19th century, however, labor organizations in Mexico had developed their own identity, and were functioning as a major political force. Persistent repression during the dictatorship of Porfirio Díaz, who ruled from 1876 to 1910, could not stop labor union development, or the upcoming revolution.

The Mexican labor movement first played its political hand in the revolutionary movement to overthrow Díaz's dictatorship. The most significant revolutionary organization, the anarchist Mexican Liberal Party (PLM) of Ricardo Flores Magón, oriented its activities towards workers and organized unions as part of its movement. The PLM published manifestos on workers' rights which would have an important impact on future labor legislation. In 1906, in an attempt to detonate a revolution against Díaz, the PLM organized strikes at the Cananea Copper Company and at the Río Blanco textile mill. While the strikes were successfully put down by the government and failed to set off the revolution for which the PLM

61

leaders had hoped, the PLM unions and strikes established the workers' movement as an important participant in Mexico's political development.[1]

When the revolution finally broke out in 1910, its leaders badly needed the support of the working class and the unions. Between 1910 and 1920, the most important national center of labor organization was the anarchist labor movement's House of the World Worker (Casa del Obrero Mundial, hereafter Casa) with its center in Mexico City. To win support from the organized labor movement, President Carranza, leader of the Constitutionalist forces, signed a decree on December 12, 1914 recognizing the rights of the labor movement, and designating Casa as the organization of the working class.

A few months later, on February 17, 1915, the Constitutionalist faction signed an actual agreement with Casa at a meeting in the port of Veracruz. The pact provided that in exchange for the Constitutionalist government's promise to pass labor laws, the Casa would form "red" worker battalions, along the lines of the Russian revolutionary Red Army, to fight with the Constitutionalist armies, and they would carry out propaganda activities in the working class to win its support.[2] The pact of Veracruz between the Constitutionalists and Casa is the origin of what Mexican union leaders call the "historic relationship between the working class and the state."

The Constitution of 1917 and Article 123

To legitimate its rule, Carranza's government convened a Constituent Congress to reform the Constitution of 1857. The Congress met between December 31, 1916 and January 31, 1917 and, rather than revising the old Constitution, finally wrote an entirely new one. Included in the Constitution of 1917 was Article 123 establishing labor rights. Adopted under pressure from the anarcho-syndicalist labor movement, and with support from peasant agrarian reformers and revolutionary troops in the field, Article 123 is often said to be the most advanced charter of labor rights of its time in any country in the world. Article 123 gave workers the right to organize, strike, and boycott; it guaranteed a minimum wage and overtime pay; it established the eight-hour day; and it decreed that workers must share in the profits of industry. It included limits on night work, established protection for women and children workers, banned wage payment in company scrip and the company store, and set health and safety standards. It also required employers to pay workers for wages lost during strikes.

At the same time that Article 123 promoted labor rights on such broad issues, it also included a legislative loophole that would undermine any real power the labor movement had; it established the state as the supreme arbiter of labor conflicts through the Boards of Conciliation and Arbitration. These tripartite Boards were made up of equal numbers of representatives from management and labor, but gave the government one member and the tie-breaking vote. As one of the leading historians of the Mexican labor movement in this period wrote, these Boards were "an imposition from above" that "weakened the combativity of labor."[3] While the state appeared to be a neutral arbiter, in fact it had all the power. The Boards of Conciliation and Arbitration had the power to declare strikes legal or illegal, and through this to influence the outcome on issues such as strike-pay following a strike, or even whether issues would be negotiated at all. The fate of the workers thus rested in the Boards' hands.

The First "Official" Union: The CROM of Morones (1918-28)

Adoption of the Constitution of 1917, with Article 123 regulating labor relations, created the legal framework for the post-revolutionary labor movement. While labor unions continued to espouse anarchist or socialist views, it was during the next decade that the labor movement divided into two factions, one pro-government and one independent. The pro-government labor movement, founded at a labor conference on May 1, 1918 in Saltillo, took the name Regional Confederation of Mexican Workers (CROM), and was led by General Secretary Luis N. Morones. The independent union movement, first known as the Great Central Body of Workers, was founded on November 7, 1918, but in 1921 changed its name to the General Confederation of Workers (CGT). At this time, sections of the anarchist left split off to form the Mexican section of the Industrial Workers of the World (IWW) and the Mexican Communist Party (PCM). Between 1918 and 1925 a struggle for domination of the labor movement was waged between these forces.

The CROM, led by Morones, entered into an alliance first with Mexican President Alvaro Obregón, and then with his successor Elías Plutarco Calles. Morones depended upon the government for support for his union federation, and the government came to depend upon the CROM and its political organization, the Labor Party (PL), for a popular base of legitimacy. With the support of the government in the Boards of Conciliation and Arbitration, by 1925 the CROM had become the dominant labor organization. The CROM continued to receive support from the Obregón-Calles governments until about 1928 when a falling out occurred over a murderous turn of events.[4]

The Second "Official" Union:
The CTM of Fidel Velázquez (1935-1991)

During the late 1920s and early 1930s, Mexico fell into severe political and economic crisis. In response, a Roman Catholic uprising known as the Cristero Rebellion broke out against the state, and plunged parts of the country into renewed civil war. Alvaro Obregón was assassinated on July 17, 1928, the eve of his re-election to the Mexican presidency, by a Cristero fanatic. Morones, though never charged, was accused of being the "intellectual author" of the assassination, and the new government of Portes Gil (controlled from behind the scene by Calles) withdrew support from the CROM. These events were followed by the Crash of 1929 and the beginning of the Great Depression, which devastated Mexican industry and commerce. This combination of economic and political crises led to the crumbling of the CROM and to the appearance of new labor organizations.

In 1932, one of the leaders of the disintegrating CROM, Vicente Lombardo Toledano, pulled his unions out of the CROM to form a new federation called the General Confederation of Workers and Peasants of Mexico (CGOCM). Several other new union organizations appeared on the scene as well, one of which would become particularly important, led by Fidel Velázquez. Meanwhile a split developed in the ruling National Revolutionary Party (PRN, today the PRI) between Calles, former president and power-behind-the-throne, and the PRN's newly elected president, Lázaro Cárdenas. In the summer of 1935, Calles launched a verbal attack on Cárdenas which was clearly intended as a call to arms to overthrow the Cárdenas government. In response, the unions of Lombardo Toledano, Fidel Velázquez, the Communist Party, and other union federations formed the Committee of Proletarian Defense to support Cárdenas against Calles. With support from the unions, Cárdenas succeeded in defeating Calles politically and established a new and powerful connection between the state, the ruling party, and the unions.

The unions which had come together to defend Cárdenas' government now merged, and on February 24, 1936 they formed the Confederation of Mexican Workers (CTM). Two years later when Cárdenas reorganized and renamed the ruling party, now calling it the Party of the Mexican Revolution, the CTM, the CROM, the CGT, and the electrical workers union became the "labor sector" of the ruling party. The CTM had by then emerged as the dominant labor organization. Fifty-five years later, it still is, with Fidel Velázquez, now more than 90 years old, remaining its head.[5]

The Institutionalization
of the Mexican Labor Movement (1938-1946)

In the calm after the storm, President Cárdenas, with the support of Lombardo and Velázquez, began the process of institutionalizing the mechanisms of state-party control over the labor unions. His first concern was to keep the new and powerful CTM from organizing the peasantry and the public employees, fearing that that would make the labor organizations too powerful to control. The President forbade the CTM or other unions from organizing peasants, and on August 28, 1938 he created the National Peasant Confederation (CNC) as the "peasant sector" of the ruling party. Likewise, on December 5, 1938, he created a separate labor federation for public employees called the Federation of Unions of Workers at the Service of the State (FSTSE), which also became a part of the ruling party. Thus the party controlled all labor organizations, but kept them separated from each other. When the ruling party was reorganized on January 18, 1946 as the Institutional Revolutionary Party (PRI), this relationship was maintained.

Meanwhile other developments contributed to the subordination of the labor movement to state control. The outbreak of World War II led the CTM, in June 1942, to propose a labor-management pact to win the war, which included a no-strike pledge. It was not until April 1945 that the pact was signed by the CTM and other labor federations with representatives of the National Chamber of Industry and the National Chamber of Manufacturing Industry, and the final agreement did not contain the no-strike pledge. Still the very signing of a labor-management pact indicated the willingness of Mexican labor to cooperate with management and the government in the post-war period.

Equally influential in establishing state control of labor was the creation of the Mexican Institute of Social Security (IMSS) in 1942, which went into operation in 1943. This national health program was overseen by a tripartite board made up of equal numbers of union, industry, and government members. While the creation of the IMSS national health system was an important social benefit, the tripartite board that governed IMSS also served as another important means of drawing the unions into an institutional relationship with both employers and the government.

The *Charros:*
Bureaucratization and Corruption (1947-57)

With the outbreak of the Cold War in 1947-48, the recently institutionalized Mexican labor unions were further deformed by their transformation into huge bureaucracies with corrupt leadership. The process may be said to have started with the 33rd National Council Meeting of the CTM in January 1948, at which time the council voted to exclude Communists from the union. After the Communists were ousted, other leftists and union activists were purged as well. Union dissidents or oppositionists could be driven from the union simply with allegations of Communist Party membership, Communist sympathies, or Communist beliefs. The leader of the movement to expel the Communists from the union was Fidel Velázquez, who had risen to become the dominant figure in the CTM, and who from that point forward was also the PRI's chosen leader of the union movement.

When, during the late 1940s, several other labor union leaders began to organize a new federation to rival the CTM, the government moved swiftly and violently to impose new leadership on several important unions. The first was the railroad workers' union (STFRM). On October 14, 1948, the government, using the police and the military, forced the union to name a new General Secretary, Jesús Díaz de Leon, better known as *"El Charro"* because he wore fancy cowboy or dude *(charro)* clothes.[6] In December 1949, the government carried out a similar process in the petroleum workers union, coercing the union to name as its head a corrupt official named Gustavo Roldán Vargas. In May 1950, the government imposed Jesús Carrasco on the Miners and Metal Workers Union (SNTMMSRM).[7]

With the success of these impositions, the government became confident of the effectiveness of this tactic and adopted it with increasing regularity in the years that followed. The government continued to use the Mexican Army, the police, the Secretariat of Labor, the Ministry of the Interior, and the Boards of Conciliation and Arbitration to illegally impose new leadership on the unions. Frequently, the government organized bogus conventions made up of phony delegates, with policemen and Labor Department officials posing as union members. Often these officials were corrupt gangster figures who engaged in job selling, the misappropriation of union funds, and other such activities. The government's main criterion for choosing the union officials that it imposed violently and undemocratically on the "official" unions, was that they be loyal to the PRI. The name *charro,* used by workers and the public to describe the leadership of the Mexican labor movement to this day, carries this connotation of union leaders who are not only bureaucratically minded and corrupt, but also committed to violence and dependent upon government use of force for their positions.

This new corrupt and dependent union leadership naturally became the union representation to the government's tripartite labor tribunals, the Mexican Institute of Social Security and the Boards of Conciliation and Arbitration. These Boards had the power to grant or deny labor union registration and to declare strikes legal or illegal. The imposition of the *charros* on the unions completed the government's control over the mechanisms for representing worker interests.

By 1950, Mexican labor unions had congealed into their present state. They are institutional unions incorporated into the state's governing apparatus, through representation on the tripartite organizations such as the Boards of Conciliation and Arbitration and IMSS. They are also directly affiliated with the party as its "labor sector." Most "official" union leaders owe their positions of power and influence to the state, which may have used the army and the police to put them in power, and which certainly used the Secretary of Labor's office and the Boards of Conciliation and Arbitration to ratify their legitimacy in office.

The Use of Massive Military and Police Force

One characteristic response of the Mexican government to movements for union democracy and independence from the ruling party which have sprung up since the successful subjugation of the unions has been the use of massive military and police force. Such use of coercion goes beyond a "chilling effect," as labor lawyers sometimes say; it freezes labor union activity for years and sometimes for decades. In order to understand the behavior of the Mexican labor movement today, it is important to know that on several occasions in the past, workers' movements have been suppressed by the police and the army, union leaders have been arrested, convicted, and jailed for "political" crimes, and this show of force has generally been accompanied by the firing of a large number of workers. It is only with the knowledge that violent suppression is the likely consequence of dissent, that the reticence of some Mexican workers to participate in unions can be fully understood. Such government repression continues, as can be seen in the use of troops in 1989 and 1990 against the Petroleum Workers Union and the Cananea Copper Company strike, as well as government complicity in the CTM thuggery at the Ford workers' strike.

An analysis of three separate occurrences over several decades—the Nueva Rosita strike of 1950, the railroad workers' strike of 1959, and the electrical workers' movement of 1976—will illustrate the consequences for workers of real union reform activity.

Nueva Rosita (1950)

In 1950, the Nueva Rosita mine was owned by the American Smelting and Refining Company (ASARCO), a U.S. corporation that had been operating in Mexico since 1916, and that in 1950 controlled about 65 percent of all mining firms in Mexico. ASARCO and its subsidiaries, such as Carboníferas Sabinas and Mexican Zinc, were the dominant economic power in much of Mexico. In Spring 1950, the contract between the Nueva Rosita mine and Local 14 was up for renegotiation. The 5,800 union miners at Nueva Rosita wanted a wage increase, better mine safety, recognition of occupational illnesses, improved benefits, more days off, construction of roads between the mine and local towns, construction of housing, and they wanted the company to create a farm.

The government, anxious to establish and maintain control over the miners' unions, had staged a phony convention of the Miners and Metalworkers Union in May 1950, putting in place a leader named Jesús Carrasco, and barring from participation the elected leadership of Local 14 and other reform-minded locals. These locals then held their own convention to form a new dissident union, the National Miners Union.

After the workers at Nueva Rosita failed in their attempts to negotiate an agreement, a strike was called on June 12, 1950. The next day, the local Board of Conciliation and Arbitration declared the strike illegal. A few days later the company and the union signed an agreement which included only a few of the miners' demands. However, a problem arose when ASARCO subsequently refused to recognize or deal with the union officials anymore, making it impossible to implement the new agreement. The Nueva Rosita miners warned the company in September that if their union was not recognized, they would strike again. A month later on October 16, 1950, the strike began.

The company used a variety of tactics to deal with the recalcitrant workers. Economic pressure was used. Of course, the miners had no income, and most had no savings, so they were without money for basic necessities. The utility companies then cut off gas and electricity to the miners' homes, and the Nueva Rosita Chamber of Commerce forbade local merchants from selling them food.

The government then took actions against the union. The government seized the union's funds, closed the local consumers' cooperative, and closed the local medical clinic. Finally, the army occupied the town and established martial law; soldiers with machine guns patrolled the streets; meetings were forbidden; residents were registered and interrogated. Strike leaders José Díaz and José Alvarado were arrested in Nueva Rosita and taken to unknown locations. As one Mexican labor historian wrote, Nueva Rosita "was turned into an enormous concentration camp."[8]

In the meantime, ASARCO brought in scabs to operate the mine. Gradually the solidarity of the miners broke down and many returned to work. Nevertheless, on January 17, 1951, the strikers decided they would march 800 miles to Mexico City to ask for the help of President Miguel Alemán. A group of 4,000 men, 100 women, and 30 children left Nueva Rosita on January 20 and began the 800-mile, 50-day trek. The governors of Coahuila, Nuevo Leon, and Tamaulipas called President Miguel Alemán and urged him to reach a reasonable agreement with the strikers. However, when they reached Mexico City on March 9, 1951, the President refused to meet with them, and some of the strikers were beaten by the police and arrested.

Finally, a special government commission ordered the company to rehire 1,000 strikers and others as jobs became available. The commission also offered land to miners who wanted to become farmers, and government jobs to others who were qualified. The government provided a train to take the strikers home. In the end, only about 800 were rehired, while the rest who were blacklisted were forced to emigrate to other mining areas or the United States.[9]

The government's role in squelching the Nueva Rosita strike was part of a campaign of violent repression of labor unions conducted between 1948 and 1950, in response to the demands of U.S. employers in key industries such as mining, whose investment was necessary for Mexico's industrialization policy to succeed. The attack was motivated in part by a desire to crush independent forces in the Miners and Metal Workers Union and in the independent National Miners Union. However, the implications of the strike's failure went far beyond the town of Nueva Rosita; as the spirit of the miners was broken, an example was set. The use of massive military and police power in the mining town sent a clear message to others who considered collective action a viable means of expression.

The Railroad Workers' Strike of 1959

As was described previously, the government had imposed the leadership of General Secretary Jesús Díaz de Leon, the original *charro*, on the railroad workers. Under Díaz de Leon, the union had become a gangsterized organization, where paramilitary groups and union goons carried out a reign of terror among the rank and file. Nevertheless, falling real wages forced the railroad workers to organize and demand improvements. In 1958, rank and file workers pressured the union to convene a Grand Commission for a General Salary Increase. However, when General Secretary Samuel Ortega Hernández found that the members of the Commission were prepared to oppose the union leadership, he called upon the government to send in the police and army and then dismissed the Commission without taking action on its recommendations.

During the course of these events, Demetrio Vallejo, a rank and file activist in Railroad Workers' (STFRM) Local 13 of Matías Romero, Oaxaca, emerged as the preeminent leader of the Commission, and subsequently of the union reform movement and the strike. Local 13 issued a call for a wage increase of 350 pesos a month, and this became known as the "Plan of the Southeast." This demand won the support of tens of thousands of railroad workers, though it was opposed by Ortega Hernández, head of the union.

Vallejo and the other leaders of the rank and file movement decided to implement a series of escalating strikes against selected railroads. The first, lasting two hours, was called against the Mexican National Railroad on June 26, 1958; 60,000 railroad workers responded, shutting down the system. The second strike on June 27 lasted four hours. The third strike on June 28 lasted six hours and was joined by petroleum workers, teachers, and students. At that point, President Ruiz Cortines intervened in the strike, proposing a wage increase of 215 pesos per month. The Commission voted to accept the president's proposal.

Following this victory, the Railroad Workers' Union met in its Sixth Extraordinary General Union Convention on July 12, 1958. Demetrio Vallejo was elected General Secretary of the union. However, the Secretary of Labor and the company both refused to recognize the new leadership. The convention then voted on July 23, 1958, that if its committee was not recognized, it would strike the railroads on July 26, 1958. At that point the Ministry of the Interior intervened, demanding that the previous union leaders be reinstated, which would have contravened the will of the elected union convention.

Consequently, the union struck on July 31, 1958 for two hours. Meanwhile, the Electrical Workers Union (SME) and some members of the teachers union (SNTE) agreed to support the railroad workers. On August 3, 1958, the government sent in the police and soldiers to seize Railroad Workers' Union halls in various cities. Vallejo and other leaders who had escaped arrest called for a strike by Mexico City locals, which in a few hours became a general strike of the entire Mexican railroad system. The government, in an attempt to end the strike, offered the workers a bonus and a raise if they would return to work, but they refused to do so. Union workers not only struck, but they and their families also blocked trains when others attempted to run them. The government was forced to negotiate and, on August 6, 1958, agreed to hold new elections.

One hundred thousand workers were eligible to vote, and about 60,000 actually voted. The final vote is recorded as having been 59,749 for Vallejo to 9 for the government's candidate. In December 1958, General Secretary Vallejo presented the government with a proposal to restructure the state-owned Mexican National Railroad system to make it more profitable, suggesting that rates be raised for the U.S.-owned mining and metal companies which used the railroad. At the same time, the union leadership proposed wage increases for workers at the National Railroad, and at several smaller lines. The union strategy was to threaten a general strike of the industry as each contract came up. No progress was made in negotiations, and on February 25, 1959, the Railroad Workers' Union struck the Mexican railroads over the issue of the National Railroad contract.

The Federal Board of Conciliation and Arbitration immediately declared the strike illegal. The union sought an injunction, but it was denied. The government deployed police and soldiers to the railroad yards and terminals. The union officially called off the strike, but unofficially it continued the work stoppage. Vallejo contacted Mexican President López Mateos, who offered a wage increase of 16.66 percent. The union accepted and a contract was signed. Meanwhile, negotiations continued over contracts at the smaller lines, and on March 7, 1959, the union threatened a general railroad strike if its demands were not met. In retaliation for the strike threat, the National Railroad, which had previously settled, reneged on the 16.66 percent settlement.

In response to this, and to the refusal of the other lines to meet the union's demands, the Railroad Workers' Union called a general strike on March 25, 1959. However, President López Mateos declared state seizure of the industry and sent the military to take over all railroad installations and all Railroad Workers' Union halls. Massive and brutal repression by the army led to the killing of several workers. At the same time, the railroad companies fired approximately 10,000 workers from their jobs. The government arrested many railroad worker activists, and claimed it held 800 prisoners, 150 of whom it accused of being communist agitators. A recent historian says that a total of 3,039 people were arrested of whom 2,600 were released conditionally.

Eventually, about 500 workers were tried. The strike leaders (Valentín Campa, Dionisio Encina, Alberto Lumbreras, González Godínez, and Miguel Aroche Parra) received sentences of 11 years. Demetrio Vallejo was sentenced to 11 years and four months, plus five years for another offense.[10]

The Electrical Workers' Movement (1976)

In the early 1970s, Mexico had three electrical workers' unions. The oldest was SME, representing workers employed by the Light and Power Company in Mexico City, the Federal District, and the states surrounding the Valley of Mexico. The second, SNE, represented some employees of the Federal Electrical Commission in the rest of Mexico, and the third, STERM, was the result of the fusion of several smaller electrical workers' unions, and also represented some employees of the Federal Electrical Commission. In addition to these main bodies of representation, each union represented other miscellaneous electrical workers in various companies and geographical areas of Mexico.

STERM was headed by Rafael Galván, a long-time labor leader, former senator, and one of the important founding figures of the Congress of Labor (CT). Galván's STERM was fast becoming independent, raising the slogan of democracy in the unions, and becoming increasingly militant. In an attempt to thwart the aims of STERM, the government gave aid to SNE, which was headed by Francisco Pérez Ríos. In 1971, the Board of Conciliation and Arbitration ruled that SNE—and not SME or STERM—had the right to represent electrical workers. In 1972, SNE union members attempted to seize by force the Franke electrical plant in Gómez Palacios, Durango, and drive STERM members out of the workplace. The Federal Electrical Commission (CFE), one of the largest and most important employers, attempted to bribe workers to leave STERM and join SNE. The CT, controlled by Fidel Velázquez, expelled STERM.

To strengthen their position Galván and STERM began to mobilize the union's membership and to reach outside the union for support. STERM organized a "First Day for Union Democracy" in 1972, in alliance with the radical Railroad Workers Union Movement (MSF). Tens of thousands of workers in cities across Mexico participated in demonstrations demanding union democracy. STERM followed up the demonstrations by organizing a Struggle Committee for Union Democracy with its union allies, and created a Committee for Popular Insurgency to mobilize the urban poor and the peasantry. Nevertheless, despite this mobilization and outreach, Galván and his union felt they had to accept a merger of STERM and SNE proposed by President Luis Echeverría. The new union formed on September 27, 1972 and took the name SUTERM.

While they had been organizationally joined in SUTERM, the two factions of the union remained deeply divided, and in June 1974 conflict erupted. The issue was a collective bargaining agreement with the U.S.-owned General Electric company. Pérez Ríos negotiated the contract, but it was rejected by the rank and file who struck. Galván supported the strikers. Pérez Ríos and the local union officials introduced 500 scabs to break the strike. One of the local officials allied with Pérez Ríos was murdered, and Pérez Ríos accused Galván of the murder. At that point Fidel Velázquez intervened on the side of Pérez Ríos, and they called an unrepresentative convention of SUTERM. At that convention SUTERM voted to expel Galván and his associates from the executive board of the union. Hundreds of Galván's supporters were also driven out of the union by Pérez Ríos and Fidel Velázquez, and then quickly fired by the employers.

Galván and his followers continued their movement nevertheless, and in February 1975 founded the Democratic Tendency (TD), a broad union reform movement made up of activists from many labor unions. The TD published a manifesto entitled *The Declaration of Guadalajara* calling for union democracy and a broad social program to fight for the original goals of the Mexican Revolution. The TD organized numerous demonstrations around the country throughout the spring and summer of 1975. Under pressure from this movement, the Secretary of the National Patrimony and the CFE agreed to reinstate the fired electrical workers who supported Galván and the TD, but Pérez Ríos and other SUTERM leaders refused to allow them back into the union or to return to their jobs, and beat and threatened those who attempted to return. Under pressure from Pérez Ríos, Secretary of Labor Carlos Gálvez Betancourt revoked the reinstatement of Galván's followers.

Galván and the TD, pressing their case, organized a demonstration of 150,000 electrical workers, nuclear workers, railroad workers, university union members, peasants, and slum dwellers on November 15, 1975. Two weeks later, on November 28, the TD organized another series of demonstrations in cities across the country. In many cities, the TD demonstrations were attacked by CTM gangs armed with clubs and other weapons. Several demonstrators were wounded in confrontations in San Luis Potosí and Zacatecas. On March 20, 1976, a demonstration of 100,000 was held in the National Plaza in Mexico City. The TD then attempted to broaden the movement, organizing the National Front of Popular Action (FNAP) on May 14, 1976, which was supported by 300 local unions, peasant leagues, community groups, and student organizations.

On June 12, 1976, Galván and the TD called for a strike against the CFE for June 28, 1976. They demanded the reinstatement of the fired workers, they called upon the CFE to remove itself from internal labor union affairs, and they called for new democratic elections in SUTERM. Mexican President Luis Echeverría called for dialogue between SUTERM and the TD, and Galván agreed to postpone the strike until July 16, 1976 at 6:00 p.m. The dialogues were unsuccessful and the strike was indeed called, but it never had a chance to happen. Early on the morning of July 16, hired thugs and army units occupied the CFE plants, preventing TD members from entering while thousands of workers were replaced by scabs. In this sweeping act, the movement was crushed and defeated. The Attorney General of Mexico later reached an agreement for all fired workers to return to work, but the agreement was not honored in many places. In some cities, returning workers were met by CTM goon squads and forced to renounce the TD before they were allowed to punch in for work. The TD was formally dissolved on November 12, 1977.[11]

The use of massive military and police force against workers, as at Nueva Rosita in 1950, against the railroad workers in 1959, and against the electrical workers' movement in 1976, is a recurring and persistent theme in Mexican labor relations. Most recently the current president, Carlos Salinas de Gortari, used the army in 1989 against the Petroleum Workers Union and against the Miners and Metal Workers Union, and in 1990 against the Ford workers. The use of such massive military might is almost always accompanied by random violence, which threatens and intimidates workers, union activists, and union leaders. In any form it is delivered, violence limits freedom of union action and inhibits workers from exercising their rights. Moreover, as the historical pattern makes clear, anti-union violence is neither an aberration nor a particular president's policy decision. It is an intrinsic part of the Mexican system of control of the labor unions and the workers, a system maintained by the embrace of imposed leadership and the strangling of all reform.

Chronology of Mexican Labor Laws

1917   Constitution of 1917 with Article 123 is established. Mexico's labor charter grants workers the right to organize and strike, minimum standards and protective legislation, and tripartite Boards of Conciliation and Arbitration.

1924   The Mexican Supreme Court of Justice rules that Boards of Conciliation and Arbitration are genuine labor courts with the power to resolve individual and collective conflicts and make binding decisions.

1927   The Federal Board of Conciliation and Arbitration is created.

1929   Constitutional Article 73, Section X, and Article 123 are reformed, restricting individual states from enacting labor law.

1931   The Federal Labor Law is adopted as the fundamental Mexican labor law implementing Article 123 of the Constitution.

1937   The Regulation of Credit Institutions and Related Organizations enacted, denying all bank workers the right to organize, bargain collectively, or strike.

1938   The Statute of Workers at the Service of the Powers of the Union enacted, establishing separate and different labor union rights for federal employees. Their right to strike becomes more restricted.

1960   Constitutional Article 123 is divided into two parts: Part A for workers in the private sector, and the more restrictive Part B for federal employees.

1963   The Federal Law of Workers at the Service of the State enacted, extending the restrictions on federal public employees to state and municipal employees as well, and to workers for other public service organizations.

1970   The New Federal Labor Law is established, incorporating the Federal Labor Law of 1931 and subsequent revisions, and adding certain new benefits for workers.

1982   A Government Announcement gives bank workers the right to organize, but reform of Federal Labor Law restricts them to one "official" union. Subsequently state bank workers are confined to Part B.

A Case Study of Modernization: The Steel Industry

Many industries have been severely affected by the Mexican government's economic program of privatization and modernization. The steel industry provides one example of the dire consequences workers face when a government-dominated industry slides into uncompetitive oblivion. Whether the economic collapse of an industry is due to a lack of profit reinvested into technology, or to a simple drop in demand for the materials produced, as long as workers have no say in the restructuring process, their interests will be the last to be served.

The Mexican government came to dominate the steel industry during the 1970s and 1980s by buying up older privately owned plants and by building new ones. In 1977, the government created Sidermex as its holding company to oversee its three main facilities: Altos Hornos de México, Lázaro Cárdenas, and Fundidora de Monterrey.[1] All three steel plants were organized in the Miners and Metal Workers Union, a particularly authoritarian "official" union affiliated with the CT and the PRI. The union has been dominated by Napoleon Gómez Sada, who has held power in the union since 1958. The union's statutes give all power to the executive board, while virtually depriving local unions and members of any control over their own affairs. Locals or individual members are prevented from gathering to discuss problems common to their industry, workplace, or union.[2] Nevertheless, the heavy, hard, hot, and dangerous work led to constant rank and file rebellion challenging the leadership throughout the 1960s and 1970s. When the workers did organize to protest the dismantling of the industry in the late 1980s, they faced three adversaries: their employers, the union officials, and the local governmental authorities, all of whom were affiliated with the PRI.

Fundidora de Monterrey was the first steel mill in Latin America, which began operation on May 5, 1900. When the company ran into financial trouble in 1972, the government of President Luís Echeverría acquired 25 percent of the stock, and in 1976 became the principal shareholder. Between 1974 and 1977, the government invested in modernization with the creation of a pellet plant, the introduction of the Basic Oxygen Furnace (BOF) process, the addition of a lime plant, changes in the furnaces, and improvements in the thermo-electric plant.[3] Nevertheless, the plant remained uncompetitive due to a world over-capacity in steel.

In the late 1970s, Fundidora de Monterrey and its smaller sister plant Aceros Planos employed more than 6,000 workers organized in two local unions, Locals 67 and 68 of the Miners and Metal Workers Union. On occasion, these unions had attempted rank and file rebellion against their authoritarian leadership, but they were never very successful.[4] As Mexico began to "modernize" the steel industry and workers' rights were increasingly restricted, the workers were ill prepared to collectively deal with the problems that confronted them.

On May 9, 1986, Jaime Carretero Puga, director of Fundidora de Monterrey, informed the public that the Tenth Civil Court of the Federal District had declared the company bankrupt and the plant would cease operations permanently. In addition, he announced that the Mexican Army was taking over the facilities to prevent the workers from occupying them. As the steel mill's closing would lead to the closing of another 20 smaller factories, ultimately an estimated 60,000 people would be affected. Shocked and angry, 6,000 steel workers and their wives and children marched through the streets of Monterrey on May 12 demanding, "Work!"[5]

Leaders of Local 67 went to Mexico City to meet with the Secretary of Labor and other officials, to try to save their plant and their jobs. Arturo Quintanilla, General Secretary of Local 67, reported that the officials had "made a joke of our union...they treated us like dummies and did not show us the proper respect." As the government would not back down from its decision to close the plant, the local union, calling upon support from neighborhood organizations and political parties, began a series of demonstrations, which included blocking highways and disrupting traffic, demanding the re-opening of the plant.[6]

These demonstrations continued throughout June and into July, but to no avail. The government did not change its position, and eventually the steel workers were laid off with severance pay according to the terms of their contract. At the time, unemployment in Monterrey was at about 8 percent, and 20 percent of the workforce was said to be working part-time.

Throughout these events, Napoleon Gómez Sada and the national Miners and Metal Workers Union did little to support the members of Locals 67 and 68 who had on occasion opposed them. In any case, Gómez Sada was not likely to oppose the policies of the PRI government to which his union and his job were beholden. His silence was yet another reason why the closing of Fundidora de Monterrey allowed the government to rid itself of an out-dated plant, and incidentally two rather unruly local unions.

With the closing of the plant, 6,000 steel workers joined the ranks of the unemployed. The government-employer had made no transitional provisions for their employment elsewhere, nor for their retraining for other jobs. They were from that point on denied their right to an income on which they could survive. It is unlikely that workers laid off from the relatively high-paying steel industry could expect to find wages as high in other industries. The denial of their right to effective union organization indeed cost the workers a tremendous amount. The PRI-affiliated national Miners and Metal Workers Union was unwilling to oppose the economic policy of its party. Workers within this very authoritarian union had never had the opportunity to build a genuine democratic labor organization which could defend their interests. The stifling of their right to self-organization over decades made it impossible for them to mount an effective protest when the plant closing was suddenly announced.

While the closing of Fundidora de Monterrey is an example of the most extreme outcome of modernization of the steel industry, many other groups of workers suffered problems as well. During this same period, at the Altos Hornos de México (AHMSA) steel mills in Monclova, Coahuila, thousands of workers were temporarily laid off and 300 of the plant's 3,500 workers were permanently terminated in 1986.[7] Thousands more steel workers were laid off at companies such as Aceros de Ecatepec and Constructora Nacional de Carros de Ferrocarril. Between 1982 and 1989, 71 mines were closed. As a result of these closures, the Miners and Metal Workers Union is said to have lost 50,000 members.[8]

Monclova, Coahuila in northern Mexico was one area particularly hard hit by steel industry layoffs. Father Pedro Pantoja, a Catholic priest in the San Antonio de Padua parish in the steel workers' neighborhoods in Monclova, Coahuila, works with an organization called the Movement of Christian Workers, whose members are steel workers or former steel workers in the state-owned Altos Hornos de México working to make the state-controlled union more democratic and representative of the workers. Father Pantoja describes today what mill closures and partial closures have meant to the hundreds of his parishioners who have been laid off over the past few years, and their communities:

> Of the labor and union problems the workers here have confronted, the most important and hardest has been the death of the factory. The industrial modernization process, what they so elegantly call "industrial reconversion," has posed the most difficulties and the greatest crisis in terms of the workers' survival. This process has also revealed all of the vices and inadequacies of the union, the incompetence of the union leaders, and their corruption. Precisely because the problem is one of industrial reconversion, workers have been affected materially, morally, socially, and economically.

A whole series of legal developments in the service of reconversion or modernization were detrimental to the workers. The union and its highest officials, at least the biggest local union, were on the side of the government. They obediently supported the process without questioning, and without identifying themselves with the workers. I would say they were facilitating the process. The workers, who were left totally abandoned, did not even know how to use the little money they had received from the so called "readjustment" [layoff].

The economy of this whole steel region sank completely. The workers were completely taken by surprise, and some who had no consciousness and no education were completely helpless, and after the layoffs, useless. Unfortunately, the steel worker does not know how to deal with this. He knows how to weld, he knows how to work in the foundry. He knows how to work, but he doesn't know how to run his life. For a long time he has been completely socially neglected as a person, neglected in everything that has to do with his human development.

...The worker didn't have the slightest idea of the economic games that were being played...they lost their source of employment, and could not even work like a peon, taking up a pick or a shovel... So these men had social problems, with their families, housing, the problems of a region completely devoid of services and politically abandoned—particularly for having been an opposition city which had dared to question the official party. It had dared for two terms to elect mayors from the opposition party. This was the general situation.[9]

Father Pantoja testifies further that the workers were told that Monclova was going to be the location for new "mini-industries" and that the state and private investors were going to collaborate to ensure that the workers who were now unemployed would not fall into a void. The government promised that there would be an "industrial corridor" in Monclova. None of this happened. Monclova, a city whose citizens, most of whom were steel workers, had repeatedly voted for the conservative National Action Party (PAN) rather than for the PRI, received even less help with unemployment and the resulting social problems than did those from other areas.[10]

The reality is that what Father Pantoja describes here has been the case in many cities in which industrial plants have closed, eliminating the jobs of thousands of workers. The Mexican state, which controls the workers' source of employment, does not bother to make a show of following through on its rhetoric with even minimal services. Beyond the paltry severance mandated by union contracts negotiated behind the backs of the workers, no services are provided by the state, which has received the profits from the workers' labor. The complicitous relationship between labor union leaders and the state, in the case of the steel industry and in many others, allowed the workers' lives to be demolished by the organs which were to protect them. One could say that the Mexican state exists not for the people but on top of them.

Chapter Four

Labor and the Privatizing State

The Mexican government's policies with regard to the state-owned sector of the economy during the two previous administrations of José López Portillo Pacheco and Miguel de la Madrid Hurtado abrogated workers' rights in many significant ways. Lasting from 1976 to 1988, this period is characterized by a reversal of the role of the state in the Mexican economy. The residual effects of these policy changes have left their mark on workers and their labor unions. While government policy during these administrations was not always consistent, it nonetheless tended to move toward certain identifiable objectives.

Prior to this period, basic changes in the Mexican economy and in the structure of international trade had led the Mexican government to alter its fundamental economic design. Beginning during the era of Lázaro Cárdenas (1934-40), Mexico attempted to stay on a course of national economic self-determination. During the 1930s and 1940s, the government took control of some of the commanding heights of the economy, most importantly petroleum. The nationalization of industry was meant to stop foreign, particularly U.S., domination of the Mexican economy, and the enormous influence foreign investment had wielded on Mexican politics.

Throughout the 1940s, 1950s, and into the 1960s, Mexico fortified nationalized industry with an import substitute development policy. Import regulations and tariffs protected infant industries which attempted to substitute Mexican-made goods for imported products. The substitution of imports was intended to lay the basis for Mexico's gradual industrialization. Both strategies for modernization, the nationalization of industry and the substitution of imports, bore some fruit for the Mexican economy, but basically failed to bring about the intended growth and self-sufficiency.

Consequently, during the 1970s, the government changed strategies. Mexico, they decided, would pump more petroleum and use oil revenues to pay for industrialization. With this oil-based development model Mexico could, and did, use its vast oil wealth as collateral for billions of dollars in loans for modernization programs. Once again, however, success was limited. The oil income did pay for some industrialization projects, but by the early 1980s, falling oil prices made it impossible for Mexico to service the debt. This led, of course, to the severe economic crisis of 1982-83.

The economic crisis of the early 1980s, combined with the creation of the global assembly line, forced Mexico into another shift in strategy, this time putting all emphasis on manufacturing for export. In Mexico, as elsewhere, the decade of the 1980s heralded the consolidation of a new era of "world production," with multinational corporations establishing manufacturing and assembly plants in foreign countries throughout the world. This internationalization of production was made possible by advances in microchip and computer technology, robotics, containerized transportation, fiber optics, and other new technologies. At the same time, transnational conglomerates and corporations sought lower wages for production throughout the world. U.S. transnational corporations in particular turned to Mexico for many of their assembly and manufacturing operations. With a hungry workforce, close proximity to the United States, and relative political stability, Mexico was the corporations' ideal location for such labor-intensive operations. Some Mexican businesspeople and politicians agreed, turning to U.S. investment as the most viable means to industrialize their nation. Mexican entrepreneurs viewed themselves as economic partners in a lucrative joint venture.

However, in order for Mexico to enter into the world of the transnational corporation with its industrial demands, several obstacles had to be overcome. One was a large and growing political opposition to the PRI, rooted in Mexican nationalism and embodied by 1988 in the break with the PRI led by Cuauhtémoc Cárdenas, son of former President Lázaro Cárdenas, to form the Party of the Democratic Revolution. Other obstacles included the decrepit state bureaucracy which ran the nationalized industries and the labor unions which were rooted in them. For an export-based development model to work, nationalized industry had to be dismantled. This did not bode well for labor unions, the most important of which were based in state-owned industries. Moreover, Mexican labor was a staunch defender of nationalization. So, beginning in the 1970s but especially after 1983, the government intensified its efforts to break the power of labor unions, particularly in the nationalized industrial sector.

During the López Portillo and de la Madrid administrations, the state mobilized towards the goal of privatizing basic industry. Economic auctioning, as it turns out, solved more than just the problem of stagnation in state-owned industries; it also provided an impetus and means for the state to weaken virtually all independent labor unions in industry. Mexico's export-based development model mandates a cheap workforce, against which goal independent unions are a constant threat. The solution of choice appears to have been to thwart any democracy in the unions or to destroy the unions altogether.

The three following case studies of the Mexican government's campaign against labor rights during this period of privatization show the detrimental impact of the absence of a system of checks and balances within this development model. Furthermore, the experiences of the nuclear workers, fish industry workers, and aviation workers also demonstrate how the violation of labor rights is exacerbated by a climate devoid of protection of other, more general human rights.

The Nuclear Workers Strike for Fair Wages

With economic reorganization as its goal, the Mexican government has frequently found it expeditious to eliminate independent and militant labor unions which opposed government policy. The example of the Mexican atomic energy industry and the Nuclear Workers Union (SUTIN) is a prime case in point. Founded in 1964, SUTIN was made up of the 1,417 employees of the Mexican Uranium Company (URAMEX) and the National Institute of Nuclear Investigations (ININ), both of which were state-owned companies. The union was headed by Arturo Whaley Martínez and Antonio Gershenson, a member of the union and a congressman for the Unified Socialist Party of Mexico (PSUM, which at the time was Mexico's Communist Party), who defended the union in the national legislature. The union was an outspoken defender of nationalized industry and of organized labor.[1]

Although numerically small, SUTIN played an inordinately large role both in the CT and among the independent unions. As Raúl Trejo Delarbre writes:

> In the union movement, as they defended their own rights, the nuclear workers teamed up with unions both within and outside of the CT. In particular, they reached agreements with the Mexican Electrical Workers Union (SME), the Telephone Workers, and the union at UNAM [the Mexican Autonomous National University], among others. Together with these organizations, they frequently published manifestos critical of the government's economic policies. [SUTIN called for]...the expansion of the state sector of the economy, an increase in taxes for those who could afford to pay more, the defense of natural resources such as petroleum and uranium, and the participation of workers in the management of their firms...[2]

These positions were a frontal challenge to the government's policy. Moreover, the Nuclear Workers' ties both within the CT and with some of the independent unions made the union a potential threat to the government's absolute control over the labor movement.

In Spring 1983, having suffered through the first phase of austerity measures imposed as a result of the debt crisis, and in an attempt to regain some of their lost purchasing power, hundreds of thousands of Mexican workers struck for higher wages. The strike wave, the biggest in Mexican history, involved both the official and independent unions, who conducted legal and illegal strikes. On May 31, 1983, SUTIN went out on strike, joining this national wave. Government and employer response to this massive upheaval was to offer most of the unions wage increases of 15 to 20 percent, but to deny increases to the most militant or independent unions in order to punish them for their recalcitrance.

By the end of June, most labor unions had settled their strikes, either taking their wage increase, or accepting their punishment. SUTIN also decided to settle, recognizing that it would not win a wage increase at that time. On June 23, it filed a formal statement that the strike was over, but the URAMEX authorities refused to acknowledge the end of the strike. As Trejo Delarbre described it, this was "a virtually unique case in the history of labor relations in Mexico: a union wants to end its strike, but the employer is not in agreement."[3] In effect, the strike became an employer lockout. Employer lockouts in response to worker strikes are forbidden under Mexican labor law (Article 123, Section XIX). Nevertheless, the Federal Board of Conciliation and Arbitration upheld URAMEX's right to refuse to recognize the end of the strike.

Regarding this decision as opportunity's knock, the company went on the offensive. On July 16, 1983, URAMEX's director, Alberto Escofet, announced that URAMEX no longer needed 2,000 employees, that it could operate with 400, and that it was offering generous final severance pay to all workers who wanted to take advantage of the offer. Very few responded, and the "strike" continued for more than another month until a decision of the Federal Board of Conciliation and Arbitration finally ended it on August 8, 1983. The moment the strike ended, URAMEX announced that it was "suspending relations" with all of its workers due to the economic crisis—URAMEX was ceasing operations and all workers were laid off.

SUTIN's situation was complicated by a factional division within the union which had been allegedly promoted by the government-employer. In the middle of 1983, a faction led by David Bahena attempted to have the employer, ININ, break off relations with SUTIN's National Executive Committee and establish relations with his rump leadership. (Most of Bahena's followers were employees of ININ, not URAMEX.) However when SUTIN held a National Assembly on January 28, 1984, the Bahena faction was defeated and the Whaley faction upheld by an absolute majority. Nevertheless, Bahena and his group continued to work against the union's leadership with the apparent support of the government. In October 1984, Bahena suggested that SUTIN become part of the "official" SUTERM electrical workers union, a proposal which was readily accepted by SUTERM's leader, Leonardo Rodríguez Alcaine. This proposal shocked even Bahena's followers, and their outspoken opposition forced him to drop the idea.

By this point, SUTIN was an organization in name only. The union's 1,400 members were now mostly laid off, and had been without work since the strike broke out at the end of May 1983. No longer in the workplace, they had no economic power. The only strategy open to them was a political one.

The Whaley leadership of SUTIN sought support from the official unions and from the Mexican House of Representatives. Within the CT, SUTIN received only nominal support from the CTM and the CROC, while the independent unions rallied behind it. In the House of Representatives, the union was able to get legislation passed calling for "a quick resolution, which does not harm the interests of the public enterprise in question or the workers...a prompt solution to the problem of the suspension of activities in [URAMEX]...that is most in accord with national interests, the interests of the firm, and of the workers."[4] Although this seemed like a positive development, the SUTIN leadership had mistakenly put stock in the "official" labor unions and the PRI-dominated House of Representatives. This resolution in no way benefited the workers. On November 15, the President presented the National Congress with a new Nuclear Law which called, among other things, for the elimination of URAMEX altogether, and the division of the atomic energy industry among several other government agencies. This opened the nuclear industry to the involvement of private firms, both Mexican and foreign.

The immediate consequence of this law was the disappearance of the union.[5] The new Nuclear Law was approved by the House of Representatives on December 19, 1984. Approval in the Senate, all of whose members were members of the PRI, was never a question.

Not long after passage of the new law, those URAMEX employees who had not already done so accepted final severance pay and termination. The SUTIN official union registration passed into the hands of David Bahena's followers who controlled Locals 2 and 8 and who were employed by ININ, and therefore had not lost their jobs. Under Bahena, SUTIN became another "official" union.

In the case of URAMEX and the Nuclear Workers Union, the government's policy of economic reorganization and privatization proved to be fortuitous in eliminating a militant union. Aside from the illegality of the lockout, workers' rights were not technically violated. For the workers, however, one more chance for self-determination had been wrested from their hands. A strong independent-minded union was erased and a new compliant one established, not simply as a result of privatization, but through the government's active pursuit of direct control over the union.

The Tepepan Fish Industry Union Cast to the Wind

The experiences of the members of the Tepepan Refrigeration Workers and Employees Union bear many similarities to those of the nuclear workers in SUTIN.[6] STERT, though affiliated with the CTM, was an independent-minded union which not only took autonomous initiatives within the CTM and the CT, but was also involved with the independent union movement. As an anomaly it created a problem, albeit a small one, for the state-controlled unions. The government, in carrying out its policy of privatization and modernization, once again found that it was simultaneously able to eliminate an unusual independent labor organization.

Until recently, the Mexican fishing industry was divided into three parts: 1) the cooperative or social sector, 2) the private sector, and 3) the state sector. Fishing was historically an export industry; its center was shrimp fishing. During the presidency of Lázaro Cárdenas (1934-1940) a Fishing Law (*Ley de Pesca*) was enacted which set aside seven species of sea life which could only be fished by peasant cooperatives. Among those species was the shrimp. Later an eighth, the turtle, was added to the list. The fishing cooperatives numbered more than 800 and accounted for between 80,000 and 100,000 jobs.

The private sector, because it was excluded by law from catching the most desired fish, was primarily involved in fish processing. The private sector also provided fishing boats and equipment to the cooperatives, with the understanding that the cooperatives would in turn provide fish for the processing plants. This arrangement created inter-dependency; while the cooperatives held a monopoly over some of the most important species, they came to depend on the private sector for equipment.

The state sector came to play an important role in the fishing industry as well. First, it began to dominate certain other species such as octopus. Second, it came to control 80 percent of the fish canning industry. Lastly, the state controlled the importation of dried fish, such as cod, which were traditionally very important during Lent and the Christmas season.

The state fishing industry expanded during the 1970s when the government created a holding company called Productos Pesqueros Mexicanos, S.A. to oversee a consortium of 22 state-owned fish product companies. Nineteen of the state's companies were processing plants for the canning, freezing, smoking, drying, and salting of fish, and all were located along the Mexican coasts. The state also had a fishing fleet which it made available to some of the coopera- tives, providing fish for its processing plants and distribution net- works. The state created two export companies, Ocean Garden Products, Inc. (a Mexican transnational headquartered in San Diego, California in the United States) and Exportadores Asociados, S.A. de C.V. With these state-owned companies the Mexican govern- ment became the most important exporter of shrimp to the United States and Japan. The Mexican government also had its own domes- tic fish marketing company, which was Tepepan. Tepepan, the story has it, began as a restaurant in the Federal District, but over the years grew to become the state-owned fish distribution and marketing company. Between 1964 and 1983, Tepepan expanded until it owned more than 100 centers of distribution throughout the country, including restaurants, fish cocktail stands, outlets, and warehouses.

Most of the workers and cooperative members involved in the fishing industry were associated with the "official" unions or other "official" organizations which were affiliated with the PRI. All of the 800 cooperatives were part of the National Confederation of Co- operatives (CNC). The CNC, in turn, was affiliated with the Na- tional Confederation of Popular Organizations (CNOP), one of the pillars of the PRI. (The CNOP recently changed its name to UNE.) There were also a number of peasant groups engaged in river fish- ing on a part-time basis who belonged to "production societies" which were affiliated with the National Peasant Confederation (CNC), yet another pillar of the PRI. Finally, most of the workers be- longed to labor unions such as the CTM, CROC, and CROM, all of which were part of the CT and part of the PRI. Essentially, all those who labored in the fishing industry, whether peasants, cooperativists, or workers, were controlled by the state-party.

The first organizing efforts at Tepepan were democratic and in- dependent, but they did not result in recognition from the labor au- thorities as such. In fact, the "official" unions and the state labor authorities moved in to impose their own leadership on the rank and file workers. The union's short history of democratic internal organization and independent labor and political positions came to an abrupt end when it was forced to affiliate with the CTM and the PRI in order to avoid being eliminated. The Tepepan Refrigeration Workers and Employees Union was "officially" formed in 1977 and became part of the CTM. The union eventually came to represent about 1,200 workers. Despite its affiliation with the CTM, the union retained its democratic and independent attitudes, continually at- tempting to influence other "official" unions in the fishing sector. It did so plagued by constant altercations with management.

Following the creation of the holding company, Productos Pesqueros Mexicanos, S.A. in 1971, a series of reorganizations began which threatened Tepepan's existence. First, in 1979, 20 Tepepan distribution centers were removed from the company and put under the control of other state organizations. This made it difficult for Tepepan to ensure product availability for its retail outlets. In 1980, in a twist of fate, Tepepan was given responsibility for a new product—Pepepez boneless breaded fish, an item well suited for its popular domestic market—which temporarily revived its retail sales. However, in 1982 and in 1984 the administration again redesigned Tepepan's mission, first emphasizing wholesale over retail, placing Tepepan's retail outlets in jeopardy, and then eliminating the Pepepez line of products altogether, at the same time giving Tepepan new warehouses and distribution centers.

Throughout these developments, the Tepepan union, never consulted on reorganization, was attempting several changes on its own. First, the union developed and promoted an alternative program for a state-owned fish industry which would serve the needs of poor and working-class people. Second, the union attempted to reconstitute itself as an independent union with free membership. Third, the union worked to create an alliance of unions in the fishing industry. Although the Tepepan union worked to organize within the CTM out of necessity rather than desire, the intended outcome was a strong coalition of unions representing all facets of the industry. Towards the end of 1988, the new union was inaugurated by the fusion of eight unions, almost all of which were in the state sector of the industry.

These efforts, organizationally based in the state sector of the industry and ideologically defending a state-owned industry which would serve the needs of the poor and the working class, were antithetical to the privatization policies of the de la Madrid Administration. Moreover, some of the workers in the Tepepan union and in other fish workers' organizations were influenced by the example of the Authentic Labor Front (FAT), a genuinely independent labor organization. Consequently, as the state moved towards privatization, the Tepepan workers became an organizational and political barrier to dismantling the industry. The state steamroller was called in to clear the path.

At the end of 1985, a final reorganization led to the decentralization and partial elimination of Tepepan. Sixty percent of the workers were terminated and Tepepan facilities were eliminated from all but eight states. In 1988, another contraction left Tepepan in only four states, with personnel reduced to just 325 workers. By the time Tepepan was closed down by the government in 1989, there were only 260 workers remaining. The cutbacks and finally the closing of the Tepepan fish warehouse, distribution, and retail outlet system eliminated the union which had been 1,200 workers strong. Manuel García Urrutia, coordinator of FAT, who was a former leader of the Tepepan union, says of his experience with the destruction of the network and then the union: "I believe that the fundamental reason for the government's actions was its political economy, and that was the priority and the fundamental axis. But clearly the government took advantage of the situation to get rid of a militant union."[7]

The PRI policy of privatization coincided nicely with its antipathy to this democratic, independent-minded, and activist labor union which was a threat to its monopoly control of the fishing industry. Nationalized in the name of the people, for the benefit of the people, the state-run industries never gave the people or workers a chance to participate in the reorganization process. Tepepan workers' rights under Mexican law were not violated. Nonetheless, because workers had no say in how the company was managed, they had no chance to determine the course of events in their favor.

The elimination of the Tepepan union is not significant because 1,200 workers lost their jobs, but because it was dismantled as part of the systematic elimination of independent or independent-minded unions from the landscape of Mexican labor relations. Privatization of the fishing industry did not mandate Tepepan's demise or the end of the union. The profitability of the Tepepan network could have ordained its survival, and the workers could have negotiated what their share would be from the fruits of their labor. For economic mismanagement to survive as an integral part of the Mexican system, workers must have no share in the decision-making process.

Aeroméxico Workers Abandoned in Flight

Aeroméxico, formerly Aeronaves de México, was founded as a privately owned company in 1934 with an inaugural flight between Mexico and Acapulco by a Stinson de Luxe five-seat aircraft. In 1940, Pan American bought up 40 percent of the line and expanded Aeroméxico by absorbing other airlines, including Aeronaves de Michoacan in 1942, Taxi Aereo de Oaxaca in 1943, Lineas Aereas Jesús Sarabia in 1944, and Aeronaves Reforma in 1954. Aeroméxico began its first international flights in 1957. The company did well for many years, but by the late 1950s found itself on the verge of bankruptcy. It was then taken over by the Mexican government on June 28, 1959.[8] During its first decade, the newly nationalized company standardized its operations, bought new equipment, and became one of the principal components of the Mexican transportation system. It also provided, as it always had, free airline service to both government officials and leaders of the PRI.

Aeroméxico ran smoothly until the decade of economic crisis, the 1980s. Since then, the company has seen several changes in management and many problems in its administration. Many critics of the airline pointed to its top-heavy supervision with 2,500 administrative employees out of a total of 12,000 workers. With President de la Madrid calling for a reduction of the role of the nationalized companies and for more private enterprise, there was speculation that the company would soon be sold off.

It became clear that something was amiss when, in August 1987, the Mexican government did not turn over a subsidy of 75 billion pesos which had been promised to Aeroméxico earlier, and instead advanced the airline only 25 billion. The money was to have been used to rent five MD-80 aircraft so that Aeroméxico could update its aging fleet of 20-year-old planes. Just after the Pact of Economic Solidarity—a program of wage and price controls—was signed on December 15, 1987, the Secretary of the Budget ordered the payment canceled for the renting of those five planes. Between 1987 and 1990, management also called for many more aircraft to be sold.[9]

Other problems were surfacing as well. In 1987, the Association of Aviator Pilots protested the suspension of flights to three South American capitals, which were subsequently turned over to a Venezuelan airline.[10] Then in early 1988, Mexico and the United States signed a bilateral agreement dealing with civil aviation issues, expanding mutual concessions of routes between the two countries. Critics feared that this would mean the invasion of Mexico's airspace by foreign airlines, and saw the agreement as a threat to Mexican sovereignty.[11]

At the end of March 1988, the Union of Technicians and Workers, 7,500 strong, and the 1,800-member Union Association of Flight Attendants filed an intention to strike with the Federal Board of Conciliation and Arbitration. The threatened strike was to protest the state-owned company's sale of 13 airplanes, which they viewed as a menace to their continued employment. At that time, Aeroméxico had 43 airplanes, 24 of which it owned and 19 of which were rented. The sale of 13 aircraft, the unions argued, would result in the elimination of routes, the closing of terminals, and the reduction of the workforce by 18 percent. The union particularly feared that it would lead to the termination of flights to Toronto and Montreal in Canada, and to the cities of Chetumal and Ciudad Victoria in Mexico.[12] The union called upon management to consider other alternatives.

The next day, Fidel Velázquez, head of the CTM and CT, announced that the CT would give unconditional support and solidarity to the two airline workers' unions. Velázquez said he would call an emergency meeting of the CT to look at specific measures which might be taken to aid the airline workers.[13] The unions also received support from CANACO, the Mexican Chamber of Commerce, which also protested the sale of the airplanes and the cancellation of routes. CANACO's president, Abraham Farah Wejebe, argued that the Mexico-Chetumal route was profitable.

At the beginning of April, Aeroméxico announced that it was canceling its Mexico City-Chetumal flights, and immediately informed 28 workers that they would be severed, though the workers demanded that they be reassigned to other routes. The union predicted that eventually some 2,000 workers would be affected.[14] The two airline workers' unions took the position that it was illegal for the airlines to proceed with the planned sale of the aircraft while their intention to strike was before the Federal Board of Conciliation and Arbitration. They also indicated their desire to negotiate with their employer, and even proposed that the unions could help pay for the cost of rehabilitating some of the airplanes which the company proposed to sell. However, at the same time the unions made it clear that if no progress was made in negotiations following the legally indicated procedure they would strike on April 12.[15]

On April 11, 1988, 4,000 members of the Union of Technicians and Workers held a meeting to discuss whether or not to strike. Union leader Melchor Montalvo Guajardo explained to the workers that the union had scrupulously adhered to labor law in filing the strike notification. He indicated that he believed the government would seize the company and that the workers would probably then be required to work under government supervision, while the union continued to negotiate an equitable settlement. In past years, the Aeroméxico union had gone on strike several times, usually triggering government seizure on the grounds that it was essential to the economy or national security. Based on their past experiences with government takeovers, after four and a half hours they voted to strike. They cited "the intransigence of the employers" as sufficient grounds for this action.[16]

Also on April 11, the day before the strike was to begin, Aeroméxico announced its "temporary" withdrawal from the Mexican stock exchange, a measure which stock analysts attributed to the likely possibility that the government was negotiating the sale of Aeroméxico to private investors, a possibility which the company did not deny.[17]

Aeroméxico braced for the strike, announcing that it was prepared to replace strikers with management employees and workers from other airlines.[18] The company put an advertisement in newspapers which said that Aeroméxico was only exercising its legitimate management prerogatives in buying and selling equipment, and that it had not laid off one union worker. The company indicated that a strike would result in the cancellation of 223 daily flights moving 15,000 people between some 42 cities. In that same advertisement, the company claimed that the unions' strike was unreasonable and without legal justification and the company would seek to have the strike declared illegal.[19]

Likewise, the Union of Technicians and Workers placed an advertisement in the papers in which they explained to President de la Madrid, Secretary of Labor Farell Cubillas, Secretary of Communications and Transportation Díaz Díaz, President of the CT Velázquez, and to the general public why they had gone on strike. First, the union asserted that Aeroméxico had refused to participate in any dialogue with the union. Second, the union explained, "we are convinced that our source of employment must be restructured, but that the workers should participate in this restructuring just as you, Mr. President, indicated to us in our interview last year." Unfortunately, said the union, the other side had shown no desire to cooperate. The union indicated its willingness to discuss all issues with the employers, and its desire for cooperation.[20]

On April 12, 1988, the 7,500 members of the Union of Technicians and Workers struck Aeroméxico for violations of the collective bargaining agreement. They were striking solo, however, because at the last minute the Union Association of Flight Attendants withdrew its announcement of intention to strike from the Federal Board of Conciliation and Arbitration. The leader of the flight attendants' union, Patricia Esnarriaga, said that her union had decided not to strike after Secretary of Labor Arsenio Farell Cubillas stated during a meeting that if the workers struck, the government would get rid of the airline altogether. Since there was no time for negotiations between the two unions to occur, each took its own route. Both sacrificed equal amounts by the end.

There were many surprises over the course of this strike. For one, the Secretary of Communications and Transportation did not use government seizure to take over the airline as expected, declaring that the strike was not a threat to the national security or economy. The strike forced the airline to cancel 260 flights affecting 17,000 passengers and the strike was estimated at costing the company about five billion pesos daily. As soon as the strike broke out, the company went to the Federal Board of Conciliation and Arbitration to demand that the strike be declared illegal on the grounds that the union was basing its strike "on suppositions and not on actual facts." Detachments of the Mexican Army were sent to guard the various Aeroméxico locations both in the Mexico City International Airport and in other airports throughout the country. In addition, according to the union, police prevented the union's picket lines from access to the workplaces.[21]

The striking Aeroméxico groundworkers received immediate support from unions at 18 nationalized industries, including the electrical workers (SME), autoworkers (SNITIA), sugar workers, and fishing industry workers. These unions declared that the airline workers' strike was "in defense of national and popular sovereignty."[22] A few days later these unions also convoked a "Second Forum of the Unions of Nationalized Industry."[23]

Surprisingly, by the second day of the strike, the Federal Board of Conciliation and Arbitration had still not issued a decision on the legality or illegality of the strike. On the third day, Melchor Montalvo Guajardo, General Secretary of the technicians and workers' union, and Patricia Esnarriaga, head of the flight attendants' union, met with Fidel Velázquez, head of the CTM, to ask for the support of the CT in fighting for a restructuring of Aeroméxico which would preserve their jobs. Montalvo Guajardo argued against the privatization of Aeroméxico, contending that routes formerly served by Aeroméxico had been turned over to Canadian Pacific and to American Airlines.[24]

Simultaneously, many opponents of the strike, particularly from the private sector, called vigorously for doing away with the state-owned airline. Luis M. Farias, the mayor of Monterrey, Nuevo Leon, spoke out to insist that the best thing that Aeroméxico could do under the circumstances was to "declare itself in bankruptcy, because it can't keep losing five billion pesos a day." Likewise Raúl Cadena Cepeda, the president of the Monterrey chapter of the National Chamber of Commerce, called for the privatization of Aeroméxico. Businesspeople in several cities called for a quick end to the strike, which was having a deleterious effect on tourism.[25]

On April 16, 1988, the Mexican government decided that it would file for bankruptcy on behalf of Aeroméxico, which would then lead to the sale of the company and its reprivatization. Meanwhile, in the period since the strike had begun, Aeroméxico had retired 13 aircraft and rented out 20 others with the option to buy, leaving only seven aircraft in its fleet. Sergio Higuera Mota, the First Judge of the Bankruptcy Court of the Federal District, declared the company bankrupt and appointed Banobras (the Bank of Public Works and Services) as the receiver. At the same time, the judge refused to release to the public financial information proving the airline was bankrupt because, he argued, such matters were secret, even though Aeroméxico was a state-owned company.

The organized labor movement protested strongly against the declaration of bankruptcy. Joining the protests were the CT; the Board of Labor Union Cooperation, a coalition of the electrical workers unions (SME) and a number of independent labor unions; 18 unions of the nationalized industries; and the National Front of Democratic Lawyers. The Democratic Lawyers argued that the company could not legally be declared bankrupt before resolving the labor dispute between the groundworkers' union and the company.[26]

Faced with an unexpected set of circumstances, on April 17, 1988 the Union of Technicians and Workers called a general assembly to discuss whether to continue the strike. In a show of solidarity, representatives of many other unions also attended the meeting, among them: unions at other airlines, workers from nationalized industries, members of independent unions, and representatives of the CT. After a discussion, the workers voted 4,995 to 5 to continue the strike.

At that meeting, the union also discussed a number of alternatives, including the possibility that the workers might use their $90 million in severance pay to acquire part interest in the airline. The union asserted that the declaration of bankruptcy on the part of the airline was "fraudulent," and that if their strike was declared illegal, they would file a new strike notification while seeking an injunction against the Federal Board.[27] The union called for the creation of a union-management commission to restructure the airlines.

Juan Moisés Calleja, legal advisor to the CTM and a former minister of the Supreme Court of Justice, supported the union's demand for a mixed commission to discuss the future of Aeroméxico. He also urged the Federal Board of Conciliation and Arbitration to make a decision on the legality of the strike, so as not to leave the workers in suspense. He warned that a decision to find the strike illegal would allow the company to declare bankruptcy and pay off the workers with a very reduced severance pay, which ironically had the effect of indicating to the employer a way to win the strike and also to eradicate the workforce cheaply and effectively.[28]

With the Federal Board of Conciliation and Arbitration still issuing no decision on the legality of the strike, and with the possibility that bankruptcy would mean the end of their jobs, Patricia Esnarriaga, the leader of the Union Association of Flight Attendants, announced that her union, which had not agreed to join the strike but whose members were out of work anyway, might return to work even before the Federal Board made a decision.[29]

The Association of Aviator Pilots had not joined the strike against Aeroméxico, nor had it cooperated with the other two unions, groundworkers and flight attendants, in their attempt to find a solution to both the strike and to the airline's economic problems. In addition, they did not support the workers' aims on April 19, 1990, when the pilots announced that they agreed with President de la Madrid's decision to refuse to operate an inefficient airline, that they supported his declaration of bankruptcy, and that they were prepared to buy the airline and make it an efficient and profitable operation. Otherwise, said the pilots, Mexico would be invaded by foreign airlines.[30] The pilots' unions also proposed to buy Mexicano de Aviación, the other state airline which was also up for sale.

Meanwhile, the striking groundworkers continued to put pressure on the government. On April 20, several thousand Aeroméxico workers and their supporters planned to march to Los Pinos, the presidential residence, to ask President de la Madrid to intervene personally in the issue. However the march was canceled after the President promised to meet with representatives of the union. The Union of Technicians and Workers had met with Oscar Elizundia Treviño, the President's appointment secretary, on April 19, and received some encouragement from him. Elizundia Treviño told the workers that "there is a desire to resolve the conflict on the best terms." Montalvo Guajardo and other union leaders took this to be an indication that the President would grant the workers an audience and would attempt to bring the company and the union together.[31]

A coalition of leaders of opposition parties on the left and the right—the PRT, PARM, PFCRN PPS, PDM, and PMS, led by former presidential candidate Rosario Ibarra de Piedra—signed an open letter to President de la Madrid on April 20, asking him to intervene and resolve the dispute.[32] In addition, various unions and organizations placed advertisements in the newspapers supporting the Aeroméxico workers and criticizing the government for declaring bankruptcy, for failing to consider a worker buy-out, and for failure to rule on the legality of the strike.[33]

As the workers continued to pursue a solution through the government, the company took its case to the Federal Board of Conciliation and Arbitration. On April 22, 1988, the official receiver for Aeroméxico, Ismael Gómez Gordillo, and the representative of Banobras asked the Federal Board to terminate labor relations between the company and the 7,200 ground employees. The petition was dealt with immediately, and a hearing date was set for May 9, 1988.[34]

That same day, Fidel Velázquez, head of the CTM, and Jorge Sánchez, head of SME—the recent past president and the new president of the CT—visited President de la Madrid to invite him to lead the May 1 Labor Day parade, as is the custom. The two labor leaders asked de la Madrid not to close Aeroméxico.

De la Madrid responded by explaining that from now on "public enterprises must be profitable and must not constitute a burden for the people of Mexico who have so many needs which we have not been able to attend to because of a lack of resources." The President promised that he would give the Mexican people a full and detailed accounting of the reasons for Aeroméxico's bankruptcy, as well as a plan to overcome the company's problems. He added that "the government of the Republic did not want to make full and detailed explanations until dialogue with the workers was concluded, but at the right moment we will have to render clear, precise, and detailed accounts of why we have arrived at this situation." President de la Madrid told the CT officials that he had asked Secretary of Labor Arsenio Farell Cubillas and Secretary of Communications and Transportation Daniel Díaz Díaz to keep lines of communication with the unions open and to continue the dialogue with the workers.[35] What all of this meant was and still is unclear, since there had never been any dialogue with the unions.

The Union of Technicians and Workers continued to look for legal avenues to resolve its difficulties. On April 22, 1988, they went to the District Judge for Labor Issues to seek an injunction against Sergio Higuera Mota, the First Judge of the Bankruptcy Court of the Federal District. The union argued that the application for bankruptcy was a violation of the federal labor laws because the company was involved in a strike. At the same time and on the same grounds, the union asked the Federal Board of Conciliation and Arbitration to suspend any demand for breaking off labor relations between the company and the union.

At the same time it attempted to stop the bankruptcy in the courts, the union continued to try to open up negotiations with the company. René Arce, the union's press secretary, indicated that the union "would continue to look for a dialogue and a path toward cooperation, in order to achieve the restructuring of Aeroméxico with the participation of the workers, and that when that restructuring took place, the company would be profitable and productive without losing its social purpose." Among other things, Arce indicated the union was willing to talk about layoffs of personnel and making contracts more "flexible." "If the bankruptcy is for a good purpose, so that a new, profitable, and more capable Aeroméxico can come out of this, then we are in agreement; but if it is to destroy the collective bargaining agreement, in order to hand the business over to private enterprise or even to transnational companies, then we are not in agreement." Arce expressed thanks to the CT for their intervention with President de la Madrid, and voiced his belief that the company and the union would soon sit down to talk, thanks to the mediation offered by Presidential Appointments Secretary Elizundia Treviño.[36]

Acting as though there was no strike and no possibility for negotiation, the company went ahead with its plans for liquidation. On April 22, 1988, Ismael Gómez Gordillo returned to the Federal Board of Conciliation and Arbitration, this time to request that it terminate Aeroméxico's collective and individual labor relations with both the Union Association of Flight Attendants' 600 members and with its 2,500 exempt employees. Hearings on the former were to be held on May 13 and on the latter on May 20.

In addition to the groundworkers, other Aeroméxico employees were being affected by the bankruptcy. Seventy employees of the Aeroméxico dining rooms, who had been laid off the day after bankruptcy was declared, formally demanded to be rehired. They expressed shock that the government-owned airline had offered them severance pay far below that to which they were entitled under the Federal Labor Law. Their attorney, Manuel Fuentes, said that the concessionaire of the dining rooms, Dulce María Oliver, had told the workers that they would get nothing if they did not accept the severance pay which had been offered. Fuentes also accused the CTM Union of Culinary Workers, headed by Daniel Mejía Colín, of having colluded with the employer to deprive the workers of their rights.

In spite of the hard-line reaction to their resistance, the groundworkers continued the strike. Melchor Montalvo Guajardo reported that only 15 percent of the groundworkers had indicated that they were willing to accept their severance pay.[37] Then, apparently as a result of pressure from the CT, on April 24, 1988, the government let it be known that it would put forward a new proposal to be worked out in the next 90 days. The terms of this new proposal were the following. First, Aeroméxico would not go out of business. Second, all three union contracts would be thrown out, and new contracts would be negotiated. These contracts would be based on a new employer-worker relationship, with changes in job titles, and reductions in wages and benefits. The groundworkers' new contract would eliminate 36 clauses. Third, there would be a reduction in the workforce by as much as 60 percent. It was also believed that as part of the agreement the groundworkers' strike would be declared illegal.[38] Presumably the government still intended to sell off the state-owned company to private enterprise. President de la Madrid was to announce the government's proposed reorganization of the airline on April 26. The government continued to meet with both the flight attendants and the pilots, while holding no discussions with the groundworkers. In response to the indications that a deal was in the offing, the groundworkers continued to put forward their proposal for the reorganization of the airline which would continue to be a state-owned company.[39]

On April 26, 1988, two weeks after the strike began, the Federal Board of Conciliation and Arbitration declared the strike illegal. Simultaneously, Secretary of Labor Farell Cubillas announced that the bankrupt company would terminate 90 percent of its workers and reopen as a private company. The new company would be privately owned, with 33 percent of the stock held by the pilots and the other 67 percent held by private investors. A Mixed Cooperation Commission would be created to oversee the restructuring of the company, and the Association of Aviator Pilots would coordinate the unions involved in the process. The existing labor union contracts would be eliminated. For the first 90 days of operation of the new company, there would be no union contracts or protections of any kind, other than the Federal Labor Law. Fired workers would receive the usual severance pay: three months' salary, plus 12 days' salary for every year of work.

With many of its routes already let to private airlines, the successor company would represent only a small part of what had been Aeroméxico. Several routes were assigned to four other airlines: Aero Caribe, Aero California, Aero Cozumel, and Aero Mar. Among the owners of these companies were Sigfrido Paz Paredes, Miguel Alemán, Enrique Loaeza Tovar, and Captain Armando Victoria. Others routes had gone to Pan Am, American Air Lines, and Continental Airlines.[40] It was reported in the press that the director of Aeroméxico, Rodolfo Gasca Neri, was a major stockholder in Aero Mar and Aero California, two of the companies which had profited from the collapse of Aeroméxico.[41] The pilots union, which the government had made the center of its reorganization, was also involved in business partnerships with two private companies: Camino Real and Holiday Inn.[42]

On May 3, 1988, the new Aeroméxico began operations with a workforce of approximately 1,200, about 10 percent of its former size. Of the ground personnel, only about 700 of the 7,200 were rehired, but with no contractual protection. One of the attorneys for the groundworkers' union, Antonio Argüelles, said that workers were rehired not on the basis of their experience or qualifications, but only because they were docile or anti-union. The airline reopened operations with only five of the 43 airplanes it had at the time it went bankrupt, and critics complained that its best lines had been taken over by Aero California, Aero Mar, Aero Caribe, and American Air Lines.[43]

Fidel Velázquez, head of the CTM, announced that the Aeroméxico workers "have no reason to be unhappy" since an agreement was signed with the government before May 1. Those who are not back at work, he said, "would be indemnified according to the law."[44] But René Arce, one of the leaders of the groundworkers' union, reported that his members were having problems getting jobs at other airlines. He asserted that "they are immediately rejected for having worked at Aeroméxico."[45] They were in effect blacklisted for having been union militants.

Frustrated with their situation, the union workers and exempt employees marched to Los Pinos on Friday, May 13 to demand that the President intervene to bring about a solution to their problems, while the flight attendants, wearing their uniforms, organized a protest at the Federal Board of Conciliation and Arbitration.[46] Ironically, it was the 28th anniversary of their union contract.

Nestor de Buen, the union's attorney, met with officials of the Official Receiver and with the Federal Board and laid out the flight attendants' case. First, said de Buen, Aeroméxico cannot be bankrupt because it is a state company and the state cannot go bankrupt. Second, the President cannot dissolve or liquidate a state company without first conferring with the Secretary of the Budget, which he failed to do. Third, the bankruptcy judge declared the company bankrupt simply on the basis of the strike, without ever examining the company's financial records. Finally, said de Buen, another "atrocity" committed was that the judge ordered the termination of labor relations with the unions because the company was no longer in operation; immediately after labor relations were terminated, however, the company was back in business.[47]

Among the workers in the worst position were some 2,300 exempt employees, who had a hearing before the Federal Board of Conciliation and Arbitration on May 20, 1988. With no union to fight for them, some 350 of them had, either in groups or individually, contacted Federal District Attorney for the Defense of Labor Alfredo Farid Barquet, who personally undertook to represent them. He was joined by another 15 private lawyers.

The exempt employees objected to the proposed severance pay of three months salary plus a seniority bonus. Several employees with 35 or 40 years of service were in the process of applying for pensions when the company folded. They, in particular, objected to the termination settlement. A number of other exempt employees said that Jorge Cervantes, the head of industrial relations for Aeroméxico, had said he would withhold their severance pay for as long as two years if they took their case to the labor courts. Workers complained that they had no income, and Mrs. Nieves López Pastrana said that in addition to having no money, they had been blacklisted, so no other airline would hire them.[48]

On May 27, 1988, the Federal Board of Conciliation and Arbitration approved Aeroméxico's termination of both its individual and collective labor relations with the groundworkers, flight attendants, and exempt employees. Labor relations with the pilots' union continued, as they had never been called into question by the employer. The 11,000 workers were awarded final severance pay of three months salary, and 12 days more for each year they had worked.[49]

During the course of this struggle, which continued for many months after the final termination of labor relations, several union activists were arrested and jailed on trumped-up charges. Miguel Angel Mejorada Sánchez was arrested for fraud and held for 35 days in the Eastern Prison of Mexico City. Others were arrested on similar charges, including René Arce Islas, and Crisanto Solís Guzmán. Finally, Melchor Montalvo Guajardo, who had been the leader of the union during the union's struggle throughout 1988, was jailed for fraud. Union activists believe the government arrested and jailed these men on false charges only to prevent them from leading the union's continuing struggle.[50]

Every legal decision handed down pertaining to the Aeroméxico strike by the Bankruptcy Court and the Federal Board of Conciliation and Arbitration was an aberration of Mexican labor law. Moreover, the final settlement of the strike clearly received support from President Miguel de la Madrid and Secretary of Labor Farell Cubillas. It can be inferred from this breakdown of justice that the Mexican legal system does not serve adequately the entire population, since it exempts labor unions and workers from access to due process.

The Aeroméxico groundworkers' union, in complete accordance with the law, filed a notification of its intent to strike. Yet for two weeks there was no ruling on the legality of the strike. This allowed much mischief to occur. As so often happens in Mexican labor relations, while the Federal Board delayed and drew out the proceedings, other government officials became involved in the strike. In this case, Oscar Elizundia Treviño, President de la Madrid's secretary, told the workers that they would have a meeting with the President which could resolve their problems. Encouraged by this, the workers canceled a mass march to the presidential mansion. In reality, the President was working on a plan to terminate their employment.

Then Aeroméxico declared bankruptcy to rid itself of two of its three labor unions, as well as to get rid of more than 2,000 other workers who had accumulated seniority, vacation benefits, and pension privileges. Eventually, over 11,000 workers were terminated. As soon as the labor unions and the workers were gone, the airline reopened. Moreover, when the airline reopened operations, it rehired some of the workers, not on the basis of seniority but on the basis of their opposition to labor unions. Aeroméxico and the other airlines blacklisted Aeroméxico workers who were known to be union leaders or activists.

In addition, several union officials were arrested and charged with fraud in what union activists believe were false charges, the government's intent being to remove the movement's leaders from the struggle for their rights. Not only did the legal system fail the workers, but the system of criminal justice was used against them.

Privatization = Union Elimination

The dismantling of the unions in the nationalized nuclear, fishing, and aviation industries demonstrates that the policy of privatization of national industry not only abrogated labor rights, but also provided the occasion for the destruction of the unions themselves.

It cannot be stated categorically that the purpose of privatization was solely to destroy independent trade unionism. To be sure, many nationalized industries were financially on less than solid ground and inefficiently run. But it is surely no coincidence that one of the major effects of privatization during the López Portillo and de la Madrid administrations was to break up or decimate the most independent unions in the national sector of the economy, by means that made a mockery of the country's labor laws.

Chapter Five

The State Sector and Labor Rights Under President Salinas

In January 1989, Mexican police and military troops attacked the homes and offices of officials of the Petroleum Workers Union at its headquarters in Ciudad Madero. The police arrested the head of the union, Joaquín Hernández Galicia, known as "La Quina" ("The Boss"). In La Quina's home, the police reportedly found 300 Uzi submachine guns and 50,000 rounds of ammunition. The Attorney General said that the arms were to have been used to paralyze the Mexican oil industry, and that the attack was "a matter of national security."[1] In the assault on the house of La Quina, one police officer was killed and La Quina was charged with his murder.

In addition to La Quina, some 20 Petroleum Workers Union officials and 30 other officers and employees were arrested. In protest of these arrests, work stoppages erupted in many of the state-owned company PEMEX's facilities. The army immediately moved in, seized the oil installations, and the entire industry was put under siege. The presence of the military forced the workers to go back to work.

President Salinas de Gortari launched this attack on the Petroleum Workers Union shortly after he was inaugurated. In theory, Salinas attacked the union to put an immediate end to La Quina's corrupt 30-year domination of the union and industry. In reality, this was not only a military attack on La Quina, but also on the 210,000 members of the union. The motivation for the President's attack on the union was in large measure the union's opposition to Salinas' program of privatization.

The petroleum workers were the first to experience the cold touch of the Salinas Administration's iron hand. The Metal and Mine Workers Union at the Cananea Copper Company, the Telephone Workers Union, and the Electrical Workers Union were next. Recently, in the wake of labor strife, the government has attempted to promote a new labor federation called FESEBES, which can be considered nothing but a *papier-mâché* model of the CTM, and yet another attempt by the Mexican government to strangle labor reform by installing a new labor organization from above. With the U.S.-Mexico Free Trade Agreement in the offing, Salinas apparently feels secure enough to ignore demands for justice or legality in labor affairs.

The Short, Happy Life
of the Petroleum Workers Union

The Mexican oil industry has a sordid history. It was developed at the turn of the century by British and North American industrialists, Lord Cowdray and Edward L. Doheny, during the later years of the dictatorship of Porfirio Díaz. The Revolution of 1910 led to demands for the nationalization of this important resource, and in the Mexican Constitution of 1917, Article 27 gave the Mexican state the ownership of all subsoil minerals, including petroleum.

The intent of Article 27 was to provide a legal basis for the nationalization of the British and U.S. firms. However, because of U.S. economic, political, and military pressure on Mexico during the 1910s and 1920s, which included two invasions, the dispatch of a private army of 6,000 into the oil region, and ongoing threats of invasion, Mexico refrained from seizing the foreign-owned oil wells. In the meantime, most Mexican oil had passed into the hands of Royal Dutch Shell and Standard Oil.[2]

The oil workers had begun to organize during the period of the Mexican Revolution, always meeting strong opposition from U.S. and European firms, which employed "white guards" to subvert labor union activities and which on several occasions assassinated labor organizers.[3] Various labor organizations continued to function throughout the 1920s and 1930s, however. Some of them were led by anarchists, communists, and the Industrial Workers of the World, while others were under the control of the pro-government CROM. The first Grand Congress of Petroleum Labor Organizations was held in Mexico City on August 15, 1935. Four months later, the Petroleum Workers Union (STPRM) was formed.

It was not until the late 1930s that the Mexican government was in a position to nationalize the oil industry. The series of events that allowed the government to take control began with a two-year strike wave by the oil workers' unions starting in 1935. Perpetual failure led the oil workers to take their grievances to the Federal Board of Conciliation and Arbitration, but the European and U.S. oil companies refused to accept the Board's judgment which required them to pay workers 23 million pesos to settle the strikes. The companies remained recalcitrant even after a decision by the Mexican Supreme Court. Faced with this intransigence, on March 18, 1938 President Lázaro Cárdenas nationalized the foreign oil companies. By 1940, the Mexican government had created Petróleos Mexicanos (PEMEX), the state-owned oil company, to administer oil field, refining, storage, shipping, and sales operations.

The union's integral role in the nationalization of the oil indus-try gave it a certain amount of status in the eyes of workers in other industries, unions, and Mexican society at large. While originally it was a rather tumultuous and radical union, President Cárdenas suc-ceeded in taming STPRM to some degree by using the army to break a strike at the Azcapotzalco refinery and administrative of-fices, Local 4, in September 1940.[4] Nine years later, however, the union's independent leadership was still poking thorns in the state's side, so in December 1949 President Miguel Alemán used the police and employees of the Secretary of Labor as a strong-arm force to impose a more reliable leadership on the union.[5]

Simultaneously, the oil company's administration and the Pe-troleum Workers Union leadership were developing an alternative, symbiotic and mutually corrupting relationship. In 1946, PEMEX agreed to pay the union 2 percent of the value of all contracts be-tween PEMEX and private companies. This brought great wealth to the union bureaucracy and gave PEMEX a degree of control over its activities. Wealth for the union meant power for the union leader-ship. Ripe for the taking, the union became increasingly controlled by a caste of ambitious bureaucrats, who were put on the boards of directors of private firms which contracted with PEMEX. PEMEX administrators consciously cultivated a corrupt labor bureaucracy, recognizing that a cooperative industry was a profitable industry. Beginning in 1947, the company agreed to pay the union officials' expenses and allowances. Later, during the regime of Secretary General Pedro Vivanco García (1959-61), union officials began en-gaging in widespread job-selling. PEMEX administrators and Petro-leum Workers Union officials also paid salaries to large numbers of "ghost employees" who never showed up for work except to collect their checks.[6] Because of these corrupt activities the relationship be-tween the PRI, PEMEX, and the union officials was inextricable.[7]

In the early 1950s, petroleum worker Joaquín "La Quina" Hernández Galicia, formed a union caucus known as the Majority Unifying Group. In 1954, he became a member of the executive board of Local 1 of STPRM, and shortly thereafter the General Sec-retary. By December 1961, La Quina had risen to the office of Gen-eral Secretary of the National Petroleum Workers Union, and he and his associates continued to control the union for nearly 30 years, outwitting a bevy of heavy-handed opponents.

La Quina revolutionized corruption. He continued the practice of job-selling and the hiring of ghost employees, but added new programs which he called "The Worker Revolution." La Quina cre-ated a panoply of union-owned businesses, from farms to factories and grocery stores to movie theaters. Those who wanted temporary jobs in the fields and refineries "volunteered" time to work in the union-owned businesses, and thus became eligible for employment.

By the mid-1980s, PEMEX employed 165,000 workers of whom only 74,000 had permanent jobs while about 91,000 were casual employees. The casual employees, who were dependent on La Quina for their jobs, were not only employed in the union's businesses, but were also used to fill up union halls with supporters, or turned out as goon squads to fight La Quina's union opponents.[8]

In addition to their role as union leaders, many STPRM officials also doubled as PRI party officials, serving as city councilors, mayors, governors, state legislators, members of Congress, and senators. Their political offices increased the number and rank of "patronage positions" controlled by the union. Towns, cities, and states on Mexico's oil-rich Gulf coast were virtually controlled by STPRM.

The STPRM by-laws forbade reelection to the same union post, so La Quina did not continue in the office of General Secretary. Instead, he handpicked his successors, remaining "the power behind the throne." One of La Quina's surrogates, Heriberto Kehoe, who became General Secretary in December 1976, attempted to break away from La Quina. He was assassinated on February 28, 1977. Kehoe's successor, Oscar Torres Pancardo, was assassinated as well, on September 9, 1983.[9] Violence was not confined to the upper echelons of union leadership. Hebraïcaz Vázquez Gutiérrez, the leader of a dissident group in the union, was badly beaten by La Quina goons in June 1985.

Corruption in PEMEX and STPRM was exacerbated by the "oil boom" of the late 1970s. Between 1977 and 1982, under President José López Portillo and PEMEX director Jorge Díaz Serrano, Mexican oil production rose astronomically. Oil production rose from 165 million barrels per year in 1973 to 358 million barrels in 1977, and finally to 1,002 million barrels in 1982. Mexico produced as much oil in 1982 alone as it had between 1901 and 1958.[10] Vastly increased production made corruption possible on a grand scale, and both PEMEX executives and union officials participated in it. The number of full-time officials employed by the union and paid for by PEMEX grew from 118 in 1969 to 222 in 1979 to 952 in 1985.[11] It was also alleged that La Quina had a paramilitary force of 3,000 armed men to deal with his opponents in the union.[12]

While there was corruption and violence, there was another side to the Petroleum Workers Union under the leadership of La Quina. La Quina himself presided over improvements in wages and in the standard of living for petroleum workers. As *New York Times* reporter Joseph B. Treaster wrote, "For nearly 30 years, Mr. Hernández has been the leader of the most powerful union in Mexico, a tough, shrewd negotiator who has made oil workers the best paid laborers in Mexico and has enriched all the towns and cities in the country's oil regions."[13]

Not all PEMEX workers enjoyed equally high wages: the casual workers were more frequently neglected than the fully employed. However, despite this disparity, STPRM was one of few unions which could claim that it had improved real wages and conditions for its members. Moreover, because La Quina's economic and political power was based on the strength of STPRM and the wealth of the nationalized oil company, he had a vested interest in defending those institutions. La Quina opposed proposals to sell off PEMEX in whole or in part, which included plans to severely reduce its workforce of 210,000. While he may have done so for personal gain, his position automatically designated him *de facto* defender of the oil workers.

When one leadership group in the PRI began to talk about privatizing the state-owned companies, La Quina saw this as a threat to his power. As divisions grew within the PRI between those who wanted an economy based on private enterprise and those who wanted to maintain state-owned enterprise, La Quina naturally gravitated toward the latter. Consequently, major factions of the government wanted to get rid of him. On February 12, 1984, a document was published which revealed a government plan for an attack on STPRM. The army and navy would be used to attack the union, existing union leaders would be arrested and charged with crimes, while support was given to the opposition. The Secretary of Labor would oversee new local union elections. All systems were go, but the government decided the time was not right and did not carry out the plan.[14]

Divisions within the PRI did not come to a head until the presidential campaign of 1988, when Salinas de Gortari was the candidate of the privatizers, while Cuauhtémoc Cárdenas represented those who defended the state-owned firms, particularly the oil industry. (It was, after all, Cuauhtémoc Cárdenas' father, Lázaro Cárdenas, who had ordered the nationalization of the oil industry.) As the split between the two tendencies in the PRI grew, La Quina decided to take a stand by actively supporting Cárdenas against Salinas. In October 1988, the Petroleum Workers Union filed charges against Mario Ramón Beteta, a former head of PEMEX, charging him with a multi-million dollar scheme to defraud the company. Beteta, who subsequently had become Governor of the state of Mexico, was a political ally of Salinas.

In retaliation for the action against Beteta, to secure his own power, and to crush La Quina, President Salinas launched an attack on the leadership of the Petroleum Workers Union as no President had dared before, immediately after his inauguration. On January 10, 1989, police officers and military troops raided La Quina's home in Ciudad Madero, Tamaulipas. A bazooka rocket launcher was used to blow down the door of his house, and shots were exchanged between the police and La Quina's men, resulting in the death of one policeman. Then La Quina and 20 other union officials were arrested. La Quina and the other union officials were quickly accused of "corruption and gangsterism," while government troops took positions in and near the PEMEX installations throughout the country. On January 10 and January 11, the Attorney General's police continued to detain STPRM officials on charges of fraud, tax evasion, and illegal possession of weapons, eventually arresting 50 union officers and employees.[15]

On the day of La Quina's arrest, there were unofficial strikes or work stoppages by oil workers in many PEMEX facilities, including seven of the country's nine refineries.[16] Petroleum workers and their supporters organized a demonstration in the Zócalo national plaza. Uncharacteristically, the CTM decried the attack and the arrests, saying that they were "arbitrary" and that "what has happened, if it is not corrected, opens a new stage in the life of the country which no one desires, a stage of authoritarianism which could lead, in turn, to anarchy, and to violent reaction." Fidel Velázquez, head of the CTM, stated publicly "It was 50 years ago when labor leaders were arbitrarily jailed, and we thought that was now past." Velázquez offered the CTM's full support to STPRM's leaders. In an open letter to President Salinas, the CTM leaders demanded "the immediate liberation of the brothers who have been arbitrarily arrested, against whom, if it were necessary, appropriate legal measures can be applied." The CT rejected out of hand the possibility of a national general strike to force the government to release the jailed union leaders, but said it would seek an interview with the President to discuss the matter.[17]

The conservative National Action Party (PAN) deputy Américo Ramírez supported the attack on the Petroleum Workers Union, saying that "the state cannot permit the existence of a force which is superior or equal to it," and arguing that "the action was correct because in this way certain groups can be prevented from exploiting the oil for themselves, when it is the resource and property of all Mexicans." However, Cuauhtémoc Cárdenas, the spokesperson for the Party of the Democratic Revolution (PRD), condemned the attack, arguing that "the violent arrest of 'La Quina' and the use of the army to take control of the oil installations are violations of the law which ought to be prosecuted." He also pledged the support of the PRD for "the oil workers union and the working-class base of that organization."[18]

Ironically, January 12 was also the date for the traditional New Year's greeting from the Mexican President to the official labor unions. Despite the gravity of the assault on the petroleum unions which had taken place only two days before, representatives of the state greeted labor organizations according to traditional rituals and formulas. Salinas told the union leaders that the historic alliance between the Mexican state and the labor unions remained firm, "based upon the promise of the Federal Executive Power to respect the autonomy of the unions and labor organizations, and cemented as well in the promise of undertaking the transformation of Mexico in a nationalist, democratic, and popular spirit."[19] Arturo Romo, head of the Education Department of the CTM and the house intellectual of the official labor movement, responded by saying that "the alliance between the labor movement and the government is of an historic nature. This rises above any incidents which might arise from the arrest and trial of the Petroleum Workers Union leaders."[20]

La Quina and 37 other top union officials were arraigned on January 12, charged with weapons-trafficking and murder, resulting from the death of the policeman. At the arraignment, La Quina admitted to smuggling the machine guns, other weapons, and ammunition across the border from the United States. "I myself asked for [the arms] to defend my union members because of the situation the country is in," said La Quina at the hearing. He denied, however, that he was responsible for the death of the policeman. With La Quina in jail, local union officials chose La Quina associate Ricardo Camero Cardiel as interim union leader. Camero Cardiel was a PRI senator and the head of the union affiliate which owned 130 supermarkets.[21]

In the meantime, while those proceedings were taking place, the leaders of the CT and the CTM had the opportunity to rethink their position. Their criticism of the government began to waver. The CT issued a press release saying that the government should release more complete information about the events so that "organized workers can be relieved of any uncertainty which may be disturbing them." The CT maintained that "the law had been seriously affected" because laws had not been followed exactly as they should have been.[22] CTM second-in-command Blas Chumcero also toned down the CTM's earlier criticism, asserting that "the arrest of the Petroleum Workers Union leaders does not endanger the political stability of the country. The Republic finds itself in social and political peace."[23] Within a few days, the official labor unions had given up their initial criticism and verbal protests to reaffirm their traditional support for the PRI and the President. Within the labor movement, only the independent unions continued to be critical of the government's role in assaulting STPRM.

The Salinas Administration next moved to impose on the Petroleum Workers Union the leadership it desired. First, Secretary of Labor Arsenio Farell Cubillas refused to recognize Ricardo Camero Cardiel as General Secretary, arguing that his choice as the new union leader had not followed the union's constitution and by-laws, which it assuredly had not. Second, the Labor Department indicated that the union's Secretary of the Interior, José Meléndez, should become the acting head of the union.

Within about a week, the government had arrived at its choice for leader of the national union, to which both CTM and STPRM officials acquiesced. Following an "Extraordinary Convention" of local union leaders on January 22, 1989, the delegates issued a press release which stated the union's position in four points: STPRM supported President Salinas; it remained loyal to the CTM; it remained loyal to the PRI; and it supported the candidacy of Sebastian Guzmán Cabrera for head of the union.[24] The union officials who participated in this special convention and who made these decisions were local union officers who had held office during the era of La Quina; in most cases they were supporters and followers of La Quina, or at least had held office at his sufferance. The fact that the convention had made no fundamental changes in union leadership or in the organization's by-laws, and that they had overwhelmingly deferred power to their former adversary President Salinas and his cadre, were signals to the members that the union's relationship to authority was unlikely to change, though the authority figure had.

Guzmán Cabrera himself was a former high official of the union and a close associate of La Quina. His choice as the PRI-CTM candidate for General Secretary was peculiar as he had already retired from the company and the union, and was not eligible to become a union officer. Extraordinary efforts had to be made before he could be reinstated by the company and the union in order to stand as a candidate for local and then for national office. With the help of union officials and the Secretary of Labor, all legal obstacles were swept swiftly aside, so that on February 1 Guzmán Cabrera took office as head of STPRM. The ousting of La Quina "was a real liberation for the workers," said Guzmán Cabrera, who promised to continue the historic alliance with the Mexican state guarding against subordinating the workers' interests to those of the government.

The transformation of STPRM was remarkable. In less than a month after taking office, President Salinas had succeeded in removing one of the most powerful labor officials ever to appear in Mexican history, replacing him with a man who would toe the government line. President Salinas had used the police and the army in a violent attack on the union with little opposition from other sectors of society. STPRM, in fact, had raised only short-lived and feeble opposition, which only slightly outweighed the opposition from other labor unions, the CTM, or the CT.

Following the installation of Guzmán Cabrera as head of the union, meetings were called for STPRM locals to choose new executive boards and general secretaries. These elections provided a rare opportunity for rank and file petroleum workers to organize movements to democratize and reform their unions. In some cases, they organized on their own. In other cases they worked with various political parties active in and around the Petroleum Workers Union, including dissident factions in the PRI, the PRD, the PRT, and others. The groups which formed included rank and file workers, members of long-standing opposition forces in the union, out-of-office former union officials, and dissident officials.[25]

Secretary of Labor Farell Cubillas, however, did not take advantage of this opportunity to ensure that democratic and fair elections were carried out in the union. Rather, elections were carried out as they always had been under La Quina, with victory secured for the chosen candidate by stacking the union halls with unauthorized supporters. In Local 30 in the city of Poza Rica, for example, opposition to Guzmán Cabrera led by a dissident PRI official, Reyes Betancourt, was strongly supported both in the union and in the city at large. Nevertheless, this opposition was overwhelmingly defeated by the machinations of the Guzmán Cabrera forces and the Secretary of Labor's office. Local election rules did not call for secret and universal elections, but simply for elections on the basis of who showed up for the meeting at the union hall and raised their hands. So the Guzmán Cabrera faction was able to stack the meeting with its supporters, including many individuals who did not work for PEMEX and were not members of the union. Despite protests, the Secretary of Labor recognized the Guzmán Cabrera faction as the winner.[26]

Similarly, in Local 35 in Mexico City, workers from the "18th of March" refinery in Azcapotzalco and from the "Miguel Hidalgo" facility in Tula, Hidalgo succeeded in forming an alliance of opposition groups. "The election in Local 35," said one Mexico City petroleum worker, "was carried out in the same way as always, using the casual workers to stack the meeting, without allowing for a clear vote."[27] To protest the results of the election, some workers engaged in a hunger strike, while others distributed leaflets. A group of these workers was attacked by a goon squad, and some were seriously injured. The Secretary of Labor did nothing to protect the opposition or to investigate protests; instead, he immediately recognized the election of officials loyal to Guzmán Cabrera.

In Local 34, several groups opposing La Quina had long existed. The "Lázaro Cárdenas Independent Movement," the Movement of Technical and Professional Workers, and two others organized an opposition slate called the Petroleum Workers Coalition, which had thousands of supporters. How the Guzmán Cabrera forces won in Local 34 is an instructive example of what the state calls a democratic election. One witness described what happened:

> The general executive committee of the local which supported Guzmán Cabrera did not call a union meeting for the election. So the opposition group seized

and occupied the union hall. Negotiations occurred, as a result of which the opposition left the union hall and a date was set for the election. The day of the elections Antonio Medina's people, who supported Guzmán Cabrera, took over the union hall with casual workers. PEMEX was even involved, because it let these workers leave during working hours. The union officials put all these casual workers who supported their election in the hall. When the opposition workers arrived, they found that the hall was full, locked, and that it had been taken over by the supporters of the Guzmán Cabrera slate. By the time the union meeting was supposed to start, there were two groups facing each other in direct confrontation. At this point the Coalition succeeded in moving the casual workers out of the hall... The auditorium was full, there must have been six thousand workers... The Petroleum Workers Coalition easily had over 90 percent of the people who were inside... They waited for the arrival of a representative of Guzmán Cabrera's general executive committee [to conduct the election]. Later, representatives of the Secretary of Labor arrived, they came in and then they left. They never called an election, they never organized anything... The Secretary of Labor said afterwards that there had been an election, that it had been legal, and that Antonio Medina's group [the supporters of Guzmán Cabrera] had won. They gave the figures for how many votes there had been for each one, when there had never been any vote.

That is how it always is in Mexico... I have to make clear that the removal of Hernández Galicia [La Quina] did not mean clean elections for the petroleum workers: it did not mean counting the vote, it did not mean listing eligible voters according to the by-laws. The Secretary of Labor, the governmental representative and the representative of Guzmán Cabrera behaved as they always behave, making a mockery of the union meeting.[28]

The significance of the events in STPRM after the fall of La Quina is described by that same petroleum worker:

La Quina was a political opponent of the current governing group in Mexico, for his own very special reasons. The blow that struck down La Quina on January 10 was not only a blow at him and his interests, but rather at the entire oil workers union, as was shown in all the local union meetings held after January 10. They had promised that there was going to be union democracy, that elections were going to be clean, but none of the elections were clean. There were no democratic union meetings, there were no voting lists, there were no secret votes.[29]

The corruption and cynicism which spawned the imposition of Guzmán Cabrera on the national union leadership, and then the imposition of his supporters in the local elections, left the union membership utterly disheartened. Many observers felt that this demoralization led to a drop in participation by members in the union and allowed the government to take total control of the organization and squash it.[30] As one disgruntled worker said:

Today more than ever, workers are not participating in any kind of union activity. There is demoralization, there is fear, as there always was, but today the people perceive that there is no alternative to the leadership. During the La Quina years there were always little [opposition] groups. In almost all of the locals these groups published little newspapers, but today none of that exists. Any opposition group that arises is blasted.[31]

The Guzmán Cabrera leadership negotiated a new relationship between the workers and PEMEX. The nature of their formerly symbiotic albeit corrupt relationship drastically changed for the worse. First, the union gave up the 10,000 technical and professional workers. The technical and professional workers, organized in 1974-75, became members of the union in 1976, during the La Quina years. As a group of worker-intellectuals, they provided valuable expertise and information to other union activists, and they were frequently found in the leadership of opposition movements to La Quina. According to several PEMEX technical and professional workers, no vote was ever taken to decide if they should leave the union, and they were given no voice in the decision-making process. Once out of the union, they were given dramatic salary increases, in some cases almost doubling their salaries at a time when most other Mexican workers' salaries were being cut in half.

Second, while the technicians and professionals were receiving raises as a "reward" for leaving the union, thousands of casual workers were laid off. The combination of these losses weakened the union tremendously vis à vis the employer.

Third, the collective bargaining agreement was rewritten and several important clauses were deleted or changed. For example, petroleum workers previously had the right to be involved in decisions regarding changes in operations or the introduction of new technology. In the new contract, management advises the workers of what the changes, made by the management, will be. A highly symbolic change was the deletion of an historic clause which said that all PEMEX orders must be given in the Spanish language, a reaction to the old days when British and North American supervisors and foremen spoke English. Lastly, petroleum workers report that since Guzmán Cabrera took power, the shop floor presence of the union has virtually disappeared. Supervisors and foremen are no longer mandated to deal with union representatives, so they don't. All of these factors add up to a devastating defeat for STPRM. In most of the recent elections, there was no opposition to the PRI-CTM-chosen incumbents.

Why did the government engage in such a violent attack on the union leadership when the company was successful, and the relationship between the union and the employer worked? Reorganization from outside of the union, weakening it to bear the blow, was part of a national plan, and attacks were carried out on many unions. As an article in *Business Latin America* proposed:

> The thesis held by de la Madrid, and now by Salinas, is that the state must reduce the strength of the old-line union leaders without destroying the unions themselves, so that they do not become a power that can rival the government and sabotage its efforts at economic modernization. In his choice of hard-liners for some cabinet officials [Secretary of Labor Farell Cubillas and Secretary of Education Manuel Bartlett], Salinas exhibited his intention to control union power and eventually change the nature of the unions.[32]

Specifically, Salinas wanted to change PEMEX, and that required the destruction of La Quina and STPRM's monopoly on power. As *Wall Street Journal* reporter Matt Moffett wrote:

> Mr. Salinas' plan to modernize Mexico's economy required an overhaul of Petróleos Mexicanos, or PEMEX, which accounts for 40% of state revenue and more than 10% of total national output. Experts have contended that the biggest obstacle to such modernization was the 210,000-member oil workers union.[33]

Unfortunately for the workers, the "experts" led the company on a rampage. In the name of profit, cost-cutting measures had devastating effects on their lives:

> Cost-cutting at PEMEX shows up in a number of ways. The Petroleum Workers Union once controlled the construction contracts awarded by PEMEX; now they go up for competitive bidding. The PEMEX labor force has shrunk from 213,000 in 1988 to 150,000 today. The

number of children in PEMEX-operated secondary schools has dropped by 5,000 since 1988, to fewer than 50,000.[34]

The destruction of the union allowed the company and the aspects of production La Quina had sectored off for the profit of the union bureaucracy to be put on the auction block. PEMEX allowed foreign investors to process crude oil into petrochemicals, and planned to allow foreign investors into other aspects of operations.

It may be that reorganization of the industry was necessary. Attacking and destroying the union leadership and reorganizing the union, however, made it impossible for the workers to participate in that reorganization as they had in the past. Without a union that represents their interests, the workers had no vehicle to put forward alternative plans for the reorganization of the company that might have benefited them as well as the new owners. In the end, they were left without the safeguards that it took years of collective action to gain.

The Salinas Administration's attack on the Petroleum Workers Union with the army and the police was devastating to the workers, who not only lost a union, but a livelihood. La Quina's personal brand of corruption was always festooned with Robin Hoodesque bestowals of jobs and meaningful wages. In contrast to the state, which mandates total control and excludes workers from a share in the profits, La Quina was a better alternative for labor. The willingness of the state to make extraordinary use of the army and the police in order to deal with a labor union inevitably has had a chilling affect on all labor union organizations. In this case, it set a tone for the Salinas Administration, which would continue to use troops to "resolve" labor disputes.

It is not clear how serious were the violations of the petroleum workers' rights according to Mexican law as it is practiced, because of the denial of due process to examine the union elections that followed La Quina's removal. Nonetheless, the attack on La Quina decreased worker power and made workers less likely to exercise their rights. The imposition of Sebastian Guzmán Cabrera was a violation of international labor law as it is recognized by Mexico, because it was carried out with the repeated use of violence against union members, and it denied those members their right to a democratic vote. In spite of persistent pronouncements by the Salinas Administration that Mexico is in a process of democratic reform, democracy continues to be denied. As many leaders of Mexico before Salinas have learned, violence speaks louder than words.

Cananea Miners: A Century of Dissent

Cananea is the largest copper mine in Latin America, and one of the world's 10 most important, both in terms of its proven reserves and its production capacity. It is also one of the most famous companies in Mexico as the cradle of both the Mexican labor movement and the Mexican Revolution. Originally owned and developed by a North American, Col. William C. Greene, the "Copper King of Cananea," the mine was the site of a huge strike in 1906.[35] Organized by the anarchist Mexican Liberal Party, led by Ricardo Flores Magón, the strike was intended to overthrow the dictator Porfirio Díaz, but the labor uprising was suppressed after the massacre of 21 strikers. In addition to being one of the first upheavals of the modern labor movement, the Cananea strike of 1906 is seen as one of the harbingers of the Mexican Revolution, which finally erupted in 1910. After the revolution, the first industrial union was organized at Cananea in the 1930s and signed its first labor contract in 1932.

The Cananea Mining Company was eventually absorbed by the Anaconda Copper Company which remained the owner of Cananea Mining until 1971 when the Mexican government and private investors acquired a majority of the stock, leaving Anaconda holding 49 percent. Anaconda remained the principal stockholder until 1982, when the Mexican government took out loans from two U.S. banks to buy out Anaconda and then nationalized the Cananea Mining Company. In 1983, National Financial (Nafinsa) acquired the other 49 percent of the stock.[36]

Beginning in 1981, between $600 and $900 million were invested in the mine to modernize its equipment and make it more productive. With these improvements, the mine tripled its productivity during the decade of the 1980s. Cananea now competed on the world market, exporting approximately 40 percent of its production to markets in America, Europe, and Asia.[37] The company bulletin for January 21, 1989 reported that "1988 was one of the best years of our company." An editorial in that same bulletin reported that Cananea was "one of the most modern and progressive" copper mines. Its rank among the most important companies in Latin America had risen from 644th in 1986 to 208th in 1987; within Mexico, it rose from number 80 to number 16.[38]

Nevertheless, in line with the call for the reprivatization of Mexican industry, the Mexican government decided to sell the company, and turn over management of Cananea to Nafinsa, which was told to make the company more attractive to potential purchasers. Nafinsa planned to restructure the Cananea Mine, while the federal government and the government of the state of Sonora were working to promote economic development of the area by creating small- and medium-sized industrial plants and *maquiladoras*.[39]

In 1989, the mine employed approximately 3,200 full-time union employees, 600 management employees, and another 800 casual workers. The town of Cananea's 35,000 inhabitants were largely workers and workers' family members, all of them dependent upon the mine in one way or another.

The current problems at the state-owned Cananea Mine began in Summer 1989. During contract negotiations, the company, headed by Alberto Pérez Aceves, proposed a series of drastic changes in the existing labor/management setup, claiming that it needed a "new system of work." Nafinsa claimed that production costs at Cananea were 33 percent higher than at other copper mines around the world. To combat this "cost overrun," the company put forward this plan: First, the company planned to close two departments (Methods Systems and Extraction) and lay off 343 miners. Second, the company wanted to rewrite the labor contract, changing clauses dealing with work days, work hours, break times, vacations, transfers, vacancy promotions, retirement funds, and overtime work. Third, the company would break up into component parts, establishing related enterprises with new labor agreements, inferior to the existing collective bargaining agreement, and even in violation of Federal Labor Law. The new companies would operate 365 days a year, averting the existing contract language which gave workers time off on Sundays and holidays. The company felt it was particularly important to change its operations in the open-pit mining operations and the extraction-by-solvents plant. The company formally put these demands before the Federal Board of Conciliation and Arbitration.[40]

Workers at the plant were represented by Local 65 of the National Mine and Metal Workers Union. The local union rejected the company's demands for changed work rules, and also wanted a 60 percent wage increase and a number of improvements in benefits. The workers' average wage was 150,000 pesos per week, 100,000 pesos after taxes, or about 33 dollars, in a city with a particularly high cost of living due to its isolation and its proximity to the U.S. border. In terms of benefits, the union wanted the company to comply with past commitments to build hospitals and recreational parks. The workers also asked the company to improve its contribution to the housing fund and to provide scholarships for miners' children.

After negotiation proved fruitless, on June 21, 1989 the union filed a strike notification with the Federal Board of Conciliation and Arbitration.[41] The strike was scheduled to begin August 27, 1989.

On August 20, 1989, a bankruptcy court in Mexico City declared the Cananea Mine to be bankrupt because of its inability to pay its debts. The name of the judge who made the declaration of bankruptcy was not revealed, however, leading to allegations that the whole proceeding was spurious.[42] In statements released to the press, the company was said to owe 20 billion pesos to the government, 25 billion pesos to its suppliers, 67 billion pesos to the American Express Company, and 578 billion pesos to Nafinsa.

That same day at 5 a.m., between 3,000 and 5,000 soldiers of the Mexican Army arrived in Cananea to take control of the mine. About 600 night-shift workers were removed from the mine, and the 7:30 a.m. shift of more than 1,000 was not permitted to enter. As the army took possession of the mine, leaflets were handed out to the workers informing them that the mine was bankrupt. Thousands of bewildered workers, expelled from the mine and not permitted to report for work, went to the Local 65 union hall to await information. Héctor Luna, General Secretary of Local 65, and Froylan Murrieta Loreto, a member of Local 65 and a PRI Congressmember, reported that Napoleon Gómez Sada, head of the National Mine and Metal Workers Union, was asking for an interview with President Salinas in order to resolve the problem.

The next day, 3,200 mine workers met and passed a resolution demanding that Nafinsa "remove the troops within 15 days and give us the installations, otherwise we will occupy the mine peacefully with the support of the local population." The union demanded that the plant reopen immediately and that the workers be put back to work. The union blamed the bankruptcy of the company on corruption, accusing Emilio Ocampo Arenal, the son-in-law of former President Echeverría, of having "sacked the company to enrich himself, robbing the company with impunity."

Union leaders said that the troops had not only taken the mine, but were also patrolling the streets and had five helicopters flying overhead. The officials also complained that members of the Federal Judicial Police had come to investigate the union "under the false impression that we had an arsenal and guerrilla groups. We do not believe in the government nor in the PRI," said the union leaders.

While Local 65 was holding its meeting, Governor Rodolfo Félix Valdés arrived, spoke to the meeting, and was openly criticized by the workers for the role of the federal government. One union activist said the government's policy was "an attack on the union and treason to labor unionism." The governor responded by urging the workers to keep their struggle within legal channels and said he would report to the federal government the indignation felt by the people of Cananea. The director of the Cananea Mine, Carlos Torres, said the mine was losing $1 million a day, and that it would have to reopen as soon as possible, though he could not say how many workers would be rehired when it did reopen.[43]

Meanwhile in Mexico City, Napoleon Gómez Sada, head of the National Mine and Metal Workers Union, and a delegation of workers from Cananea met with Secretary of Labor Arsenio Farell

Cubillas. Secretary Farell told them there would be no retreat from the government's decision to declare the mine bankrupt, and that his department would ensure that the Cananea workers were severed "according to the law and as rapidly as possible." He also explained that the bankruptcy judge had asked that the army be sent in to occupy the mine because of the great quantities of dynamite and other explosive and combustible materials which were stored there. Gómez Sada declared that the workers were not responsible for the bankruptcy of the company, but took no action to defend union members except to demand that they be severed as provided by the contract and the labor law.[44]

The events in Cananea stunned the Mexican labor movement. The Mexican Electrical Workers (SME) placed an advertisement in major newspapers expressing its dismay:

> The events which took place at the Cananea, Sonora mine the 20th of this month are cause for indignation among Mexican workers. Just when a broad debate about the future of labor relations is taking place, as a result of the proposed modification of Article 123 of the Constitution and its regulatory law; just when in the bosom of the Congress we are hearing the demands of the labor unions on the country, that any labor legislation reform requires that the rights we already have be respected; just in these moments all of the rights of the mine worker brothers of Cananea are violated, closing and militarizing their place of work in an action that reminds us of what happened in that very location back in 1906 at the height of the Porfirian dictatorship when the rangers were used to massacre the striking workers.
>
> Paradoxically, in honor of modernization there is a return to the methods of the pre-revolutionary age. Right before our eyes, 80 years of our nation's history disappear in smoke. In the *modernization* process, cooperation gives way to armed force. It is a process of modernizing by blood and fire. And all to make Cananea attractive for its sale to private capital...[45]

The official labor movement leadership, however, was indecisive. Napoleon Gómez Sada, head of the Mine and Metal Workers Union, criticized the declaration of bankruptcy and said that the union contract had not been responsible for it. "Closing sources of employment is an attack on the working class," said Gómez Sada, but he took no action. Juan Moisés Calleja, attorney for the CTM, said that "industrial modernization should not be carried out at the cost of the working class." But neither did the CTM take any deci-

sive action. Francisco Hernández Juárez, head of the Telephone
Workers Union, declared that Cananea "is a situation which forces
the Congress of Labor to be more thoughtful about what is happen-
ing, and to act with solidarity in facing our problems." But
Hernández Juárez also proposed no concrete course of action.[46]
Fidel Velázquez, head of the CTM, said later that the CT had taken
no action to support the Cananea miners because Gómez Sada was
opposed to any such show of support.[47]

The director of Cananea, Luís Alberto Pérez Aceves, blamed the
failure of the company, among other factors, on the labor union
contracts which had forced the copper company to operate in the
red. With its high labor costs and other exorbitant expenses, he said,
the company could not be competitive in the international market.
The company, which had previously operated with 3,200 full-time
and 800 casual workers, should be able to reopen with a total of
2,500 workers, said Pérez Aceves. The total loss of jobs then would
be 1,500.[48] No mention was made of the 600 management employees who were also terminated.

Meanwhile, the bankruptcy court had appointed National Financial of the Sugar Industry (Finasa) as the official receiver for the
bankrupt company. Management assured the public that the workers being permanently terminated would be paid their severance
within two to three weeks. The workers would be paid a total of 25
billion pesos. It was not clear, however, whether workers would be
paid their severance according to their labor union contract, the
Federal Labor Law, or bankruptcy law.

Certain apparent contradictions in the government's position
bred controversy in the already suspect bankruptcy proceedings.
The Secretary General Controller of the Federation (Secogef) reported that the state would not intervene in the bankruptcy proceedings because the company was not considered a nationalized
company, since the Mexican government held only a minority of
the stock. Nafinsa, the receiver for the company, held 90 percent of
the stock.[49] All of the Nafinsa-held stock, however, presumably
came from the Mexican government's share.

The army withdrew from Cananea on August 24, 1989, after occupying the plant and town for four days. The effects of the plant
closure on the people of Cananea and on the economy of the state of
Sonora were immediate and devastating. People were left with no
source of income. Luís Donaldo Colosio Murrieta, national president of the PRI, senator for the state of Sonora, and former congressmember for the district, met with the Cananea miners and
demanded the immediate reopening of the mine and the immediate
indemnification of the workers who had been laid off in accord with
their union contract, rather than under the terms of the Federal
Labor Law or the bankruptcy law. He also called for the creation of

a temporary emergency fund for the laid-off miners, and a special solidarity program, with emphasis on creating alternative sources of employment. The federal and Sonora governments, it turns out, had been planning for alternative sources of employment for some time through the creation of *maquiladoras*.

> The party of the Mexican workers can not, must not, and will not in these moments remain far from the workers, from their worries, from their demands, and from their longing for well being... It is for this reason that in this difficult hour for the people of Cananea, their party, which carries the banner of democracy and social justice, declares itself for the defense of the workers. Our solidarity is a fighting solidarity.

Despite the radical rhetoric in his above statement, Colosio Murrieta did not oppose the federal government's decision to privatize the mine, he did not oppose the declaration of bankruptcy, and he did not oppose laying off 1,300 miners.[50]

"Praising the emperor's clothes," President Salinas spoke out on August 26, 1989. In a meeting with the nation's top union leaders, the President declared that there would be no turning back from the decision to close Cananea and terminate all its employees. Only afterwards would there be a decision about when to reopen the plant. At the same time, Mine and Metal Workers Union leader Napoleon Gómez Sada said that there could be no appeal because everything was being handled according to law. Rafael de Jesús Lozano, the head of the Federation of Unions of Workers at the Service of the State (FSTSE) said that Salinas "did not take away [the Cananea miners'] jobs" and was a President "who defends the worker and his interests." Roberto Castellanos Tovar, a leader of the CROC, said that the leadership of the labor movement was satisfied now that it understood that the government was going to deal with fundamental problems and reactivate the economy. He said that Salinas had given a talk that was "very serene, authentic, and for that reason we are optimistic. To sum up, it was about finding a fast way out of the situation with realism."[51] In short, with the exception of the electrical workers union, SME, not one important official labor leader said a critical word about the use of the military to occupy the plant and town, about the shady declaration of bankruptcy, or about the termination of 1,300 workers.

Meanwhile in Cananea, Mine and Metal Workers Local 65 went ahead with its plans to strike the closed mine. The strike was supported by the Association of Retired Miners of the Cananea Mining Company. All of the workers rejected outright a proposal made by Governor Rodolfo Félix Valdés to create *maquiladoras* in the area to provide employment. The miners asked him if he could live on the

8,000 pesos per day that the transnational companies were paying. Attempting to assuage the angry miners, Daniel Liera Castro, Secretary of the Government, promised that Cananea would reopen within 60 days, and that in the meantime food would be dispensed to more than 3,000 workers.

Reporters for *Excelsior* wrote:

> Cananea is now a town in crisis. According to the local Chamber of Commerce, sales in the 350 businesses in the city have fallen by 90 percent due to the workers' lack of liquidity, now that they have gone for a week without receiving salary... So far, sympathetic help has not arrived, and workers are now putting their furniture and electrical appliances up for sale, and some, in order to come up with some money, have even tried to rent their cars to the reporters who have come to Cananea to cover these problems.[52]

With nothing else to do the night before the strike, on the evening of August 27, workers went to the "Martyrs of 1906" baseball stadium to watch the Norte de Sonora team play the team from Magdalena. Admission for the miners was free.

Earlier that day, the Cananea miners had held a general assembly where they had elected 12 commissioners to represent them, who were sent off to Mexico City with the General Secretary of the local, Octavio Bustamante. On August 28, 1989, Local 65 struck the closed Cananea copper mine. Oscar Sainz Cota, president of the strike committee, said that the workers would not attempt to take control of the plant because they did not want to be accused of the damage which had been caused by soldiers. Sainz Cota said that Local 65 had an adequate strike fund to see it through the current conflict, and that, in addition, it had received economic support from various independent unions in Sonora and throughout the country, as well as from U.S. miners in Arizona and California. Senator Colosio sent two tractor-trailer truckers with food for 3,000 workers. A group of independent unions held a demonstration in Mexico City in support of the Cananea workers on September 1, 1989.[53] The union, however, was in desperate shape, without sufficient funds to buy gas for the union's cars and vans, and without money to pay for the airline tickets that sent their officials to Mexico City.

When the commissioners arrived in Mexico City the day the strike began, they met with Emilio Gómez Vives of the Secretary of Labor's office, who proposed that the mine could reopen immediately if the workers accepted the following conditions: 1) permanent lay-off of at least 500 miners; 2) restructuring of the labor agreement with the elimination of 115 clauses and the rewriting of 143 others.

Bustamante rejected this offer, claiming it proved the declaration of bankruptcy was fraudulent and spurious.

Local 65 representatives also went before the Federal Board of Conciliation and Arbitration. The Cananea Mining Company had asked the Federal Board to terminate all labor relations with its employees. Local 65 commissioners went before the Board to declare the strike and to repeat their objections to the bankruptcy proceedings. At the same time, Napoleon Gómez Sada reported that he had asked for an injunction against Cananea's declaration of bankruptcy and that he was asking the Secretary of Labor to investigate the basis for the declaration. He also stated that neither the national nor the local leadership had yet been officially informed that the company was bankrupt. The commissioners also met with Secretary of Labor Arsenio Farell Cubillas to seek his help in resolving the crisis. Local 65 expressed its willingness to accept voluntary lay-offs from the some 200 physically disabled miners suffering from injuries or silicosis. Secretary Farell told the miners the government's decision was final, but suggested that the workers might acquire 25 percent of the mine's stock.[54] Jorge Leypen Garay, director of the CTM Industrial Group, later said that the CTM's business organization was prepared to invest up to 100 billion pesos in Cananea stock.[55]

On August 30, Napoleon Gómez Sada held a press conference in which he declared that a judge had handed down a temporary injunction against the bankruptcy of Cananea, though he did not identify the court or the judge. "The workers' rights," he proclaimed, "have been saved."[56] Héctor Romero Sánchez, lawyer for Local 65, said he had not been informed of the temporary injunction.[57] Meanwhile, the former director of Cananea, Emilio Ocampo Arenal, had been arrested.

President Salinas spoke out again on Cananea on September 1 while in Guadalajara, Jalisco, saying that the government would protect the miners' rights, but that it would only operate efficient and productive enterprises.[58]

It was now more than a week since the government had seized and closed the mine, and the unity of the workers was in question. Some union members advocated accepting the government's proposed severance pay, while others wanted to continue the fight to reopen the mine and rehire all the workers. There was a divergence between the union's executive board and the local strike committee. General Secretary Octavio Bustamante and the union leadership now advocated accepting severance pay, while Carlos Escalante, a rank and file activist involved in the strike committee, proposed continuing the fight for the jobs of all the miners.[59] Two days later, on September 3, 1989, Bustamante announced that the workers were prepared to accept their termination if they received full severance pay according to the union contract.[60]

The strike continued, and on September 8, 1989, Local 65 placed an advertisement in the national papers expressing the deep discontent and anger the workers felt:

> It shall go down in history that only two presidents of the Republic have dared to send the army to Cananea: Porfirio Díaz and Carlos Salinas de Gortari...
>
> The miners of Cananea do not deserve the treatment of common criminals that we have been given. We feel hurt, offended, indignant and betrayed...
>
> The current government is perhaps the most reactionary that we have had for many decades, which, wrapped up in the slogan of "modernization," is actually trying to take us back to the Porfirian era. We will not permit it. We are a people with a tradition of struggle, repeatedly demonstrated during an entire century, and we are not afraid of threats.
>
> The working conditions we have were achieved with the sweat and blood of many generations of miners. We cannot give up our collective bargaining agreement. We would be betraying ourselves.

Local 65 called for four essential points:

> 1) Complete respect for the collective bargaining agreement; 2) Immediate reopening of the Cananea Copper Mine; 3) Payment for lost time; 4) Reopening of negotiations on the new contract.

Finally, Local 65 called upon President Salinas, Secretary of Labor Arsenio Farell Cubillas, and Secretary of the Treasury Pedro Aspe Armella to come to Cananea to negotiate a settlement directly with the local union.[61]

The Cananea Mining Company made another offer on September 11, 1989, saying it would rehire 2,500 of the 3,295 union miners, leaving 795 unemployed. Napoleon Gómez Sada did not directly respond to the offer, but merely said that all miners laid off would have to be compensated according to the union contract. He also said that there had been no movement of the injunction which the national union had placed before the judge of the Fourth District Court of civil matters.[62]

That same day, Special Board number 13 of the Federal Board of Conciliation and Arbitration approved the termination of both individual and collective labor relations at the Cananea Mining Company. The Board also ruled that both union and management employees would be indemnified according to the Federal Labor Law.[63] It was subsequently announced that the management employees would be indemnified according to federal bankruptcy law.[64]

Nevertheless, the strike continued with support coming from steelworkers in Arizona, from the telephone workers, from employees of the University of Sonora, and from other sources. The head of the strike committee, Oscar Sainz Cota, said that the workers rejected the idea of accepting their termination in exchange for part ownership of the company, calling it a "smoke screen." The miners considered taking their case to the United Nations and said that Amnesty International had offered to bring their representatives to Washington, where Presidents Bush and Salinas would meet on October 2.[65]

The Cananea Mining Company offered the miners severance pay amounting to 8,772 million pesos, the amount due them according to the Federal Labor Law. Napoleon Gómez Sada rejected this settlement, demanding the 25,000 million pesos due to the workers under their current contract.[66] Likewise, Oscar Sainz Cota, head of the Local 5 strike committee, said that no Cananea worker would accept the severance pay which had been offered "because it is treason to the workers' movement." Any worker who accepted such a settlement, he said, would be expelled from the union immediately.[67] The union workers were joined by the management employees in rejecting the government's proposed settlement.[68] Local 65 stepped up its activity on September 14 when workers blocked the highway leading to Cananea.[69] The next day the general secretaries of 14 locals of the Miners and Metal Workers Union signed a statement protesting the government's action in closing Cananea.[70]

In Cananea itself, a group of mine workers, their wives, children, and supporters seized the offices of the Federal Board of Conciliation and Arbitration, cut the telephone lines, and kidnapped the receiver's agents who were paying out severance pay. The receiver's employees were released a few hours later. Those who seized the offices said they had done so because union employees were being severed and paid off, though the union officials had not been fully informed as the law requires. Workers and their wives also seized the *Voz del Norte* newspaper as part of their attempt to bring their case to public attention and put pressure on the government. Leading the seizure of the newspaper was Luz Marina Morales, the former candidate of the Mexican Socialist Party (PMS) for Mayor of Cananea. The conservative National Action Party (PAN) also organized a march and rally to protest the government's decision to declare bankruptcy.

Perhaps in response to this continued pressure, Secretary of Labor Arsenio Farell Cubillas promised to recommend to the bankruptcy judge and to the receiver for Cananea that the workers' severance pay be increased. Under the auspices of Secretary of Labor Farrell, another session of negotiations was held. On September 25, Salvador Trueba Martínez, director of Nafinsa (the Nationalized Bank of the Sugar Industry), the receiver for Cananea, proposed to Local 65's negotiating committee and Napoleon

Gómez Sada, head of the national union, that the mine reopen and operations resume at the same salary levels that existed before the bankruptcy, but that many clauses in the collective bargaining agreement would still be eliminated.[71]

In fact, the company presented the workers with a new labor contract, completely rewritten, eliminating some 152 contract clauses. Behind all of the changes was consistent affirmation that the company could use the workers in any way it deemed profitable to the company. In other industries, this kind of renegotiation was called "flexibility." The contract also allowed the company to contract out work to third parties, with no compensation to union employees who had formerly done such work. The employer's new draft contract also specified that "the mining enterprise can freely administer its business, and, consequently, the workers shall not meddle in the administration."

The union rejected the proposal and negotiations continued.[72] Workers were still demanding that the mine be reopened, all full-time miners be rehired, and casual employees be severed according to the terms of the labor contract. The union presented an alternative collective bargaining agreement, eliminating many antiquated clauses, but retaining others which it said protected the workers' historic achievements.[73]

In response, at another session arranged through the Secretary of Labor, the receivers of the Cananea Mining Company told the workers that they were willing to reopen the mine if it was possible to guarantee a certain level of productivity. However, said the receiver, the termination and severance of the 3,200 workers was an accomplished fact and would not be reconsidered.[74] Back in Cananea, the frustrated workers debated the possibility of seizing and occupying the mine, though in the end they decided not to do so.[75] The company returned to the table with a counter-proposal, telling the union representatives that if they accepted it, the mine could be opened and the workers back at their jobs in 48 hours.[76]

A solidarity conference in support of the Cananea miners was held in Hermosillo, attended by more than 50 labor union, civic, and political organizations from Mexico and from foreign countries. The conference condemned the "anti-national politics" of President Salinas, demanded that the Cananea mine be turned over to the miners, and called for a "national civic work stoppage" for October 24.[77]

Meanwhile, in Mexico City the talks continued. On October 16, an agreement in principle was finally reached, though the details of the agreement had yet to be spelled out.[78] In the end, the company did not go bankrupt, and all of the miners were not terminated. The final agreement released the next day provided that some 400 job titles would be eliminated, and that thenceforth there would be only three job titles for both maintenance and production workers. The

the Telephone Workers Union (STRM) which at the end of the 1980s had 49,000 members. Like most major Mexican labor organizations, throughout the 1940s, 1950s, and 1960s it was controlled by *charro* leaders loyal to the ruling PRI. However, during the turbulent 1970s various opposing political forces began to be organized within the union and succeeded in building a base of support among the union's rank and file. In April 1976, a rank and file rebellion among the telephone operators led to the ousting of the old *charro* leadership and to the election of an apparently more militant and democratic group led by Francisco Hernández Juárez.[85]

Under Hernández Juárez, the Telephone Workers Union was more democratic internally, with various caucuses active within it. For a while at least, Hernández Juárez attempted to maintain the union's relative independence from the state-party. Between 1976 and 1987, the Telephone Workers Union carried out five strikes at TELMEX (as well as several other strikes at other companies related to the telephone industry); most of the strikes called for higher wages. However, on each occasion, the government used Article 112 of the Federal Law of General Routes of Communication to declare government seizure of TELMEX, under which the telephone workers were required to continue working. With these declarations, TELMEX facilities were seized by military or police units or by company guards, and the workers were forced to return to work under their supervision. In each case, "the union ended up accepting the proposals that the company had made before the work-stoppage began."[86]

Not only did seizure allow the state-owned company to successfully defeat these five strikes, but it was also used to intimidate the workforce on the shop floor. As Raúl Trejo Delarbre writes, "The seizure ended, but not the strict supervision and extra-legal intervention against the telephone workers." For example, on January 4, 1985, 30 armed guards ordered about 100 operators at the San Juan Telephone Exchange to leave the facility. Having no orders from their superiors, and fearing that if they did leave the building they might be charged with negligence, the operators refused to do so. At that point, armed guards "who were part of the 'exempt personnel' of TELMEX, took out their guns, and then used fire extinguishers against the operators, as well as roughing them up."[87] Thirty telephone operators had to be taken to the emergency room. One of the operators later said, "The TELMEX facilities are concentration camps for their workers. In general, the union continues to be under attack. But it is the operators who are most closely watched, repressed, and controlled."[88] The repeated use of seizure and the associated violence were part of a process of taming a union that might otherwise have become dangerously independent and democratic.

Repression was not the only means the government used to deal with worker militancy; in addition to the stick, there was also the carrot. Hernández Juárez's political ambitions made him amenable to the blandishments of the Mexican ruling party. First, Hernández Juárez made peace with Fidel Velázquez, head of the CTM and still the dominant figure in the Mexican labor movement. In 1986 Hernández Juárez served as vice-president of the CT, and in 1987 he served as its president. Second, Hernández Juárez made peace with the PRI. At the end of 1984, Hernández Juárez announced that he was asking the telephone workers to vote for the PRI. In August 1987, he announced that he was personally affiliating with the PRI. On April 15, 1988, Hernández Juárez and other Telephone Workers Union officials received President Salinas de Gortari at union headquarters and announced that they wanted to collaborate with the government in carrying out the modernization of Mexican industry. Hernández Juárez became a vocal supporter of Carlos Salinas de Gortari. In fact, as Salinas toured Mexico and visited the United States to promote his new Mexico, he took Hernández Juárez along as an example of a model labor leader.

The combination of seizure and repression on the one hand, and cajolery on the other, succeeded in bringing a union that seemed to be headed away from the PRI back under party control. Originally opposed to the privatization of the company, Hernández Juárez eventually came to accept and welcome it. In December 1990, TELMEX was sold to Carso, a Mexican group associated with France Cable, Radio Francia, and Southwestern Bell, headed by Carlos Slim. The Slim group acquired 20.4 percent of the government's stock in TELMEX. Hernández Juárez praised the deal because the telephone workers would control 4.4 percent of the stock. The union signed a Quality, Productivity and Training Pact, giving the workers co-responsibility for carrying out the modernization of the company. At the same time, the company guaranteed job security for some 5,000 operators whose jobs were jeopardized by the modernization program.[89] At this time, it remains unclear what the telephone workers have gotten out of the privatization of the phone company, but it is clear that the whole process was influenced by years of repeated government takeovers of the company, military and police occupation of the facilities, and occasional violence. As the fate of the workers is primarily resting in management's hands, how much of the carrot they will actually eat remains to be seen.

The New Union Federation—FESEBES

From the first day of his presidency, Carlos Salinas de Gortari recognized that "official" labor unions were at best a mixed blessing. On the one hand, the official unions were an essential support system: they provided a social and ideological basis for the state as the organized working class; they were important for influencing public opinion; but most importantly, they turned out votes for the PRI on election day. On the other hand, the official unions were an obstacle to Salinas' program of privatization and modernization of national industry. The official labor unions were rooted in the nationalized industries, and were based on what had become "traditional" forms of organization, involving bossism and patronage. Salinas' plans to sell off state industries and put in new technologies which would shake up existing worker relations were a threat to the official unions of the CT, and were opposed by the union bureaucracy.

It was for these reasons that immediately upon taking office Salinas launched an attack on the unions, using the police and the military against the Petroleum Workers Union and the Cananea copper miners. CT and CTM responses proved that they were unprepared to fight the government, and the way was opened for Salinas to remodel the labor movement in the form of a new labor federation which would be in line with his privatization and modernization program. The chief figure in carrying out the Salinas program would be his ally Francisco Hernández Juárez, head of the Telephone Workers Union. Another major figure in this project was Jorge Sánchez, head of the Electrical Workers Union (SME).

These two large unions, and four smaller ones, came together in 1990 to form FESEBES (Federation of Unions of Goods and Services).[90] However, after Salinas promoted the organization of FESEBES, he did not know what to do with it. He still needed the CT and the CTM to get out the PRI vote, and within those organizations there was resentment against the new union federation. The new union federation, made up of only six unions and representing less than 200,000 workers, was not sufficiently large or important to act as a counter-weight to the other federations. By early 1991, it seemed as if President Salinas would allow FESEBES to atrophy, and that, perhaps, he was hoping that it would biodegrade, as *papier-mâché* is prone to do.

Whatever eventually happens to FESEBES, it was an important development, even if it turns out to have been but an experiment or an approximation of what a new state-run labor organization would be. Students of the Mexican labor movement refer to FESEBES as a neo-corporativist project, an attempt to reform the system from above, maintaining government control over labor organizations. The important point to be made regarding FESEBES and labor rights is that this paper tiger, like the CROM and the CTM before it, is another government-party inspired initiative, and therefore is inherently a violation of the right of workers to self-organization and determination.[91]

President Salinas has been willing to systematically suppress some sectors of the labor movement while attempting to entice others into his fold. In another era this type of policy was known in

Mexico as *pan o palo*—the carrot or the stick. Neither the government's bribes nor its bludgeons, however, have served to protect the interests of, or the internationally recognized rights of, Mexico's working people, whose revolutionary gains of the 1910s and 1920s continue to erode under the aegis of the Party of the Institutionalized Revolution.

Chapter Six

Private Industry and Labor Rights Under President Salinas

If labor activity in the state-owned sector of the Mexican economy during the Salinas de Gortari Administration posed the question of what role workers would play in a newly privatized society, workers demanding their rights be respected in the private sector answered it. The Salinas Administration has consistently encouraged the abrogation of workers' rights in the private sector, as it has no use for labor organizations outside the umbrella of the state. The three cases presented in this chapter show that workers employed in the private sector are an even greater detriment to Mexico's "modernization" program based on a cheap wage-labor force and production for export than are public sector workers, and are therefore at greater risk. The strikes discussed in this chapter at the Modelo Brewery, the Tornel Rubber Company, and the Ford Motor Company are not "typical" of Mexican history; in some ways they were even extraordinary. All involved large workplaces and affected thousands of workers. They became huge media events in the labor movement and in society at large. These three upheavals put employers, "official" labor unions, and government labor authorities to the test, to prove they were capable, under Salinas' so-called "reform" administration, of protecting and enhancing worker rights. Not surprisingly, the Salinas Administration failed the test miserably, violating labor rights at every turn and tolerating, even encouraging, violence.

The Modelo Brewery Strike

The Cervecería Modelo (Modelo Brewery), founded in 1925, is a well-established Mexican corporation owned by the Diblos Group. One major stockholder is Juan Sánchez Navarro, an important Mexican industrialist, who founded the Council of Businesspeople (Consejo de Hombres de Negocios) in 1962. By 1990, Modelo had operations in six different regions: the main plant is in the Mexico

City area with some seven warehouses in the Federal District, as well as other plants in Mazatlán, Sinaloa; Tuxtepec, Oaxaca; Guadalajara, Jalisco; Mérida, Yucatán; and Torreón, Cuahuila.[1] During the 1980s, the company was very successful in promoting its Corona brand beer which was exported to over a dozen foreign countries and had become very popular in the United States.

The 5,200 workers in the Mexico City plant had been represented for decades by the Modelo Brewery Workers Union, affiliated with the CTM. The Modelo union was by Mexican standards a relatively decent union. Executive Boards were democratically elected, and workers had succeeded in winning what they considered to be some of the highest wages in Mexico: base pay before taxes of 26,905 pesos (about 7 dollars) per day and top wage of 47,689 pesos (about 16 dollars) per day. Seventy percent of the workers made 32,030 (about 10 dollars) per day.[2] In spite of their relatively high wages, like all Mexican workers, the Modelo workers watched with despair as the purchasing power of their wages deteriorated throughout the 1980s. More important from the workers' standpoint was that during this same period, with the exception of periodic wage increases, there had been no improvements in their contract. As the expiration date of their contract, February 15, 1990, drew near, they wanted tangible improvements.

In 1989, the workers voted out Secretary General Isidro Guzmán, who had been supported by CTM leader Fidel Velázquez, and democratically elected a new union leadership headed by Germán Reglín. In general meetings of local unions the workers then adopted a set of contract demands. The union was asking for changes in nine clauses in the contract:

- A 100 percent wage increase, subject to negotiation.
- An increase in the vacation bonus.
- An increase in life insurance payments.
- Elimination of tax deductions on the Christmas bonus.
- Improvements in health and safety conditions.
- Improvements in food programs.
- Retirement at any age after 30 years of service.

Health and safety standards were of particular concern as many workers had suffered injuries resulting from electrical accidents, explosions of beer bottles, broken glass, long-term side effects from working with dust and powerful acids, and back injuries as a result of heavy manual labor. Something needed to be done for them.[3] Perhaps the thing the exhausted workers desired most was the flexible retirement age.

Talks between the company and the union began in late 1989. According to union activists and officials, the company rejected virtually any improvements in the contract language. Talks were going nowhere. The union, scrupulously adhering to Mexican labor law, presented a list of demands and strike notification to management and to the Federal Board of Conciliation and Arbitration on December 5, 1989. A first conciliation meeting was held on February 1, 1990, but no agreement was reached. On February 8, the company challenged the union's right to strike. There was another eleventh-hour conciliation meeting on February 14, 1990, but again to no avail.

Unsuccessful negotiations led the union to strike the plant on February 15, 1990; the company immediately demanded that the strike be declared illegal. Within 24 hours, the Federal Board of Conciliation and Arbitration ruled the strike illegal and gave the workers 24 hours to return to work. That same day, February 16, Fidel Velázquez, the head of the CTM, also announced that the strike had been declared illegal, that the relationship between the company and the union had been ended, and that "those people were still in the street."[4] Velázquez's statement was understood to be a threat that the strike workers would be replaced by workers provided by the CTM. Despite this provocation, the Brewery Workers Union leader, Germán Reglín, indicated that he always had been and continued be a member of the CTM and that he expected the support of the CTM and of Fidel Velázquez. Neither Reglín nor any other member of the union executive board suggested any desire to leave the CTM, to form an independent union, or to join any other organization.

On February 17, 1990, the Modelo Brewery workers held a general assembly and decided that they would continue the strike, despite the fact that it had been declared illegal. That same day, Modelo Brewery management announced that the 5,200 striking workers had been fired. The Modelo Brewery Workers Union decided to seek a writ of protection or injunction in the courts to overturn the ruling of the Federal Board. Meanwhile, Miguel Angel Pino de la Rosa, the president of the Federal Board of Conciliation and Arbitration, demanded that the striking workers remove their picketlines and encampments at the plant and warehouses and return the facilities to the company.[5]

Seeing that the Federal Board was firmly set against them, some of the workers walked picket lines at the plant, while another group marched to the offices of the Secretary of the Interior and sought an interview with Interior head Fernando Gutiérrez Barrios or with his head of human rights, Luis Ortiz Monasterio.[6] With tension at the Modelo Brewery now threatening to erupt, the opposition parties in the Mexican Congress called upon the Congressional Labor and Social Welfare Commission to intervene in the dispute and attempt to resolve it. Leaders of the CT claimed that the Modelo Brewery Workers Union was a member of opposition parties and that it was carrying out the strike with political motives. Reglín and other strike leaders denied the charge of political motivation and asserted that they simply wanted a better union contract and remained loyal to the CTM. As one worker said, "We're CTM members, but Fidel Velázquez has turned his back on us."[7]

Meanwhile, the brewery continued with its plan to eliminate the workforce. On February 23, 1990, the company informed the Mexican Institute of Social Security (IMSS) that it had fired the workers. At the same time, Salvador López Lee, one of the directors of the company, indicated that the company would no longer recognize the union executive committee as representing its employees.

The workers continued the strike, accompanied by a series of marches and demonstrations. Thousands of strikers demonstrated at the management office of Cervecería Modelo with supporters from the Chicago Teamsters who deliver the imported beer. Reglín said that if the strike was not resolved, the Modelo Brewery Workers Union would attempt to extend the strike to at least five other companies producing bottled refreshments which were owned by the Diblos Group.

At a press conference in front of the company headquarters, the legal advisor to the union, Tonatiuh Mercado, stated that the workers did not consider their employer to be the enemy. The workers, said Mercado, understood that both the employers and the workers produced, and that the employers created a source of jobs. But without a labor force there would be no production. All the workers wanted, said Mercado, was retirement at any age with 30 years service, while the other union demands were negotiable.

The Modelo strike was affecting other labor and community movements, drawing them into the struggle. Housewives in the working-class community of Naucalpán, organized in the Association of Tenants and Neighbors, offered to block beer trucks attempting to enter the neighborhood of Tacuba where the plant was located. Drivers on "Ruta 100," a major public bus service in Mexico City controlled by an independent union, promised that they would collect no fares from workers who presented their Modelo identification cards. Chrysler auto workers donated one million pesos (300 dollars) to help the brewery workers.[8]

The Modelo Brewery workers continued to broach other methods of resolving the dispute, turning to President Salinas. Reglín and a contingent of workers went to the presidential residence, "Los Pinos," to ask the President to intervene. "We believe in the line of cooperation which President Carlos Salinas de Gortari has been pushing with such success," said Reglín. At the presidential residence, Reglín then presented a petition to the Chief of Presidential Audiences, Jorge Valadez Castellanos.[9]

As the 111th Council of the CTM convened on February 25, 1990 in Campeche, Campeche, the CTM leadership made clear the strategy it would follow with regard to the strike. First, the Modelo workers were called provocateurs and were criticized for striking when they were among the best-paid workers in the CTM. Second, the CTM leaders indicated that they held General Secretary Germán Reglín and the legal advisor Tonatiuh Mercado responsible for the strike. Third, the CTM leadership proposed that Reglín and other members of the executive committee be removed, and that new elections be held to provide a new local union leadership. Fourth, it was suggested that in order that the CTM not lose the contract at Modelo, the CTM should cast names for a new local union leadership. These positions were put forward by CTM leader Neyra Chávez, head of the Union of the Bottling Industry, who was apparently interested in bringing the Modelo workers under the control of his organization.[10]

In a press conference held on February 26, 1990, Fidel Velázquez, head of the CTM, told reporters that he agreed with the Federal Board of Conciliation and Arbitration in its ruling that the Modelo Brewery strike was illegal. Velázquez declared that the Modelo Brewery Workers Union executive committee had lost all of its rights, and that this cleared the way for the CTM to take responsibility for settling the strike. Velázquez attributed blame for the strike to "outside" advisors who had "led the workers on this adventure." He also named Porfirio Muñoz Ledo of the Party of the Democratic Revolution (PRD) as responsible for the strike, because he had a group of lawyers who were helping stir up trouble among the workers. (Mercado denied this allegation.) Only the CTM could solve the problem, said Velázquez, now that there was "no union, no representatives, no work, no collective bargaining agreement, no nothing."

At a union rally involving thousands of workers from 11 labor unions and three community groups, Reglín declared that he was a member of the PRI, a member of the CTM, and that if it would help the workers' cause, he was prepared to resign in order to make a settlement possible. In response, the Modelo workers shouted, "No, because we elected you."[11]

The workers won a legal victory of sorts on March 2, 1990, when the Judge of the Third Court of Labor Issues, María Edith Cervantes Ortiz, granted a temporary injunction which reversed the previous decision of the Federal Board of Conciliation and Arbitration declaring the strike illegal. The decision forbade the company from firing the strikers and from replacing them.

However, Judge Cervantes also called for the workers to place a bond for possible damage to the company in the amount of one billion pesos (about 300,000 dollars) in cash to be deposited with the judge within five days. The next hearing was set for March 8, 1990. The enormous amount of money mandated for a bond of this type was unprecedented.

Despite this ruling, CTM leader Fidel Velázquez declared that from his and from a legal point of view, the Modelo Brewery Workers Union no longer existed because the company had broken off relations with the union. When the officers of the Modelo Brewery Workers went to the CTM headquarters to see Velázquez, he refused to see them as long as they were accompanied by attorney Tonatiuh Mercado, whom he again accused of being controlled by Porfirio Muñoz Ledo. The union officers refused to see Velázquez unless Mercado could accompany them. Therefore, no meeting took place.[12]

While the judge's decision overturning the Federal Board's declaration of the strike's illegality was a victory, the demand for a bond of one billion pesos was an enormous burden, one that most observers believed impossible for the union to meet. One newspaper editorialist observed a huge flaw in this mandate. If the workers were able to get together one billion pesos, their rights would be recognized, and if they could not get the money, they had no rights.[13] The Modelo Brewery Workers Union called upon all political parties (PRI, PRD, PAN, or others), all labor unions, and other organizations to come to their aid with financial assistance.[14] Immediately, the contributions began to pour in: housewives from the Anahuac neighborhood contributed several million pesos; workers from the Tampico Brewery agreed to donate 16 million pesos; 1,200 workers from the Modelo Brewery itself took out a loan for 240 million pesos; workers at the Pato Pascual bottling company donated 550 million pesos; General Motors workers contributed; Local 22 of the teachers union (SNTE) made a contribution; the university workers unions (SITUAM, STUNAM) donated significant amounts, as did the electrical workers union (SME), the RUTA 100 workers union (SUTAUR), and two political parties (PFCRN and PRD). Other money was collected on the metro trains, on the streets, and in public plazas.

While the workers spread out across Mexico City and across the republic to ask for contributions for the billion peso bond, Fidel Velázquez tried again to take control of the situation, and of the union. On March 5, 1990, he met in his office with a group of 20 workers from Modelo. Velázquez reiterated that the Modelo Brewery Workers Union no longer represented them and that the situation could only be resolved with the involvement of the CTM. "The company," said Velázquez, "would surely prefer to deal with the CTM, which is a serious organization, and not with irresponsible people such as the advisors to these workers, Tonatiuh Mercado and others."[15]

On March 7, 1990, the Modelo Brewery Workers Union deposited one billion pesos with the Third Court of Labor Issues, the result of tremendous solidarity from the Mexican labor movement and society at large. (The company then asked that the amount of the bond be increased, because it had not included an estimated 187 billion pesos reported as profits.) The workers sense of satisfaction for having raised the bond was short-lived. On March 12, 1990, the judge decided not to grant a permanent injunction, and consequently the previous decision of the Board of Conciliation and Arbitration that the strike was illegal remained in force.

A few days later, on March 16, 1990, Fidel Velázquez created a new Modelo brewery workers union and a new executive committee. Early in the morning of March 18, riot police armed with clubs and firefighters using fire hoses attacked the workers encampment in front of the Modelo Brewery. Pushing some and beating others, they succeeded in removing the workers from the area. Workers were put on buses, driven to the outskirts of Mexico City, and let out by the side of the road.[16] Hitchhiking, taking buses, or hiring taxi cabs, the strikers soon returned to the plant, put up their picket lines, and reestablished their encampment. (Workers later complained to the Attorney General of the Republic that they had been illegally removed.) The next day, Modelo Brewery, the CTM, and the Federal Board of Conciliation and Arbitration announced that there was a new contract and called upon the workers to return to work.

By now the Modelo strike had become one of the central political issues of the day, and on March 18, the opposition Party of the Democratic Revolution led by Cuauhtémoc Cárdenas demonstrated in support of the Modelo workers. Cárdenas attacked the government for carrying out a policy which was inimical to the workers' rights. The next day, the Modelo Brewery workers voted to continue the strike. On March 20, a debate over the Modelo strike was held in the Mexican Congress, with delegates from the conservative PAN, the nationalist PRD, and the Popular Socialist Party (PPS) arguing that there was collusion between Modelo and the CTM. As a result of this debate, the next day three opposition parties—the PRD, the PPS, and the Authentic Party of the Mexican Revolution (PARM)—formed the "Front of Parties in Defense of Labor."

On March 26, Judge María Edith Cervantes Ortiz conducted another hearing on an injunction to overturn the Federal Board of Conciliation and Arbitration's ruling that the strike was illegal. The next day, the judge announced that the illegality of the strike had been upheld. The court's ruling was not the only setback. The attack on the striking workers continued as CONCAMIN, an employer association, implied that the workers were carrying out the strike against Modelo at the instigation of North American, Canadian, Dutch, and German brewers.

At this point, another party became involved in the dispute. On March 29, Manuel Camacho Solís, the governor of the Federal District, a leader of the PRI, a close associate of President Salinas, and a likely successor to Salinas as the PRI presidential candidate, intervened in the dispute and proposed a number of conditions to end the strike. While there was no legal basis for the governor of the Federal District to intervene, Camacho Solís was a very powerful political figure and his intervention had to be taken seriously by all parties involved.

Camacho Solís proposed that the conflict between Modelo, the CTM, and the workers be resolved on the following basis:

1) That Alfonso G. Calderón, General Secretary of the CTM, act as a special advisor to mediate the interests of all parties, including both the Modelo Brewery Workers' old executive committee (the committee elected by the workers and headed by Reglín) and the new executive committee (the committee Fidel Velázquez had appointed), and to protect the rights of the workers who worked in the Modelo plant before the strike broke out.

2) Once the workers were back to work and the situation had stabilized, and within a period of less than six months, the CTM would call a general assembly so the workers could elect a new executive committee.

3) With the goal of determining the state of the older workers' health, the Secretary of Labor and Social Welfare would name specialists from the Office of Occupational Medicine and Safety to examine older workers so that those who were physically incapacitated could be retired with a one-time payment.

4) Up to 100 workers could voluntarily resign or could be terminated by the company, and would be compensated with their full legal severance pay without regard to their political or labor union views.

5) All of the workers would return to work with their seniority and all of their rights.

6) The bond which had been given to the Judge of the Third Court would be returned to the complainant.

7) The company would accept that within one year it would reduce the retirement period by 2.5 years (without any age limit regarding years of service).

8) The company would create a social welfare fund to be controlled by the CTM into which would be put 50 percent of the wages workers lost while on strike. The fund would be used for the benefits of Modelo workers.[17]

There was no confusion among Modelo management, the CTM, or the workers as to what the Camacho Solís plan tacitly proposed: 1) the company could fire 100 workers, which would mean the old executive committee and other union activists; 2) the old executive committee would have no further control over the union, while the CTM advisor and CTM-appointed executive committee would now run the union; 3) the CTM and not the workers would control the workers' lost wages; 4) production could start up using the skilled and experienced workers.

While the Modelo workers were looking for some basis to end the strike and return to work, they were unwilling to give up their right to elect their union leadership. The workers informed Camacho Solís, the CTM, and Modelo management that they were willing to accept the Camacho Solís plan with one exception: Germán Reglín and the current executive committee would have to remain the leadership of the union. The next day, Fidel Velázquez rejected the solution proposed by Camacho Solís, though talks arranged by Camacho Solís with officials of the Federal District and all of the parties continued. On April 2, 1990, Jesús Martínez Alvarez, one of the heads of the Federal District government, warned the workers who were still camped in front of the Modelo plant that if they did not accept the plan proposed by Camacho Solís, their picket lines and encampments would be removed.

On April 3, the Modelo workers held a general assembly. At this meeting Gerardo Cavazos Cortés, a CTM leader and PRI congressmember, proposed that the workers return to work gradually on the basis of a list of employees worked out by the company and the CTM, with the obvious intention of removing union activists. Germán Reglín, the union executive committee, and the union advisors Tonatiuh Mercado and Jorge García Ramírez recommended that the workers accept the proposal with the understanding that they would attempt from the outside to help protect the workers' rights. Nevertheless, the workers, shouting "all or none," refused to accept the CTM proposal and voted to continue the strike.[18]

Ignoring the strike and the demands of the workers, the Modelo plant reopened on April 4, 1990, with Fidel Velázquez claiming that thousands of workers had showed up and the plant was running normally. Germán Reglín claimed that only 200 or 300 of the 5,200 workers had crossed the picket line and that the strike continued to be effective. Newly hired replacement workers reported that they were being offered 32,000 pesos (about 10 dollars) per day, which was approximately the average wage paid the Modelo workers before the strike.[19]

The next day, April 5, there was a near confrontation when an estimated 5,000 Modelo workers and another 5,000 supporters, including workers from the Revolutionary Workers Confederation (COR), marched toward the Modelo plant, which was surrounded by hundreds of riot police.[20] When police stopped the workers from entering Lago Alberto street, Reglín told them, "We will take another path, we're not going to be provoked. But in any case, sooner or later, we will be back."[21]

That same day, Modelo manager Salvador López Lee reported that 2,000 workers were in the plant and producing at 33 percent capacity; however, journalists (denied access to the plant) reported that the plant was empty. Reglín stated he did not believe the plant was running and doubted that they had been able to produce a single can of beer. López Lee also announced that workers would return to the plant during that week or lose their jobs and be replaced by workers from among the 6,000 who had applied for jobs, among whom were many professional brewery workers.[22]

The government continued its pressure on the workers. On April 7, 1990, Jorge García Ramírez, one of the attorneys of the Modelo workers, was arrested by the Judicial Police of the Federal District on charges resulting from an incident in a restaurant bar a year and a half earlier when he supposedly refused to pay his check. Tonatiuh Mercado and other attorneys immediately went to the Attorney General of the Federal District to protest the arrest, arguing that it was a politically motivated attack on the workers and their labor union. Various opposition parties and union leaders went to protest to the Secretary of the Interior. García Ramírez was also supported by the COR.[23]

Once again, the Modelo workers held a general assembly and once again Reglín and Mercado urged the workers to return to work on the basis of the eight points proposed by Camacho Solís, with the understanding that the points be put in writing. Reglín suggested that neither union executive committee should continue to hold office. It was understood that Reglín and his committee would never be allowed to return to work. Reglín also demanded that all other workers be returned to work within seven days. Attorneys Mercado and García Ramírez volunteered to bow out of the talks so that their involvement would not be an issue. On this basis Reglín attempted to renew talks with the authorities of the Federal District, the Modelo company, and the CTM, while the strike by an estimated 4,500 workers continued.[24]

At the beginning of April 1990, CTM chief Fidel Velázquez celebrated his 90th birthday. In the course of a press conference to publicize the event, he declared that the Modelo strikers were being supported financially by U.S. breweries. At the same time, he declared that drug dealers were sponsoring Mexico's opposition parties, which he had earlier accused of being behind the Modelo strikers. It was, from Velázquez's point of view, a conspiracy.[25]

Modelo workers, hanging in limbo, continued to challenge the original decision of the Federal Board of Conciliation and Arbitration which had ruled their strike illegal. On April 13, the Modelo union filed an appeal with the Circuit Court for Labor Issues asking that court to overturn the earlier ruling of Judge María Edith Cervantes, who had denied its injunction.[26]

These workers, who had begun their strike affirming their loyalty to the CTM and the PRI, were now furious with the entire system of Mexican labor relations. On April 14, they held a rally at which they burned in effigy those they held responsible for the sacrifices they had been forced to make over the last two months: Fidel Velázquez, leader of the CTM; Arsenio Farell, Secretary of Labor; Judge María Edith Cervantes Ortiz; Perfecto Galicia, the CTM-appointed head of the new Modelo union executive committee; and Juan Sánchez Navarro, the head of the Modelo company.[27]

The strike, which had been going on for two months, was strengthened when a small and select group of workers known as *Fuerza Motriz* (Motor Force) decided they would no longer continue to work in the plant. The Motor Force workers were in charge of the electricity, gas, steam, and water used in the plant, and, as the Federal Labor Law provides, they had continued to work through the strike because their work was key to the safety of the plant. When four of their members were fired for refusing to sign a statement supporting the new CTM-appointed executive committee, headed by Perfecto Galicia, 11 other Motor Force workers decided they would also strike the plant. One of them said he decided to strike because he was tired of having police inside the plant, riot police outside the plant, and having to work around the clock. Other Motor Force workers complained that they had been threatened by the police when they were observed conversing with their co-workers.[28]

The strike became increasingly confrontational on April 17, when thousands of striking workers succeeded in blocking access to the plant for two hours, making it impossible to start the afternoon shift. The Modelo union demanded that Manuel Camacho Solís, governor of the Federal District, intervene in the strike. At the same time, workers threatened that if there was no progress in resolving the strike, they would seize the factory and occupy it.[29] During this same period, Salvador López Lee acknowledged that sales to the United States, Canada, Australia, New Zealand, Japan, France, Italy, England, and other countries had fallen off as a result of the strike.

The calendar was now putting pressure on the government to resolve the strike. President Salinas wanted the strike resolved before the annual May 1 labor day parade, when hundreds of thousands of workers parade before the President as he stands on the balcony of the National Palace. The Mexican government fears each year that this event will get out of hand, that the labor union radicals will succeed in using it to embarrass and put pressure on the President, or that, at worst, there will be riots and violent clashes between the "official" unions and the radicals. Consequently, negotiations were renewed on April 18 under the auspices of Camacho Solís and other officials of the Federal District.[30] With the possibility of a resolution in sight, there were more support rallies, with 50 labor, community, and political groups rallying in support of the Modelo strikers, among them the COR, major university unions, sections of the teachers' union (SNTE), and many others.[31] On April 23, 1990, Germán Reglín told the 5,000 striking Modelo workers that he felt that the talks held under the auspices of Camacho Solís were making great progress, that he had been told that President Salinas himself had ordered that the strike be resolved, and that he was sure that it soon would be.[32]

Now 68 days old, the strike was finally resolved on April 24, 1990 according to the agreement arranged through the intervention of Camacho Solís. All of the 5,100 workers would be allowed to return to work with seniority and other rights. They would receive 50 percent of their lost wages and the company would be allowed to fire 100 workers, including both executive committees headed respectively by Reglín and Galicia.[33]

It was not clear that either Modelo or the CTM would abide by the agreement. First, when the workers returned to the plant, they were told they would have to sign a statement professing their loyalty to the CTM and they found Perfecto Galicia at the plant gate, claiming to be the head of the union.[34] Second, the company, rather than accepting all 5,100 workers as promised, slowly and selectively rehired workers, with thousands still remaining outside waiting to be recalled. CTM leader and PRI congressmember Gerardo Cavazos even announced that some 2,000 former workers would not be rehired because their jobs had been filled by replacement workers hired during the strike.[35] Workers who had been rehired complained that former strikers would have to march together with the scabs before the presidential palace to give thanks to President Salinas for having resolved the problem, and those who refused to march were informed they would be fired. Nevertheless, most of these threats were never carried out.

In the end, most of the 5,000 or so Modelo workers were returned to work. The company did pay final severance pay to the previously agreed 100 workers, and to another 234 workers as well, who may have voluntarily decided not to return to work. The workers did win retirement, not after 30 years of service, but after 32. They did not win the 100 percent wage increase they sought, but rather 20 percent, which was typical of the wage increases which were being given by the government and by private employers at the time. Germán Reglín and all other members of the union executive committee were fired and given their final severance pay, ceding in full their posts as heads of the Modelo workers union.[36]

Through this strike, the government, the agents of justice, and the protectors of the working class were all given an open opportunity to justify themselves. In all of their statements and actions, hypocrisy won out. Decades of rhetoric were revealed to be bunk. The

CTM never acted as the labor arm defending the interests of its constituents—the Modelo union and workers. Even though the Modelo union and leaders like Germán Reglín proclaimed that they were loyal to the CTM and the PRI, the CTM viewed them as enemies, and did everything possible to crush them. The CTM rejoiced that the workers' strike was declared illegal, and immediately declared that the Modelo Brewery Workers Union no longer existed. The CTM leadership created in its wake a spurious local union, headed by Perfecto Galicia, to replace the democratically elected union headed by Germán Reglín. The CTM accused the striking workers of being agents of opposition political parties and of U.S. breweries. In short, the CTM did everything possible to defeat the strike and destroy the Modelo workers union.

The Modelo strike of 1990 again demonstrated the antagonistic role of the very parties which exist to protect the workers—Mexican labor authorities, the Secretary of Labor, the Federal Board of Conciliation and Arbitration, and the labor courts. These agencies make it impossible for Mexican workers to exercise their constitutional rights.

Violence was also used against the workers who were engaged in peaceful civil disobedience. The Federal District police, riot police (granaderos), and firefighters violently beat Modelo workers on March 17 and 18 when they evicted them from their encampment at the Modelo plant. This, combined with the April 7 arrest of attorney Jorge García Ramírez by the Judicial Police of the Federal District on a minor charge dating from one and a half years before, represents a gross violation of the human and civil rights of the Mexican people. This is a dangerous precedent to set in a country supposedly striving for democratic reform and deregulation. It is an especially sinister tendency of the Mexican government to arrest activists, leaders, and attorneys engaging in dissent, yet it consistently administers this form of injustice.

The intervention of the governor of the Federal District, Manuel Camacho Solís, was characteristic of Mexican labor relations. Frequently, it is not the labor authorities who settle Mexican labor relations problems through legally established channels, but rather important figures in the PRI political establishment, whether the mayor of the city, the state governor, or more typically the Secretary of the Interior. It would be a mistake to view the intervention of Camacho Solís as a beneficent act of mediation. Rather it was the characteristic intrusion of officials of the Mexican one-party state into the labor arena in an attempt to manipulate and control the labor unions and workers.

Finally, the settlement which was reached through the involvement of Camacho Solís was a violation of the workers' rights. The elected leadership headed by Germán Reglín was removed from the company and from the union, proving once again that there is no place for democratic labor unionism in Mexico.

The Tornel Rubber Company Strike

In 1989, workers at the Cia. Hulera Tornel, S.A. de C.V. (Tornel Rubber Company) decided they wanted to change their union affiliation. At the time, Tornel was the third largest tire company in Mexico, employing 1,700 workers, of whom 1,200 were union members. These employees worked at plants located in the San Antonio industrial development in Azcapotzalco, and in Tultitlán, in the state of Mexico. They produced tires for bicycles, motorcycles, automobiles, and various other kinds of vehicles.

Tornel workers were concerned about serious health and safety problems in the plant and declining real wages.[37] At the time, the minimum weekly wage was 131,000 pesos (about 45 dollars), with some skilled workers making 145,000 pesos weekly (about 50 dollars). Wages at Tornel were lower than wages at other rubber plants for workers performing the same jobs.[38] The health and safety problems posed were dust in the air, inadequate ventilation, poor masks, injuries resulting in lost fingers or hands, heavy weights, and back injuries.[39]

The CTM had run the union at Tornel for many years. Many workers viewed the union as a *charro* union and some said that it was closer to management than to the workers.[40] In the past, there had been at least one attempt by a local union leader to form an independent union; he was immediately fired.[41] In the late 1980s, the CTM perpetually refused to account for the use of union funds, refused to show workers their union contract, and made changes in the executive board without consulting the workers. In 1989, when the union officials refused to hold a meeting as the workers requested, the workers organized their own union meeting, in which they voted out of office the long-time local union boss Rubén Díaz Reynoso and decided to form an independent union. Some 950 of the plant's 1,200 workers signed the petition for an independent union and the petition was filed with the Federal Board of Conciliation and Arbitration.[42] When the Federal Board refused to allow the workers to form an independent union, they decided to leave the CTM's rubber workers division headed by Sergio Pérez Tovar and sought affiliation with the Revolutionary Confederation of Workers and Peasants (CROC) rubber workers division headed by Salvador Martínez Carrillo.[43]

The workers took their demand for an election by representation to the Federal Board of Conciliation and Arbitration, which would organize and arbitrate the vote to switch affiliations from the CTM to CROC. On five occasions, the vote was postponed. A year later, the union affiliation election still had not taken place. Meanwhile, scores of workers active in the movement were fired by Tornel management.

On May 3, 1990, five of the Tornel workers were kidnapped at gunpoint, including the movement's principal leader, Rogelio Hernández Medina. Also kidnapped were Pedro Navarro Pérez, another leader of the movement, and three other workers, Félix Guerrero, Santiago Salazar, and Victor Navarro.[44] After being threatened and roughed up, the workers were released. The kidnapping was reported to the appropriate authority, the Attorney General of the Federal District. In mid-June 1990, another kidnapping at gunpoint took place. This time, the wife of one of the workers was taken, threatened, roughed up, and then released. The workers made a formal protest before the Mexican government's newly formed National Commission of Human Rights headed by Jorge Carpizo McGregor. In addition to the kidnapping, the rubber workers complained that Dionisio Noriega Aparicio, general director of the Demetrio Vallejo Center for Worker Information and Orientation, had received anonymous threats because he was a consultant to the Tornel workers. They also reported that 25 Tornel workers had been fired.[45]

On August 4, 1990, the vote on union affiliation was finally scheduled. However, when the Tornel workers showed up to vote, they were attacked and beaten by a group of at least 200 men wearing shirts with the CTM logo. Some workers estimated the goon squad to number between 700 and 800.[46] The CTM members had arrived with an escort from the Tultitlán police, and Sergio Pérez Tovar, the head of the CTM's rubber workers division, was seen with Tultitlán Mayor Antonio Hernández, alledgedly carrying a pistol.

Newspapers reported that CTM thugs appeared to be drugged or intoxicated and were seen drinking alcoholic beverages. Many of them were believed to have come from the Good Year Oxo and the Chaparritas plants, which were organized by the CTM and under the direct control of Pérez Tovar. Nine workers from both sides were injured, some of whom were hospitalized. Two newspaper photographers and a reporter also were beaten by the CTM goons, Martin Salas Sabina of *Graph Prensa*, and Francisco Mata and Judith Calderon of *La Jornada*. As a result of the riot, the union election vote was suspended. The CTM union members had claimed that they were attacked by CROC supporters.

Charges were filed by Tornel workers and various reporters against Sergio Pérez Tovar of the CTM, Tultitlán MayorAntonio Hernández, and the PRI congressmember for Tultepec, Gonzalo Ortiz Ugalde, for organizing the beatings. Several workers reported that Wallace de la Mancha, the former leader of the CTM shock brigades, was among the group that carried out the beatings. In addition to filing charges against their attackers with the Attorney General of the Federal District, workers also took their complaint to the Mexican government's National Commission of Human Rights and demanded that the Board of Conciliation and Arbitration set a new date for a union affiliation election.[47]

It was later reported in the newspapers that the goons were part of a special shock brigade organized by Sergio Pérez Tovar, head of the rubber workers division of the CTM. The goons were known as *Los Cien* (the hundred) or *Los Tepos.* [48] Some two weeks later, Sergio Pérez Tovar denied that he had anything to do with the violent attack on the Tornel workers. [49] On August 6, 200 pro-CTM workers went to the CTM offices to shout *"Vivas!"* to CTM head Fidel Velázquez and to Sergio Pérez Tovar. That same day, Armando Tornel met with the workers to thank them for their support for the company. [50]

On August 7, Tornel fired another five workers, bringing the number of workers who had been fired since the movement began to 160. Meanwhile, groups of CTM goons continued to threaten the Tornel workers, and on August 7, some 300 CTM thugs showed up at the Azcapotzalco plant and threatened the workers on the first shift. Other workers received insulting or threatening phone calls. [51]

In separate interviews, Armando Tornel, head of the Tornel company, and Fidel Velázquez denied responsibility for the events. Velázquez denied that Sergio Pérez Tovar or Wallace de la Mancha had anything to do with the attack on the Tornel workers. He claimed that, in fact, the CTM had been the victim of the attack. [52]

The company continued to fire workers on a massive scale. On August 10, the company fired 500 workers from the second and third shifts, replacing them with CTM workers from the Good Year Oxo plant and other plants. [53] In response to the fact that the company had fired approximately 650 workers, the workers made a request through the Federal Board of Conciliation and Arbitration for the reinstatement of the workers, and organized an encampment in the plaza of the Board—a traditional form of Mexican protest. [54] The Tornel company, in a letter to the Federal Board of Conciliation and Arbitration, formally refused to reinstate the 650 workers.

Meanwhile, there were new developments regarding the workers' desire to change from the CTM to the CROC. Two other "official" unions asked to have their names put on the ballot: the Mexican Workers Confederation (COM) and another CTM union. Tornel workers believed that these two unions had come forward at the request of the CTM in order to confuse the situation. The Federal Board of Conciliation and Arbitration ruled on August 20, 1990 that the Tornel workers would continue to belong to the CTM rubber workers division controlled by Sergio Pérez Tovar, and that the workers' request for a vote be tabled. [55] In response to this decision, the workers addressed an open letter to President Carlos Salinas de Gortari, asking for his intervention so that "this problem could be resolved with justice." [56]

On November 15, 1990, the Federal Board of Conciliation and Arbitration unexpectedly reversed its decision and set November

22, 1990 as the date a representation election would take place at five locations in the Tornel Rubber Company. The Tornel workers feared that the Tornel company and the CTM would turn out goons and scabs to vote, and that the next union election could turn into another riot.[57] Consequently, the Tornel workers decided not to participate in the Federal Board of Conciliation and Arbitration's representation election. As a result, the CTM won the election, with 541 votes for the CTM and 15 votes for the CROC. As only 1,200 workers were still employed by the company, about 650 having been fired, this could hardly be called a representative election.[58] Feeling they had nowhere else to go, the workers once again took their complaints to the Mexican government's National Commission of Human Rights.[59]

The loss of the right to a free and fair election at Tornel, while it involved a more important company and a larger number of workers than at most enterprises, epitomizes the "institutional" response to Mexican workers who attempt to exercise their labor rights. The tripartite Boards of Conciliation and Arbitration either do not act expeditiously, or they force the workers to choose among "official" unions affiliated with the ruling PRI party. While the Boards prolong the procedure, putting off dates for hearings and for elections, often on the basis of fabricated violations, employers fire the movement's leaders and activists, and if individual firings fail, they engage in mass firings. "Official" unions play their role as well, using thugs or shock troops to threaten, beat, kidnap, and sometimes kill dissidents.

Finally, after several months of firings and beatings, the labor authorities may hold an election in which union goons and strike breakers are allowed to vote, but from which the long-time workers for the firm are either excluded because they organized to protect their rights, or they decline to participate because they fear further violence. In the end, the state, "official" unions, and employers succeed in destroying the movement.

Over and over, this pattern repeats itself. Inertia, it seems, has set in. The government bodies set in motion in the 1930s and 1940s, which were strike-busting even then, remained in motion, gaining momentum with a push in the 1980s from promised foreign investment. The slippery slope of repression will not stop until workers are given the right to represent themselves before their employers, the courts, and the state.

The Ford Motor Company Strike:
Open Collusion with the State

The beatings and kidnappings unleashed upon the workers at the Ford Motor Company in Cuautitlán and the murder of another worker which occurred in January 1990 originated with a series of events that began years earlier. As with the workers at Tornel and Modelo, the workers at Ford belonged to the "official" CTM Ford auto workers union which represented three locals in Chihuahua, Hermosillo, and Cuautitlán. In 1986, as a result of years of struggle by local union members, the Ford Cuautitlán plant had one of the best labor union contracts in the Mexican auto industry, with higher wages and better working conditions than in many other auto plants.

Then, in 1987, the Ford Motor Company closed its Cuautitlán plant, and paid final severance pay to all 3,400 union employees, eliminating the union contract. A few months later, Ford reopened the plant, and rehired many of the workers, but with a new contract which drastically reduced salaries and benefits, and which compacted job titles, eliminating whole categories. The "official" CTM Ford auto workers union, run at the time by General Secretary Lorenzo Vera Osorno, accepted the new arrangement, to the detriment of the workers. The workers, who had no say in accepting the contract, were understandably angry about the loss of labor standards.[60] "All of the benefits and conquests from years of struggle were erased from the contract," stated Raúl Escobar, a Ford employee and a leader of the reform movement among the Ford workers.[61]

Lorenzo Vera Osorno soon left the union, and the CTM leaders appointed Héctor Uriarte for an interim term due to end in 1989. To protest the appointment of Uriarte, a group of union reformers held their own union-wide election for leadership of the Ford workers' local in Cuautitlán. This reform leadership sought to recoup the losses suffered when the old contract was eliminated. The company and the CTM union had previously made agreements without conferring with the workers, but the new local leadership took on a different strategy entirely. They began to do unheard of things like holding union meetings and listening to union members. The Cuautitlán local was also preparing to challenge Uriarte for leadership of the national union in the 1989 elections.

Consequently, on June 22, 1989, Ford fired members of the local union executive committee, with tacit support from the CTM. The firings led to a number of protests, including actions in the plant, marches, and demonstrations. In addition, two of the workers carried out a hunger strike to demand their reinstatement. The hunger strike lasted over 30 days, but neither the company nor the union relented. The Ford workers' movement continued throughout July, August, and September, with public protests in both Cuautitlán and Mexico City.

On one occasion, the workers and their supporters occupied the area around the base of the "Angel de la Independencia," a famous statue celebrating Mexican independence located in downtown Mexico City. Because they were demonstrating just before September 15, Mexican Independence Day, they were removed by the police. Many of the workers and their supporters were beaten in the process.[62]

During the six months from June to December, the fired members of the Ford Cuautitlán executive committee continued to act as the local union executive board and to advise workers who had problems in the plant. When Ford announced that the legally mandated annual Christmas bonus would be reduced in late December—many workers who would have received 600,000 pesos (200 dollars) would only receive about 10,000 pesos (three dollars)—this leadership was prepared. On December 21, the workers engaged in a work stoppage. The next day, they demanded not only that they receive their full annual bonus and profit sharing payments required by law and their union contract, but also that their fired union leaders be reinstated, and that they be allowed to elect their own union leaders, obviously alluding to the appointed official, Héctor Uriarte, who continued to hold office as interim head of the CTM auto workers union.[63] The movement was now a direct challenge both to Ford and to the CTM.

The Ford workers began to carry out regular demonstrations in Mexico City blocking Paseo de la Reforma, one of the city's main arteries, and protesting in front of the office of the CTM. They succeeded in meeting with Fidel Velázquez, head of the CTM, and Velázquez promised to let the workers hold an election for union leaders among workers from all three Ford plants. With no signed agreement, the workers feared that Velázquez would not keep his word, and thus continued to demonstrate in various locations throughout the Federal District. They also demonstrated at the office of the Mexican Secretary of the Interior and head of the political secret police, demanding that Secretary Gutiérrez Barrios intervene on the side of the workers. The Secretary of the Interior frequently becomes involved in major labor union conflicts.

On January 5, 1990, the Ford Cuautitlán union leadership put out a leaflet calling upon the Ford workers to come to the meeting with Fidel Velázquez at the CTM headquarters. That same day a group of 30 thugs, most of them reported to be officers of the Judicial Police of the state of Mexico, and reputed to have been hired by the CTM and Ford, attacked and beat several leaders. Six workers—Marco Antonio Jiménez, Jaime Peña Silva, Antonio Galindo, Alfredo Arista, Francisco Ferrusca, and José Sánchez—were either kidnapped or arrested.

As soon as workers at the Ford plant learned of the disappearance of their co-workers, they stopped work, bringing production at the Ford plant to a halt. Union members and activists contacted the Secretary of the Interior, the National Front Against Repression, a human rights group, and Mexico City newspapers to report on the disappearance of their fellow workers.

Within eight hours, the six workers who had been detained or kidnapped were released. It appeared that they had been arrested by members of the Judicial Police, though they had been held in the town of Tlalnepantla, and apparently also had been handled by police of Cuautitlán-Izcalli. They reportedly had been beaten by members of both police forces. The workers filed charges with the Subprocurator of Tlalnepantla against CTM leader Héctor Uriarte and against Ford, accusing them of having contracted the goons to beat the workers.[64] Raúl Escobar and other workers took their injured co-workers to the hospital and then went to report the incident to Ortiz Monasterio of the human rights department of the Secretary of the Interior.[65]

During the night on Sunday, January 7, 1990, members of the executive committee of the Cuautitlán local union received numerous reports from workers living near the factory and from workers in the plant that the company was providing uniforms and identification cards to persons who were not employed by Ford. When workers went to work on Monday morning, some 70 of them, all of whom were either members of union committees or union activists, found that the locks on their lockers containing their uniforms had been changed, and that they were to go to the locksmith to receive new keys. Photographs taken that day showed a large truck parked outside of the locksmith's office. Workers believe that if they had reported there to receive their keys, they would have been kidnapped and perhaps killed.[66]

In addition, some 200 or 300 armed men had been introduced into the plant. They were reported to be drunk or drugged and they carried clubs and firearms. They ordered the workers to go to work, threatening and pushing the workers to make their point. At the same time, announcements came over the company loud-speaker system, advising the workers to do as they were told. This message was followed by a blasting noise apparently intended to encourage the goons and unnerve the workers.[67] Mexican Social Security records show that the thugs were put on the payroll on Saturday, January 6, 1990, and that most were let go two weeks later, apparently because they had accomplished their mission.

In self-defense, the 2,500 Ford workers on that shift, who greatly outnumbered the gangsters, began to arm themselves with tools, pieces of machinery, and scrap metal. They intended to drive the armed men out of the plant. However, as the Ford workers began to drive the intruders out of the plant, the gangsters fired on the workers, wounding 12 of them. One worker, Cleto Nigno, died a few days later.[68] He had been shot in the back. When the Red Cross arrived, the gangsters refused to release the injured workers. One Red Cross worker is reported to have taken out a pistol in order to protect one of the injured workers from the gangsters. At no time did any government police appear on the scene.[69]

Meanwhile, inside the plant the workers believed that some of the gangsters remained hidden, and so formed groups to search for outsiders. They succeeded in finding three men (Armando Salgado Jaramillo, Constancio Escobar Hernández, and Juan Enrique Hernández Avalos) who were then turned over to the police. Those three men subsequently made statements that they had been hired by Héctor Uriarte and J. Guadalupe Uribe, both leaders of the CTM Ford union.[70] Uriarte declared on various occasions that he was not responsible for the violence, and that the problems in the Ford plant were caused by people affiliated with the Party of the Democratic Revolution (PRD) or the Revolutionary Workers Party (PRT).[71] Fidel Velázquez, head of the CTM, supported Uriarte and accused the Ford workers of inciting the violence.[72] Wallace de la Mancha, reputed to be the head of the CTM goon squads, had also been accused of promoting the violence and shootings at Ford. In interviews and in a letter to Mexico City newspapers, de la Mancha declared that he had nothing to do with the attack on the Ford workers.[73]

After the attack, somewhere between 800 and 2,000 Ford workers occupied the plant, both to protect themselves physically and to pressure the company and the CTM to recognize their right to choose their own leaders. Over 3,000 Ford workers signed a petition sent to the Federal Board of Conciliation and Arbitration, asking the Board to protect their labor union rights.[74] The occupation of the Ford plant resulted in a loss of production of 450 automobiles per day. Because of the "illegal" occupation of its plant, the Ford Motor Company asked the Federal Board of Conciliation and Arbitration to terminate the collective bargaining agreement and the union representation in the plant.[75] Ford also announced that it would not pay the workers who were engaged in the occupation of the plant.[76]

The events at the Ford plant led to a full-scale debate in the Mexican Congress where the National Action Party (PAN), the Party of the Democratic Revolution (PRD), the Authentic Party of the Mexican Revolution (PARM), and the Popular Socialist Party (PPS) all accused the CTM and the Ford Motor Company of having been responsible for the violence. Blas Chumacero, the second highest official of the CTM, responded by saying that "The events were provoked by people from outside the union. Let us speak with clarity: the company is responsible and can always find people at its service for these kinds of illegal acts." The PRD representative, Pablo Gómez, called for an investigation by the Congressional Commission for Intergovernmental Relations and Complaints.[77]

Ford attempted to pay final severance to workers who were considered obstacles to reopening the plant. The Ford workers entirely rejected "liquidation."[78] In order to put pressure on the government and the union to do something about this problem, Ford announced that as long as the problems continued in its Cuautitlán plant, it would have to reconsider its planned investment in the plant amounting to some $300 million for the coming year. Ford announced that the workers' "illegal" occupation of the plant was not only stopping the work of 6,000 workers and the production of 450 units daily, but that it was also affecting some 300 auto parts manufacturers and 125 distributors in Mexico.

During a visit to residential neighborhoods of Naucalpán, President Salinas de Gortari met for 15 minutes with Ford workers, listened to their complaints, but finally indicated that the matter would have to be settled through the proper channels, which in this case was through the Secretary of Labor.[79]

On January 11, 1990, a wake was held for Cleto Nigno in the Ford Cuautitlán plant, which was still occupied by the Ford workers.[80] There was also a growing demand from labor union activists that Guadalupe Uribe, Héctor Uriarte, and Wallace de la Mancha be punished for their role in the attacks on the Ford workers. Several unions attended a solidarity day for the Ford workers held in Cuautitlán.[81] The Ford Cuautitlán workers also received support from Ford locals in Hermosillo and Chihuahua.[82] With this support, some 400 workers and their spokespersons met with Fidel Velázquez at the CTM headquarters on January 15, 1990 to demand that he remove Héctor Uriarte as Secretary General of the Ford workers union, and allow the workers to conduct a democratic vote for a new union leadership. Velázquez rejected the workers' demand and called instead for a referendum on the union leadership.[83] It was reported that Uriarte was offering dissident workers 500,000 pesos (about 150 dollars) each to vote for him for union general secretary.[84]

The three men who had been arrested for attacking the Ford workers (Enrique Hernández Avalos, Salvador Rojas, and Constancio Escobar) were released on bail of three million pesos (about 1,000 dollars) each.[85] At nearly the same time, Silvestre González Portillo, head of the National Union of Automobile Workers with which the Ford workers union was affiliated, held a press conference in which he called upon the Secretary of the Interior to prosecute Wallace for his criminal attacks on workers in a number of incidents, the attack on the Ford workers being only the latest.[86] On January 21, 1990, it was reported that Uriarte had been sending his gangsters to "inform" the workers that if they did not go back to work they would be harmed. The head of this goon squad was reported to be Alvaro Bizuet.[87]

On January 22, 1990 at 5:30 a.m., about 2,000 police officers from the Attorney General of the Republic, the Attorney General of Justice of the Federal District (PGJDF), the Justice Department of the State of Mexico, the state and municipal police departments, and the Federal Highway Police, together with a few helicopters, about 40 patrol wagons and police cars, 15 buses, 20 ambulances, and a number of police dogs, descended on the 300 workers who still occupied the Ford plant. After removing the locks from the doors, police entered the plant. Some workers claimed that they were threatened at gunpoint. All the workers (except for six who were allowed to stay to protect boilers and other machinery) were removed from the plant.[88]

That same day, Fidel Velázquez—who was at the time meeting alternately in two separate rooms with a group of workers from the Ford plant and with Héctor Uriarte and other officials of the CTM auto workers union—immediately announced that the company was ready to go back to work and that those workers who did not return to work within three days would be in danger of losing their jobs. Meanwhile, José Guadalupe Uribe Guevara and nine other individuals were formally charged with a number of crimes, including murder, by the Attorney General of Justice of the State of Mexico, Humberto Benítez Treviño, before a criminal court in Cuautitlán. The workers did not feel vindicated.[89]

On January 23, 1990, the day after the workers were removed from the plant, some 2,500 workers remained on strike, demanding union elections and the arrest and punishment of Héctor Uriarte. However 700 administrative employees and some 300 union employees did show up for work, according to Ford officials.

Uriarte still had not been detained, and the CTM's attorney, Juan Moisés Calleja, a former minister of the Supreme Court of Justice, stated that he doubted that the authorities would be able to locate and arrest Uriarte, but that if they succeeded, Juan Moisés Calleja was prepared to testify that he had been with Uriarte on the morning of the shooting at the Ford plant, and that therefore Uriarte would be released. Calleja characterized Uriarte as "honest, clean and tolerant" and "an excellent leader who has always handled the problems of the workers."[90]

The continued pressure on the CTM finally forced Fidel Velázquez to remove Uriarte from office and replace him. Velázquez appointed Juan José Sosa as interim leader of the Ford workers union. Sosa announced that the Ford workers union had no intention of leaving the CTM.[91]

The violence continued. On January 27, 1990 at about 8:00 p.m., Ricardo Cervantes and Héctor Hernández, two Ford workers who were handing out leaflets and collecting donations to support the movement, were surprised by six men and a woman who beat and kidnapped them. After several hours, they were released in the same neighborhood where they had been kidnapped. Their captors had told the two men to "quit making a fuss." They made a protest to Subprocurator Pineda Gómez.[92]

Company supervisors continued to call workers and urge them to return to work.[93] Simultaneously, the CTM Ford auto workers union placed a large advertisement in the newspapers on January 31 in which it urged workers to return to work "since the plant has begun operations" and workers who failed to return to work could be in danger of being disciplined. "No fellow worker should put their job at risk in this way. It is important to return to work at once," said the advertisement.[94]

By the beginning of February, a large number of the Ford workers had returned to work and were laboring under the supervision of inspectors of the Secretary of Labor who were in the plant in order to guarantee their safety. However, Ford refused to rehire some 50 workers who it claimed were the principal organizers of the event that had led to the violence a month before.[95] As a result, many of the workers decided to resume their strike, and management later reported that less than one-third of the workers had returned to work.[96]

Precisely because those 50 leaders had been excluded, the Ford workers decided that they would attempt to change their affiliation from the CTM Ford auto workers union to the auto workers union affiliated with the Revolutionary Workers Confederation (COR). The COR was another "official" union affiliated with the CT and with the ruling PRI.[97] The COR filed a demand for the entitlement of the Ford workers contract on February 6, 1990, and, in response, the Ford Motor Company sent notices to hundreds of workers advising them that they were being fired, and called upon the CTM to provide 1,000 workers to fill the vacant positions.[98]

For their part, the workers organized a number of activities to put pressure on the government, on Ford, and on the union. They carried out a mass march from Cuautitlán to the Zócalo national plaza, a five-hour walk, but riot police prevented them from reaching the plaza. They blocked the Mexico-Queretaro highway, a main thoroughfare. They demonstrated at the CTM building.

On February 7, the Ford Motor Company announced that it was firing 2,300 workers from the Cuautitlán plant because they had refused to return to work, and with the help of employees of the Secretary of Labor, firing notices were delivered to workers in the neighborhood of the plant. At the same time, the CTM began to send replacement workers to the Ford plant. "It's better this way," commented CTM advisor Gerardo Cavazos Cortés. "Now they're out of the union, and the union will continue to be in the CTM."

José de Jesús Pérez of the COR argued that it was illegal to fire the workers since the COR had already applied for entitlement of the Ford workers' contract. "It would be very unjust if a group of capable Mexican workers, who have been recognized for their productivity and who, in addition, have fought within the legal framework for the elementary right to elect their leaders, should be put out in the street."[99]

Secretary of Labor and Social Welfare Arsenio Farell Cubillas told the press that his office would not intervene in the Ford workers' movement because it was an "inter-union" conflict. Moreover, argued Farell, the Ford situation was an exception to otherwise generally peaceful Mexican labor relations.[100]

Throughout the first few weeks of February, the Ford workers continued their discussions with Fidel Velázquez and other officials of the CTM. The workers indicated they were willing to stay with the CTM rather than go with the COR if their right to elect their own leaders was recognized, and if the CTM would support them in their demands for justice from the Ford Motor Company. Tentative agreements were reached by which the workers would be returned to the plant.[101] Meanwhile, with only 162 of the strikers having returned to work, the company began to selectively rehire some of the fired workers. The Ford company brought in 300 police under Commandant Cheverhuiel from Public Security of the State of Mexico, a dozen inspectors from the Secretary of Labor's office, and some CTM officials, and rehired 140 new workers on February 12.[102] Two days later, on February 14, the plant had succeeded in getting 1,028 workers to return to work, while 2,772 remained on strike. The company warned them that they had better return within two more days, or they would lose their jobs permanently.[103]

The company continued to selectively rehire certain workers, while keeping others waiting. By February 15, 1990, the company claimed that 2,500 workers had returned to their jobs, though other sources indicated that only 1,050 workers had been rehired. The next day the company announced that it was suspending the rehiring process for 10 days, leaving at least 1,800 workers still on the street. At the same time, it became clear that the CTM, rather than recognizing the workers' right to hold local elections, intended to appoint a new interim General Secretary by the name of Elias Hernández Quintero.[104] A Ford manager took another tactic against the workers, meeting with Fidel Velázquez of the CTM to complain that there were some "dissident workers" among those who had been hired.

About this time, the Federal Board of Conciliation and Arbitration informed the Ford workers' attorney, Manuel Fuentes, that it would not act on the Ford workers' request to change their affiliation from the CTM to the COR, that they were going to "file" the request. Fuentes protested that the Board was violating the workers' rights, and said he would seek an audience with the President. He added that he would also attempt to meet with union leaders in the various political parties and seek a political judgement against Labor Secretary Farell Cubillas.[105]

Secretary Farell, however, announced that he would attempt to mediate the dispute between Ford and the workers directly, in order to resolve all difficulties. He promised to meet with Ford and CTM Ford union officials.[106] Attending the meeting were Secretary of Labor Farell, Ford director Nicholas Scheele, CTM head Juan José Sosa, CTM legal advisor Juan Moisés Calleja, and rank and file representative Gabriel Abogado leading a delegation of Ford workers. At the meeting, Scheele told the workers that they would either sign or be fired, and so the workers signed. The agreement provided that the Ford workers—but not necessarily all of the workers—would continue to be rehired slowly, that there would be no pay for lost wages accrued during the work stoppage which had gone on for nearly two months, and that in the case of any disruptions or actions in the plant, Ford would be free from all obligations. "It leaves us with a bitter taste," said Gabriel Abogado, a member of the rank and file negotiating committee, "now that the highest labor authority in the country cannot defend us from the decision of a transnational [company] which imposed on us an agreement that violates our rights."[107]

Despite the agreement, the matter was far from settled. The company continued to slowly rehire, and a week later had only rehired 200 of the 1,200 who remained on the streets. One of the members of the CTM's appointed (not elected) provisional local union executive committee, Pablo Rodríguez, was accused of having threatened the workers, and the Mexican Social Security Institute (IMSS) refused to declare that the nine workers who had been badly enough wounded to require hospitalization were "incapacitated."[108] By March 25, 1990, there were still close to 800 workers who had not been rehired by Ford. When, on April 20, hundreds of Ford workers attempted to return to work *en masse*, they were stopped by a cordon of 1,500 police from the Federal District and the state of Mexico.[109]

By this time, the Ford workers who had not been recalled to work had definitively decided that they wanted to change their union affiliation to the COR.[110] On April 20, the Mexican Supreme Court granted a writ of protection declaring that the COR's demand for the right to the Ford workers' contract was still in effect and would have to be heard by the Federal Board of Conciliation and Arbitration, which had previously ignored it. Three days later, COR leader José de Jesús Pérez announced that the Ford workers at

Cuautitlán no longer belonged to the CTM, but were now members of the COR and that he expected they would soon be joined by the Ford workers at Hermosillo and Chihuahua.[111] On April 29, 1990, 3,000 Ford workers from Cuautitlán met in assembly and formally joined the COR.

It was not until October 5, 1990 that the Federal Board of Conciliation and Arbitration met and set a date for the hearing on affiliation with the COR; the date was November 28, 1990. Nevertheless for various technical reasons, no hearing was held on that date. A hearing was held on December 6, 1990, at which the company demanded that the petition to change affiliations be thrown out on the grounds of a technicality. On December 7, the Board denied the company's demand that the change of affiliation be "filed," and denied the CTM legal representation of the local. The Board also indicated that three other unions had filed demands that they become the legal representatives of the Ford workers. These were granted. They were a CTM iron workers union, another CTM automobile workers union, and an automobile workers union belonging to the Confederation of Workers and Campesinos (CTC), which many consider to be an employer-dominated union.[112] With this decision, the Board simply skirted out of administering justice, remaining within the letter of the law while violating the workers' rights. "For me," says the Ford workers' attorney Manuel Fuentes, "the Board of Conciliation and Arbitration is a kind of freezer for workers rights. Complaints arrive there, and they are frozen."[113]

Late in 1990, the Secretary of Labor and the Federal Board of Conciliation and Arbitration had removed the leaders of the COR, replacing them with new leaders loyal to the PRI. Héctor Uriarte was never brought to trial. Wallace de la Mancha died. In early 1991, these issues were still unresolved. The company refused to re-hire the nearly 800 Ford workers who remained on the street, and refused to recognize the COR as the representative of the workers.

A court-ordered representation election was held for workers at the Ford Motor Company on June 3, 1991. It was overseen by a committee of independent observers from human rights and labor education organizations. A report on the election found a series of abuses, including:

• The vote was not by secret ballot. Instead, workers had to vote out loud in front of management and CTM personnel, and then sign their names next to their votes.
• The government allowed the company to decide which workers could vote. Supervisors chose each group of voters and brought them to the voting area.
• The government allowed the company to bring a large number of people to vote who were not eligible.
• The company and the CTM were permitted to warn workers

on their way to vote that if they voted against the CTM, they would be fired. This threat had great credibility since the company had previously fired more than 800 workers dissatisfied with agreements between the CTM and Ford management.
• The company was allowed to videotape some of the voters as they stated their names and which union they preferred.

As a result of these and other abuses documented by the committee, the following conclusions were reached:

1) There were multiple irregularities in the representation election which seriously affected the outcome of the voting.
2) The fundamental rights of the Ford workers to freely choose their union representation were denied.
3) A new election should be held under conditions which would assure a free and democratic choice.
4) Labor Secretary Arsenio Farell should be removed from office by President Carlos Salinas de Gortari due to repeated intervention by Farell and his subordinates against COR's supporters and on the side of the company and the CTM.[114]

The Ford workers at Cuautitlán suffered through one of the worst labor confrontations in Mexico during the later half of the 1980s, not a good decade for labor rights as a whole. In 1987, the company fired the entire workforce, eliminated the union contract, and then rehired the workers at a far inferior salary. When the workers attempted to win the right to democratic local union elections, and to fight for their legally mandated benefits, they were subjected to beatings, kidnappings, and murder blatantly conducted through collusion between the Ford Motor Company and CTM union officials. For years, workers were consistently terrorized by CTM and Ford hired gunmen and thugs who attacked their meetings, demonstrations, and picket lines. This tactic of terror was even taken to the workers' homes and neighborhoods. When workers attempted to redress their grievances before the Federal Board of Conciliation and Arbitration and before the Secretary of Labor, they were subjected to long delays and denied their rights due to technicalities. When the workers attempted to change their union affiliation, the labor officials did not allow the workers a vote, but mandated changes for them. Throughout this process, the Ford Motor Company and the CTM union officials, evidently with the tacit approval of the Mexican government, lied to the workers and manipulated their powerlessness, exhausting their resources and their determination. It does not seem to be enough for a profitable company like Ford to rely on inexpensive Mexican labor without ensuring that the workers live in poverty.

Raúl Escobar says of the lack of respect for labor rights:

> The Constitution exists, giving employers as well as workers the right to join together to defend their interests. Nevertheless, for a long time in Mexico the "official" confederations which are the right arm of the government have been anti-democratic. Workers who lift up their heads to demand their rights are repressed, threatened or assassinated. We might say, these rights exist in the Constitution—but they are not respected by the government itself.[115]

Conclusion

Events at Modelo, Tornel, and Ford reveal that the Salinas Administration, while attempting to reorganize the labor movement, has not brought about reform that promotes or even remotely defends labor rights. Workers at all three plants suffered violations of their rights, legally and physically. They were never free to select their union affiliation or elect their union leadership. They were never free to bargain collectively, nor were they free to strike. As case after case comes into the light of scrutiny, a rather sinister design appears: the Salinas Administration is grabbing control of the workers' lives in a way different from any of its predecessors. The difference between Salinas and de la Madrid on the one hand, and all the past Presidents since 1920 on the other, is in the government's attitude toward foreign capital and its willingness to destroy or suppress organized labor for the sake of currying favor with foreign capital. In a national self-sufficiency development model, wages must be high enough for workers to buy the goods they produce. In an export-driven model, that linkage is replaced by wage competition for the sake of foreign markets. Now that Mexico is opening up to the United States with the Free Trade Agreement, products will not necessarily be produced for Mexican consumption, and Mexican companies will not stand to lose or profit based on the domestic market.

Mexican workers and their labor movement have already felt the impact of freeing trade for an entire decade. As they have been required to reshape themselves into a cheap labor force with no rights, in order to make themselves more appealing to potential investors, they have lost their human dignity inch by inch. Anyone who doubts that 10 to 12-hour workdays in plants without the most minimal health and safety standards are detrimental to human life should study carefully the next chapter on the *maquiladoras*. Hepatitis, dismemberment, and an under-age workforce are just the beginning of the problems. The future for Mexican workers looks bleak, while a very small percentage of the population stands to gain from an agreement that forces Mexico to compete with world-class productivity levels for far less than world-class wages. One of the Tornel workers' leaders, Rogelio Hernández Medina, said of the Free Trade Agreement:

> It would be very interesting if you could explain what's happening in Mexico. We're very disturbed that many times we Mexican workers have to knuckle under to the kind of repression that is being handed out to the workers, who are facing conflicts that are prolonged by the labor authorities in order to exhaust and beat them down, wearing them out so that eventually hunger will force them to betray their struggles and their demands.
>
> We're disturbed that American or Canadian workers think that Mexican workers are scabbing on them. From our point of view, regarding the Free Trade Agreement, we think that capital has no creed, and businessmen have no country, they have no religion. The only thing they care about is money, and if the Canadian or American workers won't work for them in certain conditions or challenge their wishes, then they will bring that technology and that capital here to Mexico so that we Mexican workers can work for them.
>
> Mexican workers will continue to fight for our rights, but it is very hard to fight against the union bureaucrats of the CTM, against the bosses, and against the labor authorities. The labor authorities have repressed the workers, the bosses have fired and intimidated the workers, and the union bosses are on the other side beating us. We don't want to be scabs, we have no choice.[116]

Chapter Seven

Maquiladoras and Worker Rights

Maquiladoras, also known as in-bond or twin plants, are located primarily along the U.S.-Mexico border, where Mexican workers are employed in the assembly of parts for electronic goods, automobiles, clothing, and other industrially produced items. The number of plants has grown rapidly over the last 25 years and they are considered by many to be the leading edge of modernization in Mexico. Though plants that fall under the heading *maquiladora* can be very different, they have in common features that the U.S. and Mexican governments think desirable: they are private enterprises, highly integrated into the U.S. and world economies; and they frequently produce high-tech products, sometimes with technologically sophisticated equipment. For businesspeople in both countries, this concept seems to work so well that they are urging their respective nations to enter into a Free Trade Agreement. Considering that they might well succeed, the question naturally arises: has the development of the *maquiladora* industry also meant improvements in the standard of living, wages, benefits, and working conditions of the workers, and has their ability to exercise their labor rights been advanced? This question is particularly important because some of the *maquiladoras* are breaking productivity records, which means higher profits for the company, and this in turn *should* mean higher wages for the workers. Only higher wages can combat widespread poverty.

Looking at various aspects of life in three cities which are major *maquiladora* centers located at different points along the U.S.-Mexico border—Tijuana, Ciudad Juárez, and Reynosa—it becomes apparent that in spite of their diversity, there are features the *maquiladoras* share which are not pleasant, becoming, or humane. An example of labor-management relations in the city of Chihuahua located in the interior of Mexico further shows that no matter where the *maquiladoras* are, they function in much the same manner. General background on the *maquiladoras* will shed light on the present situation of Mexican workers in the *maquiladoras* and in Mexico as a whole.

Demographics

The Mexican Border Industrialization Program (BIP) began in 1965, and provided that on a strip of land 12.5 miles wide along the length of the U.S.-Mexico border, Mexico would allow foreign capital and primary goods free importation with no custom clearance, import duties, or most other taxes. Breaking with the practice since the Revolution of majority ownership by Mexican citizens, Mexico would allow foreign owners majority ownership of plants on Mexican soil. The only condition was that 100 percent of all products finished in Mexico would have to be re-exported. The program was intended to industrialize the border region and provide jobs for Mexican workers.

"The *maquiladora* industry is nothing other than the free import and re-export of components, free of taxes, except on the value added," explains Jorge Carrillo Viveros, sociologist, general academic director of the Colegio de la Frontera Norte (COLEF) in Tijuana, Baja California, and an authority on the *maquiladoras*. "It is not an industry but rather a tariff system, and within what is considered the '*maquiladora* industry' exist many types of industries. There is a very striking diversity of technology, of unionization, of working conditions. It is not a homogeneous industry; this is a very important point."[1]

The *maquiladora* industry is dominated by large U.S. corporations such as General Motors, Ford, and Zenith. Many of the plants employ several hundred workers. About 80 percent of the *maquiladoras* are located on the border, though this percentage has declined over the years as the Mexican government permitted *maquiladora* plants to be established in the interior of Mexico as well. The Mexican National Institute of Statistics, Geography and Information (INEGI) published a report on the *maquiladora* industries in December 1990.[2] According to the report, of the 1,909 *maquila* plants, 1,464 were located on the border and 445 in other parts of the country. The locations given by INEGI are as follows:

Baja California	763
Chihuahua	365
Tamaulipas	238
Sonora	155
Coahuila	144
Jalisco	39
D.F. and state of Mexico	19
Baja California Sur	13
Other areas	103
Total	1,839

Most *maquiladoras* are assembly plants relying on intensive, unskilled labor, with little to no high-technology equipment. In recent years, advanced technologies have been increasingly introduced, particularly in the auto parts sector, including integrated circuits, semiconductors, pick-and-place robots, and re-programable automatic systems.[3] According to INEGI, at the end of 1990, the *maquiladoras* were engaged in the production of the following products:

Food preparation, packing, or canning	46
Clothing and textile	290
Shoes and leather	50
Furniture, wood, and metal assembly	270
Chemical products	81
Transportation equipment	157
Tools, equipment, or parts (non-electronic)	34
Electrical and electronic machinery, equipment, or apparatuses	106
Electrical and electronic materials and accessories	408
Toys and sports	30
Other	354
Total	1,826

A document from the Secretary of Commerce provides another breakdown for the industry:

Electronics	38%
Transportation	20%
Textiles	10%
Metal and wood	5%
Food	1%
Chemical	1%
Other	24%
Total	99%

Workforce

According to INEGI, in 1990, some 1,909 *maquiladoras* employed 371,780 workers of whom 145,297 were men while 226,483 were women. In addition, the *maquiladora* industry employed 54,358 technicians and 33,699 administrative employees. The total number of all employees, management and labor, was 459,837. As has been frequently observed, working in the *maquiladora* plants is particularly tedious and exhausting. Most of the work is on assembly lines, in many cases in the assembly of minute parts. Many plants operate 24 hours a day, seven days a week, including holidays. The workday is generally nine or nine and one half hours.

Since the BIP program began, most of the *maquiladora* workers have been women, and though the percentage of male workers is growing, women still comprise a majority today. From 1974 to 1982, women made up 87 percent of the *maquiladora* workforce, while men made up only 13 percent. By 1983, 71.9 percent were women and 28.1 percent were men; and by 1985, 68.5 percent were women and 31.5 percent were men.[4] The growing participation of men in the *maquiladora* workforce can be directly attributed to the growing diversity of *maquiladora* products and use of high-technology equipment which necessitates more managers and technicians. In Mexican society, women are considered a second-class workforce and few are trained for high-tech or managerial positions. More than two-thirds of the *maquiladora* workers are women because women will work for low wages and they are considered a more passive workforce. In addition, most of the women workers are young, in their twenties and teens, relatively strong and healthy and therefore bear the health hazards they are exposed to with little visible damage.[5]

One of the most serious problems facing the largely female workforce in the *maquiladoras* is that of sexual harassment, a problem so pervasive, not only at work but in society at large, that it is seen as the norm in society. Since the majority of workers are women, and by and large the supervisory personnel are men, supervisors frequently use their authority to demand sexual favors from women employees. Very often women do not charge their supervisors with sexual harassment because they are likely to be humiliated and in the end they are not indemnified in any way. "There is no law that says that if there is sexual harassment the company must pay so much to a worker," Gustavo de la Rosa, a labor lawyer from Juárez, explains. Sometimes women who were fired for refusing to sleep with their supervisors will get their jobs back, arguing that they were unjustly terminated, but without raising the issue of sexual harassment. Teresa Almada, a social worker in Ciudad Juárez, also notes that the dangers of sexual harassment are not limited to the workplace. She explains,

> With regard to sexual harassment...many of the girls are between 14 and 20 years old, so it is very serious. I don't know at what level it goes on, whether it is the supervisors or the foremen, but it is a fact...also when they leave the factories they are in a lot of danger, rape occurs frequently, many of which go unreported...many young women become pregnant with no possibility of a stable family life.

The Mexican Secretary of Commerce predicted in January 1991 that the *maquiladora* industries would grow by 17 percent during 1991, and that employment would grow by 20 percent. Most of the new workers are likely to be women, and most will work for subsistence wages. In promoting the *maquiladora* industry to U.S. companies, the Mexican Secretary of Commerce pointed out that wages in 1991 would be about $.51 per hour as compared to between $3.00 to $6.00 for similar work in the United States. The Secretary of Commerce went on to point out that the price of labor in Mexico was declining.[6]

Year	Wages per Hour in U.S. Dollars
1982	$1.38
1983	.67
1984	.69
1985	.73
1986	.58
1987	....
1988	.69
1989	.53
1990	.45
1991	*(estimated)* .51

Since most of the *maquiladoras* produce parts for export to the United States, they are structurally dependent upon U.S. industry and on the U.S. economy. Consequently, employment in the *maquiladora* industry is as stable or unstable as employment in the United States.[7] Some Mexican analysts have shown concern over the slowing growth rate of the *maquiladoras*. The most recent figures show the *maquiladoras* growing at a rate of only 18 to 19 percent in the last two years, undoubtedly due to recession in the United States.[8]

Employment in the *maquiladora* industry is very unstable in other ways as well. It is estimated that about 20 percent of the workforce turns over each month, though the rate of turnover drops to 15 percent or less during periods of economic recession.[9] In 1978 and 1979 anthropologist María Patricia Fernández-Kelly worked in *maquiladoras* in Ciudad Juárez and described the working conditions that led to high labor turnover:

> Discontent over low wages, the tediousness of assembly work and frequent complaints over eye-sight deterioration, and nervous and respiratory ailments... The nature of the work performed at the plants is a contributing factor to high turnover rates. Highly monotonous, repetitive operations, accelerated work rhythms, lack of promotions and inadequate working conditions combine to prevent long-term employment.[10]

Plant managers and workers in Ciudad Juárez and Chihuahua indicated in interviews that low wages were the greatest factor in the high rate of turnover.

Pollution

The health and safety of workers and environmental contamination are serious problems in the *maquiladora* industry as well. The University of Lowell's Work Environment Program recently conducted a study of the Matamoros-Reynosa area which involved 267 workers and 25 community leaders. The Lowell report pointed out:

> What appears to be the future of working conditions in one of the most active areas of the *maquiladora* system in the Mexico-U.S. Border is in many ways a journey to the past. The working conditions identified in this study are reminiscent of the nineteenth century sweatshops of the U.S. industrial town. They are well illuminated worksites and they serve lunch in the *maquiladora* operations, but still the worst abuses of the methods of production of Taylorism are evident... The workers' survey found clear evidence that *maquiladora* workers are suffering from musculoskeletal disorders related to working conditions, including rapid pace of work, poor workplace design and other ergonomic hazards. Acute health effects compatible with chemical exposures were also identified, indicating the potential for the future development of chronic diseases in the workforce.[11]

Gustavo de la Rosa agrees that occupational health is a serious issue. "There are illnesses caused by the chemicals that are used in the plant, but they are not reported. And in practice, Social Security does not recognize occupational illnesses." The problem is much deeper, however, than exposure in the workplace. The related problem of environmental contamination is equally devastating to the workers' lives. De la Rosa further asserts that "The quantity of solvents and toxic chemicals which enter the company is very low in relation to the quantity of toxics and solvents which leave. Toxic chemicals are thrown into the canals which carry the sewer water. There is evidence that the *maquiladora* companies are not careful with disposal."

In 1987, the Colegio de la Frontera Norte (COLEF) and the Friedrich Ebert Foundation, a labor think-tank associated with the CTM, conducted a study of the *maquiladoras* and their industrial wastes. One aspect of the study was simply to document the kinds of toxic materials used in the *maquiladoras*.[12] These were the findings:

Electronics Industry
Alcohols: isopropyl and isopropanol
Aromatic hydrocarbons: benzene, toluene, xylene
Chlorinated hydrocarbons: 1,1,1 trichlorethane,
    trichlorethylene, perchlorethylene, and others
Ketone group: Acetone and methyl ethyl ketone (MEK)
Others: freon, zinc fluxes, liquid nitrogen
Metals: lead and zinc
Acids and alkalies: nitric acid, sodium hydroxide, sodium
    carbonate

Plastics Industry
Plastic waste: latex, resin, fiber glass, paint, shellac,
    dyes, adhesives
Solvents: toluene, xylene, benzene

Metal Industry
Metals: copper, bronze, tin, lead, aluminum, iron, zinc
Acids: chromic acid, sulfuric acid, phosphoric acid,
    hydrochloric acid, and alkaline solutions
Alkaline solutions: sodium hydroxide, potassium
    hydroxide, sodium carbonate, trisodium phosphate
Solvents, pigments, and resins

Auto Parts Industry
(Metal mechanical, plastic, electric, electronic)
Acids, alkalies, paints, solvents, flux, adhesives,
    varnish, resins (the specific chemicals are similar
    to those listed in the three industries above).

According to Robert Sánchez, author of the study, there are serious problems of environmental contamination from these toxic chemicals and metals. Major reasons why contamination occurs are that the Mexican government's Secretary of Urban Development and Ecology (SEDUE) does not have adequate controls, and has not established adequate industrial toxic waste disposal sites. Sánchez indicates that "clandestine industrial waste dump sites have begun to be found [in Mexico] which are imputed to the *maquiladoras*..." and that "there is a lack of strict control and adequate legislation over this type of waste in Mexico which leads to its clandestine or semilegal disposal."[13] The Lowell report also noted that there is a severe lack of governmental regulation. "The Mexican government, moreover, is economically dependent on the industry and is reticent to require research or health assessments, which may lead to unfavorable publicity."[14]

A 1989 AFL-CIO study by Leslie Kochan found that *maquiladora* use of toxic chemicals had caused the following serious environmental and health and safety problems:

• Drinking water supplies and irrigation waters are being polluted and fish and wildlife face extinction.
• The fragile ecosystem is endangered by indiscriminate dumping of waste in land dumps.
• The region lives under the threat of toxic poisoning caused by transportation or industrial accidents.
• Adequate waste treatment facilities are lacking on both sides of the border.
• Mexican workers are frequently denied basic health and safety protections against occupational illness or disease, and they risk the loss of their jobs if they protest these dangerous conditions.[15]

The lack of health and safety standards, pollution in surrounding areas, low wages, and tedious work are parts of the destitute whole that is life working in the *maquiladoras*. Only poverty-stricken human beings accept these inhumane conditions, and only because they have no power to better their lot.

Unions

Since the *maquiladoras* began in 1965, labor unions have organized contracts and strikes, and struggles have been pervasive among the various "official" labor unions—CTM, CROC, CROM—for control of plants in various cities. The level of union organization in the *maquiladora* industries is not uniform. In different border cities and cities in the interior of Mexico there are markedly different degrees of union organization.[16] In the border area in general, the unions are strongest in the East and grow weaker as one moves west. Matamoros, Reynosa, Nuevo Laredo, and Agua Prieta have strong "official" labor union organization: the level of unionization in Matamoros and Nuevo Laredo is "almost 100 percent," in contrast to the cities of Ciudad Juárez, Tijuana, Mexicali, and Nogales, which have levels "from 20 to more than 30 percent."[17]

In 1989, investigative reporter Diane Lindquist researched the labor union movement along the entire border for a series of stories in the *San Diego Union*.[18] She found the following levels of organization:

Baja California	5%
Sonora	15%
Chihuahua	20%
Coahuila	25%
Nuevo Leon	50%
Tamaulipas	85%

She concluded that the unions were failing in their attempt to organize the *maquiladoras,* not only because of management's anti-union attitude, but also because the workers were not attracted to the unions. "*Maquiladora* employees, for the most part, have shunned the country's organized labor movement, judging it useless and ineffectual. Charges of cronyism, injustice, and corruption among its ranks make it repugnant to many of the new breed of workers."

A few years ago, the Laredo Development Foundation wrote in its *Los Dos Laredos: Industrial Fact Book—Laredo Texas and Nuevo Laredo, Mexico:*

> In Nuevo Laredo, the unions are committed to new job creation. If requested by management, they perform many of the normal U.S. corporate personnel management functions, such as recruiting, training, discipline, hiring and firing of workers.

The section on "Labor Unions" continues:

> The Nuevo Laredo Chapter of the CTM recruits and screens prospective applicants according to management's stated requirements and assists management in discharging and replacing unsatisfactory employees.[19]

Those who attempt to democratize official unions or attempt to organize independent unions often find their path blocked by the legal system. As Jorge Carrillo, an expert on unionism in the border-area, explains:

> In general the role of the Board of Conciliation and Arbitration, in the case of the *maquiladoras,* has always been in one way or another to protect the industry by protecting the stronger union—the union which has the closest relationship with the government. In this sense it has served as a wall to hold back independent unionism. The Board...has never permitted independent unions to be legally registered. Consequently independent unions have had to organize within the federations. There have been democratic movements within the federations, but the Junta, we can say, has not shown itself to be in favor of helping these movements...in general we know that [the Board] is not a very efficient instrument for the workers. If one presents a demand, there is a very long process which can go on for a year or two...and in the end there is a "mediation," and so it is probably better to make a deal beforehand.[20]

Mexican workers in the *maquiladora* industry confront the same sort of difficulties encountered by other Mexican workers in industries throughout the country. The Boards of Conciliation and Arbitration, rather than helping the workers defend their rights, are used by the companies and the unions to prevent democratic and independent union movements or actions.

In addition to the traditional forms of domination, some of the larger corporations (led by the auto parts industry), have introduced new forms of labor control, such as organizing the workforce into quality circles and teams, originally pioneered in Japan and then used in the United States. Given the invisibility of the Mexican labor union on the shop floor of the *maquiladora*, these circles and teams simply become vehicles of employer intimidation and coercion.

Tijuana, Baja California

As in other border areas, the *maquiladora* program in Tijuana, which lies across the border from San Diego, California, began in 1965. In the 1970s, it grew rapidly with the creation of an industrial park known as New Tijuana Industrial City (CINT). The park was created in 1972, but plants were not in production there until 1977.[21] The number of *maquiladora* plants and workers employed by them grew quite rapidly. The growth of the *maquiladora* industry was one of several factors which led to the rapid growth in population of Tijuana, at a rate of 7 percent per year during the 1970s and 1980s, until it reached more than one million inhabitants by the late 1980s.

Before the arrival of the *maquiladora* industry, Tijuana had a labor union movement dominated by the "official" unions of the CTM and CROC. When the *maquiladora* plants opened, the CTM and CROC began to organize the new plants. Over time, the quality of union representation deteriorated. In Tijuana, there exists what Jorge Carrillo calls "low profile" unionism—the establishment of "protection contracts" which are weaker than those originally established by the CTM and the CROC. "Protection contracts" allow the company to show that it has signed a contract with a union, even though the terms of that contract may be below minimum standards of the Federal Labor Law. Protection contracts occur all over Mexico and are always negotiated behind the backs of the workers, but in the *maquiladoras* in Tijuana they are accompanied by the complete absence of any union life within the plants. In January 1991, Carrillo described the Tijuana unions this way:

> On the one hand, we have a high level of unionization at 30 percent of the work force in the *maquiladoras*, which is above the national level. But on the other hand, we have a unionism with little-felt presence:

they do not carry out strikes, there are no marches, they do not, for example, participate in demands for salary increases.

It is a kind of unionism which the union leaders themselves call "transparent." Transparent means that it does not have any color, it is neither a "red union" [government union, CT, CTM, CROC, CROM], nor is it a "white union" [company union]... Obviously they are not democratic unions and even less could they be considered independent unions. Probably they are closest to being "paper unions," because of the fact that they have on record a signed contract, so [the employer] avoids situations or contingencies in which some other kind of unionism might arise. In addition, many workers do not even know they have a union or that they belong to a national federation.[22]

The Mexican government and the employers are well aware of the labor unions' role in promoting labor peace and thus helping to keep wages low. "Both the federal and the state governments, but mostly the state, realize that Baja California is attractive for investments," Tijuana lawyer Fernando Cervantes told *The San Diego Union* in 1989. "One of the things needed to make it attractive is to say you have a healthy labor atmosphere. We don't have strikes. We don't have riots."[23] Reporter Diane Lindquist commented:

The agreement [between *maquiladora* managements and the unions] apparently discourages more aggressive unions from organizing manufacturing plants and leaves the industry open to unionization by friendly, or so-called white, unions. In return for not taking part in any tactics that would discourage further investment, the white unions are allowed to try to form contracts with plant operators to increase their membership rolls.

While the term "white union" usually refers to the company unions, reporter Lindquist uses it here to refer to the official CTM, CROM, and CROC unions.

Tijuana's workers are so stifled by this "healthy labor atmosphere" that it is as if there were no unionism whatsoever. It is not hard to understand why working conditions in the *maquiladoras* resemble those in the United States 100 years ago. When workers have no means of demanding their rights, their rights are not respected.

Ciudad Juárez, Chihuahua:
The Worker and the Union

The *maquiladora* industry in Ciudad Juárez, which lies across the border from El Paso, Texas, began in 1966, just after passage of the Mexican government's *maquiladora* decree. By 1971, the city had 52 *maquiladora* plants with 5,617 employees, making it the largest center of *maquiladoras* on the Mexican border. With the opening of the Antonio J. Bermudez Industrial Park in 1972, the *maquiladora* industry in Juárez grew even more rapidly, attracting companies such as RCA, Sylvania, Ampex, General Instruments, Centralab, and American Hospital Supply. Following the 1974-75 recession, the Mexican government made even greater economic concessions to attract employers to Mexico. This led to another growth spurt of *maquiladora* employment to 23,580 employees.

One major attraction of Ciudad Juárez has been low wages. Frequently, plants that opened in Juárez were "run-away shops" fleeing labor union wages in the United States. RCA, for example, closed its television manufacturing centers in Cincinnati and Memphis and moved them to Juárez and Taiwan. Similarly, Zenith closed its plant in Chicago and moved operations to Juárez and Taiwan. Companies like General Electric indicated that by 1978 they were saving between $10,000 and $12,000 in wages per worker per year. The continuous devaluation of the peso led to a fall in wages in Ciudad Juárez from 85 cents per hour in 1975 to 43 cents per hour in 1984.[24]

Gustavo de la Rosa Hickerson, a labor lawyer who has been practicing in Ciudad Juárez since Summer 1972, and has handled many cases of *maquiladora* workers over the years, says that between 1970 and about 1977 there was a long fight between the CTM and the CROC for control of the workers in the *maquiladora* plants. During the same period, there were also attempts by democratic movements to reform some of the "official unions" and by independent unions to organize outside the official federations. However, with the recession in 1974-75 in the United States, there was also a recession in the Juárez *maquiladora* plants and the companies threatened to leave the area unless something was done. The companies wanted all organizing by the official unions stopped, as well as the total dismemberment of independent unions. With the recession hovering, and under pressure from the employers, the government agreed that it would not support the unions in their attempts to organize the plants. "There was also a guarantee given to the *maquiladoras*," says de la Rosa, "that independent unions would not be permitted...in this way it was defending its own corporative organizations such as the CTM and the CROC."[25]

The result of all this bickering, says de la Rosa, has been very unfortunate for the workers:

> The *charro* labor unions did very little for the people all those years, so the unions had very little credibility and when they no longer had the government's support they stopped growing. Their own efforts were too sporadic to win sympathy and respect from the people. Since there were no independent alternatives, the workers prefered to have no union.

Workers continue to attempt to reform the bureaucratic unions or to organize independent unions. However, such activity goes on in opposition to the employer, the official union structure, and the government. When companies find any kind of union activity, they fire the perpetrators and their associates. There have been violent confrontations, but usually the style of repression used by the companies is to fire the workers who are the most visible.[26]

Experts on labor unions in the *maquiladoras* all paint the same picture of Ciudad Juárez:

> ...the CTM is the most important labor organization in Ciudad Juárez, both in numbers and in political power... In more than a decade of activity in the *maquiladoras*, the CTM's union practices were very similar to those of the CROC: the complete abandonment of democratic methods, such as the suppression of democratic union meetings or control of union meetings; the direct involvement of the local CTM in the internal affairs of each of the affiliated unions; the misappropriation of funds; the union's approval of temporary disciplinary suspensions by the company; and the use of the exclusion clause [expelling union members who are then fired] to get rid of any indication of discontent on the part of the workers.[27]

Today, Ciudad Juárez has about 150,000 *maquiladora* workers, but because the labor movement does not represent the workers nor attempt to defend them to improve conditions, these already very poor conditions have stagnated or deteriorated.

The average wage is about 125,000 pesos (about 42 dollars) per week for a 45-hour week (about 93 cents per hour). Teresa Almada, a social worker in Ciudad Juárez, gives a somewhat lower estimate of wages: 100,000 pesos (approximately 35 dollars per week). In either case, wages are low for long hours of work. The typical working conditions in the Juárez *maquiladoras* were described by Jorge Carrillo and Alberto Hernández in 1985:

The workdays in Ciudad Juárez are nine hours daily for five days per week, and in general, although different kinds of activities are performed, the jobs are monotonous and repetitive. A woman worker in the electronics industry, for example, in one day has to solder 2,000 pieces of a size which is hardly visible. The intensity of the work has to be hard and constant in order to achieve the established production goals, which are generally based on the standard of production of the fastest workers.[28]

The workday is usually longer than the basic nine hours, however, as a majority of workers work one or two hours overtime, and sometimes double shifts.[29]

Workers in the plants in Ciudad Juárez also complain about the lack of basic health and safety standards, and in particular about the dangerous chemicals they work with.[30] Carrillo and Hernández, discussing health and safety conditions in the Ciudad Juárez *maquiladoras*, write that there is "lack of ventilation and light, excessive use of soldering equipment, microscopes and toxic substances which seriously undermine the health of the women workers. It has also been shown that rotating shifts are a problem, although only 17 percent [of the plants] engage in that practice." The Mexican Institute of Social Security does not register occupational illnesses and is not conscientious in protecting the health and safety of the workers.[31] Combined with the toxic substances released into the air, water, and soil, hazardous exposure in the workplace chips years off the workers' lifespans.

If Ciudad Juárez can be used as an example of a successful *maquiladora* town because industry and employment has grown, then it must also be used as an example of what happens to the people who work there. The lack of meaningful unionism in Ciudad Juárez, or in any other *maquiladora* community, means not only that workers have no protection on the job, but that they have no way to defend the environment in which they live, or the social structure of their lives. As their bodies are being poisoned at work, their families deteriorate at home.

Ciudad Juárez, Chihuahua: Life in the Community

The important point to be made about life in Juárez is that living conditions as well as working conditions are sub-human. *maquiladoras* are not simply well-placed factories. In cities like Juárez along the border of Mexico, the size of the *maquiladora* industry is so great, in relation to the city, that the *maquiladoras* determine the entire reality of city life. In Juárez, there are about 340 *maquiladoras* employing about 150,000 workers, in a city of 1,300,000 workers. The rest of the jobs, for those who are not unemployed, are really extensions of the *maquiladora* industry: taco selling to the workers, teaching school, when there are schools, to the *maquiladora* children. The *maquiladora* is the axis of the economy.[32]

Because *maquiladoras* are so pervasive in workers' lives, workers feel alienated more than in other parts of Mexico, not only from their jobs, but from life itself in the *maquiladora* community. Gustavo de la Rosa calls this "industrial neurosis." Women and men hate the factories, their jobs, and even their very existence. They feel used because the days are long, the money is short, and the companies are not in the least bit concerned about what happens when the worker leaves the factory. Teresa Almada is a social worker and a member of the Independent Peoples Organization (OPI). The OPI helps residents of working-class communities in Juárez to improve their neighborhoods by fighting for their rights as residents. The hope is that if workers are provided with basic utility services such as water, sewer drains, and electricity, and if the high cost of living is brought under control and wages are brought up to a livable level, their lives will be drastically improved. "In short," says Almada, "there are a whole series of cultural problems which are closely related to the border, the *maquiladoras*, and women workers."

Almada asserts that the reason parts of Juárez remain contaminated, undeveloped slums is that the political interests of the Mexicans who are most involved in running the *maquiladoras* take precedence over the interests of the workers. The best example, she says, is the city's development plan.

> They have a plan worked out until the year 2010, which is rather unusual in Mexico...this municipal administration has given priority to main thoroughfares and to pavement...if we analyze the layout of these thoroughfares, we see that they have been planned in order to give the city an infrastructure which is functional for the *maquiladora* industry. They are going to connect the *maquiladoras*... But this is in a city where half the population doesn't have a sewer system...it is unreasonable that pavement should be the priority. It is in this sense that we say the *maquiladoras* determine the whole reality.

The standard of living in working-class neighborhoods in Juárez is quite low. In general, a family with six or seven children will live in a house of two or three rooms made out of adobe, or in rare cases, out of concrete block. In most cases, members of the family have made the adobe bricks themselves. About half of the families are fatherless.

The attendant problems of urban development in Juárez, and every other *maquiladora* city, have brought about many social problems, including child labor, rape, drugs, disease, and general familial breakdown. According to Almada, a study done in Juárez in 1988 indicated that 15 percent of the workers in the *maquiladoras* were between 14 and 16 years of age, and most of them were working full-time. "It is very common that they change their birth certificates," she says. "When we had a program in a high school, and we asked the students for their birth certificates, they said, 'Okay, but which one shall we give you, the good one or the one for the *maquiladora*?'"

Drugs are another feature of life for children in the *maquiladoras*. Because women are primary breadwinners, and there are *no* day care centers, there is no way to protect the children from the drug dealers in their neighborhoods. Children are left alone all day, abandoned in this sense, and there are no social programs to turn to. Almada believes that in the neighborhoods where OPI works, drugs are used by 60 or 70 percent of the young people. The drugs of choice are mostly inhalants—Resistol 5000, paints, thinners, shoe polish, and marijuana. Almada further asserts that drugs are only one problem that children and teenagers face, and that really their whole identity comes into question as a result of exposure to North American culture. The big problem, as she sees it, is social breakdown. "There is a whole human and social disintegration which has to do with the kind of city that is being created. We cannot technically say that *maquiladoras* are the cause of this, but there is a relationship between social breakdown and *maquiladoras*."

With a profit margin of $10,000 to $15,000 per year per job moved to Mexico, one might think that the U.S. companies reaping the benefits of these unprotected workers' labor might have some responsibility to the communities the workers live in. In other parts of Mexico, large companies that have developed in remote areas have provided social services. They have made an investment, whether adequate or not, in their future workforce. In the border region, the U.S. companies have no incentive to better the lives of the workers, and the workers have no unions to force the companies to make needed changes. The onus thus lies with the government under whose sponsorship the *maquiladoras* began, and under whose guidance the unions collude with the companies. It is a painful reality in Mexico that all possible development strategies are being scrapped for *maquiladoras*. The lives of the Mexican people will never improve while they are auctioned as labor in exchange for their blood.

Reynosa, Tamaulipas

The problems posed by the *maquiladora* industry in Mexican society are inevitably interconnected with women's issues. The breakdown of the family is devastating to everyone, but more often than not, women are left to combat the obstacles of raising children alone and in poverty. Pollution and exposure are hazards everyone in the community faces, but a majority of the workers who are trapped in the enclosed environment of the workplace are women. In addition, women living in the *maquiladora* cities "to make some good money for a few years" are particularly vulnerable to psychological and sexual harassment. Xochitl Romero Ortiz works for a non-profit, non-governmental organization called Service, Development and Peace (SEDEPAC). She is in charge of SEDEPAC's volunteer work with women *maquiladora* workers, and while she is familiar with the *maquiladora* industry in various cities in the border area, much of her work has been concentrated in the city of Reynosa, Tamaulipas. Sexual harassment and discrimination, says Romero, are issues women denounce across the board, throughout the whole industry. From what she can discern, sexual relations are used by the largely male management to control the largely female workforce. "The male supervisor gets involved with a woman on the assembly line, and then after a while he gets involved with another. This leads to bad feelings... Any woman who is involved with a supervisor also becomes his informant. He has emotional control over her, so if there is dissatisfaction or if the workers are thinking of taking action, she tells him."[33] Romero also asserts that not only have the unions failed to take up the issue, but they are accomplices to the same misdeeds. Despite the fact that the majority of workers and union members in the *maquiladoras* are women, the persons running the unions are men. These men patronize the women with "superficially emotional and paternalistic relationships, which are actually subtle forms of control...saying things to them like, 'Come along now, my daughter'."

Over and above their discrimination against women, unions in Reynosa are racked with many of the problems plaguing unions all over Mexico. They are bureaucratized organs of the state, their leaders are not democratically elected, and any attempt at reform leads to massive firings by the employer, who is collaborating with the union. In Reynosa, all industrial unions are affiliated with the CTM, and their officials are named by the CTM, rather than elected. Romero describes the unions as dysfunctional. "By law you have the right to strike, but in fact you do not." The labor union bureaucracies make the decisions to accept contracts or to go on strike without any input from the workers or a democratic decision-making process. Sometimes the workers carry out unofficial or wildcat strikes, but they are inevitably fired. "There are great limitations on the workers," says Romero. "The union itself is a block to their actions, to their demands, and to their minimal rights."

All over Mexico, the stranglehold on unions leaves workers devastated and alone, vulnerable to violation and discrimination. Reynosa is nothing more than a classic example; it is *not unique*. As in Juárez, Matamoros, Tijuana, etc., in Reynosa women are exploited, workers have no rights, and the lack of health and safety standards leads to widespread exposure and contamination problems.

No one argues that these problems do not exist. In fact, violations of health and safety standards are so widespread it would take the Mexican government over 50 years to document them with their current staff. SEDEPAC views unsafe conditions as a human rights violation, especially because in Reynosa the use of chemicals has caused damage to the workers' reproductive systems. This is not surprising. The study done by the University of Lowell Work Environment Program on Reynosa concluded that the potential for environmental catastrophe is there.

> The apparent disregard for sound hazardous waste disposal practices shows ignorance or carelessness in the management of toxic substances inside and outside the plants... Although most of the worksites in this study are assembling plants and do not produce chemicals (with few exceptions), all of the plants use and store substantial amounts of toxic chemicals. The warning signs of a potential acute environmental catastrophe should not be ignored... In April 1986 approximately 100 workers were overcome by fumes from TCE, a toxic chemical stored in a tank at a Zenith plant in Reynosa. Another incident occurred in May of 1990 when a fire at a Deltronics plant which produces parts for General Motors caused 76 workers to be sent to a Matamoros hospital emergency room for smoke inhalation.[34]

Also prevalent among the workers were symptoms such as headaches, unusual fatigue, depression, forgetfulness, chest pressure, insomnia, stomach pains, dizziness, and numbness or tingling. A large number of workers reported "a noticeable airborne substance during at least part of the workday."[35]

Xochitl Romero is also quite concerned about toxics in the workplace and their effect on the general environment. She sees the problem of toxic waste as the result of governmental neglect.

> There is a big problem with materials which were completely prohibited in the United States, but which can be used here indiscriminately because there is no

legislation to control them. This has a big effect on the women workers, and it also has an effect on the ecology of the community. The *maquiladora* industry's waste is not controlled...chemical substances are used, the waste is thrown out and contaminates the rivers, the sewer water, and the drainage system, and that same waste water is used in the countryside for farming!

In 1990, SEDEPAC organized a meeting of *maquiladora* workers from the northeastern border area (Tamaulipas, Nuevo Leon, Coahuila) to discuss conditions at work. Conditions were diverse, but the problems were universal. A worker from the Autonomous Union of Workers at Dickies in Piedras Negras said that workers there were paid the regional minimum wage of 8,405 pesos or $3.11 per day ($15.55 per week) straight time, and that "conditions of hygiene and safety in the plants are minimal or do not exist..." Workers also brought up a different point entirely:

> ...foreign investors in the *maquiladora* industry suddenly and without previous warning close the workplaces without indemnifiying their workers. The machinery and tools which are left in the buildings do not guarantee even a third of the workers constitutional indemnification, seniority, and other benefits which are due the woman worker for her work.[36]

To confront the problems in one *maquiladora* city is to confront the problems in all, because the problems all stem from an imbalance of power. As the experiment with *maquiladoras* proves, when workers have no voice they have no safety and no chance for economic survival.

Chihuahua, Chihuahua

The workers at the Wire Products and Electrical Circuits, Avalos Plant, a *maquiladora* in Chihuahua, provide an excellent example of how independent action within labor unions in the *maquiladoras* is squelched. This case is typical because the majority of the workers involved were women, and the product they produced, electrical "harnesses"—sets of electrical wires used by the automobile industry—involved labor-intensive, unmechanized work.

The union involved, which still controls the plant, is the Sole Union of Workers of Wired Products and Electrical Circuits, Plant 2, affiliated with the CTM organization, controlled by Doroteo Zapata. At a meeting on October 28, 1990, attended by hundreds of workers, union members accused their General Secretary, Rogelio Ledezma, of fraud and called for his removal. Ledezma was a close associate and supporter of Zapata, and therefore Zapata declared the meeting to be invalid.[37] He was highly unprepared to confront this type of dissent. Zapata, who had never worked in a *maquiladora* plant or as part of the labor movement, unexpectedly landed as the head of the CTM and was therefore also an important PRI official in Chihuahua.[38]

On December 1, 1990, in response to Zapata's quick dismissal of the workers' call for new leadership, over 1,000 workers from Plant 2 held a special union meeting at a local theater. The meeting was called to elect a new union executive board because of the allegations of fraud against Ledezma. At the entrance to the theater, supporters of Ledezma attempted to prevent his critics from entering. There were incidents of pushing and fist-fighting, but both factions eventually entered the hall. The microphone was in the hands of Felipe Castillo, legal advisor to the CTM. Castillo attempted to prevent the convenors from voting to remove Ledezma, but their numbers were too great. Eventually the vote occured.

The predominantly women workers voted overwhelmingly to remove General Secretary Rogelio Ledezma and replace him with a new executive committee headed by a worker from the plant named Imelda Ortega. The outcome of the vote was 950 in favor of Ortega out of a total of 1050 votes cast. Castillo, recognizing his powerlessness, said that the election would be considered temporary until another could be held in the plant. Hundreds of workers responded by shouting, "No, we have already elected her!" Nevertheless, after the meeting, Castillo told the local press that he was going to gather representatives of both factions to hold another election.[39] Zapata also refused to recognize the newly elected board.

The new leaders did not stay in power long. They were fired. Even before the election, two members of the opposition to Ledezma and Zapata, María de los Angeles Almodovar and Gonzalo Carreto, had been fired. Then at the end of December two others were fired, Imelda Ortega and Berta Alicia Sifuentes. All of the fired employees reported being told at the time of their dismissal that CTM leader Doroteo Zapata demanded that they be removed. All filed suit with the local Board of Conciliation and Arbitration, charging that they had been fired unjustly and without cause.[40]

Doroteo Zapata denied that he had played any role in the workers' termination. He also said that those who had been fired had never been duly elected to office and had never functioned as the executive board of the local union. Zapata accused them of being trouble-makers. Imelda Ortega declared, "We have never been dissidents. We are still CTM members. Because a majority voted in favor of us, we have been removed, which is illogical. When we tried to talk to Doroteo Zapata, he treated us in a humiliating way, acting like a big dictator, and refused to speak with us."[41]

The next day, January 5, 1991, the fired workers took their case to the office of the Department of Labor of the state of Chihuahua, arguing that they had been unjustly fired after collusion between the company and the CTM union. They then organized a sit-in in front of the Department of Labor building.[42] The workers also sought help from the independent labor federation Frente Auténtico del Trabajo (FAT) and from PRD Congressman Antonio Becerra Gaytan.[43] The fired executive board members complained that within the plant there was now constant harassment from the foremen at the instigation of the CTM union.[44]

Despite the workers' protests, on January 9, 1991, the local Board of Conciliation and Arbitration ruled that the four workers who had originally been fired, and another who had been fired since then, Pedro Ortega Quezada, had no possibility of reinstatement. The fired workers said the decision was due to "orders from above."[45] With a definitive ruling against them, however, they were forced to accept their final severance pay, and were eventually able to negotiate double severance pay by agreeing to give up both their jobs and their union posts.

On January 12, 1991, at a meeting of 300 union members, a new election was held, and a new executive board elected, headed by Luis Raúl Rado Piñon and Isidra Rodríguez. The new leaders were reportedly identified with the opposition to Ledezma and Zapata, though not obviously. Some saw the election as a gain for the union's rank and file anyway, even though the leaders who were originally elected were fired from the plant and the union.[46] Others were not sure what was really gained. At the time of this writing, the final resolution of these events is not clearly a win for either side. Of the workers who were fired, María de los Angeles Almodovar believes that she and the others were blacklisted in the *maquiladora* industry, but that she had been fortunate and found work in a food-packing plant.

The Sole Union of Workers of Wired Products and Electrical Circuits, Plant 2 was denied its right to independently elect its own leadership, exemplifying what happens to rank and file workers who attempt to reform their unions in order to make them more democratic or more representative. The apparent collusion between the company, the union, and the labor authorities is part and parcel of Mexican labor relations, not only in the *maquiladoras*, but also in unionized Mexican workplaces in general.

Conclusions

The unions in the *maquiladora* industry do not serve to protect workers from employer abuses, nor do they fight to improve the quality of workers' lives. They are characterized by the presence of "protection contracts," which include clauses below the standards of protection afforded by the Federal Labor Law. According to Jorge Carrillo, *maquiladora* unions "do not permit worker dissidence" and are therefore "non-representative authoritarian" unions. Carrillo argues further that "there exists no substantial difference between the practices of the various federations (CTM, CROC, CROM, etc.)."[47]

Moreover, conditions in the *maquiladora* unions are not improving, but steadily getting worse. Carrillo, who has done the most extensive work in this area, argues that the unions were more aggressive and more democratic in the period from 1965 to 1975 but that they have become increasingly unrepresentative of their members. Since 1976, he argues, there has been "a process of set-backs" due to various factors including the mobility of capital and the more aggressive stance of companies.[48] Simultaneously, many *maquiladora* workers have developed an "anti-union attitude" which varies from city to city depending on the experience of the worker.[49]

Carrillo refers to *maquiladora* unions as "regressive and functional." They are functional from the point of view of the company, since they keep the workforce under control. They are regressive from the point of view of the workers, since they do not improve their conditions. Says Carrillo:

> The kind of unionism which has been prevalent in the *maquiladoras*, at least for the last ten years [1979-1989], is a unionism which is constantly weaker in its ability to negotiate with the employer, and constantly further from the immediate interests of the workers. The tendency of this kind of unionism is to become more powerfully consolidated despite the protests of the workers.[50]

Carrillo believes that the *maquiladora* unions are having a deleterious effect on other workers in Mexico. He investigated the situation and found that *maquiladoras* had contributed to a general weakening of the Mexican labor unions, and to a general deterioration in the ability of workers to organize to improve their lot. He looked in particular at the auto industry and found that while in the 1970s the auto industry was practically 100 percent unionized, by the 1980s, the percentage had deteriorated to 60.1 percent for Ford, 79.7 percent for Chrysler, and 47.2 percent for General Motors. Only Volkswagen remained at 100 percent. Carrillo attributed the deterioration of the strength of the unions to the growth of the auto parts *maquiladoras*, what he called the *maquilazation* of the auto industry.

The contracts that still exist are inferior, benefits are less, and wages have declined. His conclusion is that:

> In general terms…it can be said that a process of de-unionization exists in the auto parts *maquiladoras*, not only because of the lower levels of unionization compared with the final production sector of the industry in the 1970s, but also because the kind of unionism which exists is far less developed. Union activity in these plants is generally non-existent, and the leaders do not come from the rank and file…in the majority of instances it is a case of imposition of the union and contract. In this sense, we are dealing with a type of unionism which…is beyond authoritarianism. In the extreme case of the CROM the union members aren't even aware that they are affiliated with a union organization.

The situation of workers in the *maquiladoras* is bad and appears to be getting worse. The most obvious indicator is hourly wages, which in the *maquiladora* industries, as in the rest of the Mexican economy, have fallen by about half in less than a decade, from a high of $1.38 in 1982 to a low of $.45 in 1990. Unions have become more authoritarian and repressive while doing less to represent their members. Women workers suffer from constant problems of sexual harassment on the job. Occupational health issues have not entered into the consciousness of Mexican labor unions. Workers and their unions tend to think about accidents, but not about issues of workplace health and safety, despite the fact that occupational health hazards, particularly to the reproductive system, are one of the greatest potential problems in the *maquiladora* industries. Likewise, related environmental hazards are growing with the use of greater quantities of toxic chemicals, with little improvement in regulation or control. As the Lowell University Work Environment Program study of Reynosa-Matamoros points out:

> It is apparent that "voluntary compliance" with internationally established occupational and environmental health standards and procedures is not being practiced by the owners of the *maquiladoras*. This demonstrated failure of transnational firms to operate responsibly—and the apparent failure of the host country to regulate effectively—raises serious questions about the desirability of further deepening of economic relations.[51]

If, as Secretary of Commerce Jaime Serra Puche has stated, the *maquiladoras* are the forerunners of U.S.-Mexico economic integration under a free trade agreement, then the conditions of workers and the limitations on unionization which characterize the *maquiladoras* today should be a matter of concern to all citizens of both countries.

Summary of Conclusions

1) Workers Do Not Earn a Living Wage. A collusive relationship between employers, union officials, and the state makes it possible for Mexico to offer among the lowest wages in the world for industrial and service work. Automobile workers at the Ford plant in Chihuahua, for example, receive a base pay of about 90,000 pesos ($30 per week), and 120,000 pesos including bonus pay for a 44-hour work week (about $40). The collaborative nature of government, employer, and union relations has also made it possible for employers to maintain the 44- or 48-hour work week.

2) Workers' Health and Safety is at Risk. The Secretary of Labor and Institute of Social Security (IMSS) do not protect the health and safety of workers. Virtually no preventative measures are taken against occupational illnesses, not even in the form of face masks. No national health and safety policy exists; there are few trained hygienists, physicians, or epidemiologists; and use of safety equipment is rare. In most cases there are no inspections; in the larger and more important industries where regular inspections take place, they are ineffective because they do not employ adequate methods or equipment. Unions deal with accidents only after they have occurred, via alternative employment, compensation, or retirement; they do not address accident prevention. Moreover, the lack of consciousness or education about occupational health among working people fosters unnecessarily life-threatening conditions.

3) Environmental Hazards Pose a Serious Threat to Workers and their Communities. In industrial areas in most of Mexico, and in the *maquiladora* areas along the border, pollution from industrial wastes causes dangerous environmental hazards. Many workers and community organizations attest to pollution in the air, soil, and water that causes visible effects in the population.

4) Women Workers Face Discrimination and Sexual Harassment. Women workers, who comprise a majority of the workforce in the *maquiladoras*, face the same difficulties as their male counterparts: lack of union democracy and representation, long hours, unhealthy working conditions, etc. In addition, they must deal with rape and sexual harassment in the workplace, lower wages for equal work, entrapment in poverty as single parents, lack of child care facilities, and institutional—including union—discrimination. Moreover, their lives are made more difficult by lack of access to contraceptives and denial of the right to abortion.

5) Child Labor is Widespread in the Informal Economy and in Many Industries. Child labor has reached socially damaging levels in the informal economy, on the streets, and in domestic production. Children are also employed in various industries, often working for even lower wages than adults, with immediate damage to their development from the same health hazards that show up as long-term diseases in adults. Thousands of children work in *maquiladoras* by acquiring false papers. Children work out of desperation in an attempt to survive. The only solution to this problem is raising adult wages to a sustainable level so that parents *can* support their families.

6) Human Rights are Not Respected by the Government or the Judicial System. Workers are routinely victims of illegal detention and torture as a result of their political activity. Extra-judicial murder remains a serious problem, despite recent attempts at reform. Recent studies by human rights groups from the United States and Mexico cite the validity accorded by the courts to confessions extracted through torture and the relative impunity of the perpetrators within the system as the main reasons why these violations of constitutional law continue. The threat of violent retaliation for dissent within an official union or unionization demands undoubtedly has a chilling effect on workers.

7) Freedom of Association is Denied. Mexican workers are systematically denied the most fundamental labor union rights. Workers may not freely form or join labor organizations. Most union members have been forced to join unions affiliated with the ruling Institutional Revolutionary Party (PRI). Membership in these state-controlled unions is often a condition of employment. The Boards of Conciliation and Arbitration and the Secretary of Labor regularly refuse to grant labor union charters to independent unions. The only important exception to this generalization are the charters granted to the "white," or company-controlled, unions in Monterrey and other parts of Nuevo Leon.

8) Labor Law Denies Workers' Rights. Mexican labor law acts to prevent workers from freely organizing or joining labor unions. The state labor authorities routinely deny independent labor unions official registration, which makes it impossible to officially hold labor union contacts. Union representation elections are occasions for intimidation by the employer or the "official" unions. The periodic recording of changes in the union officers and statutes, which should be a routine procedure, is a method by which the state either accepts or rejects these changes.

9) Labor Law Denies the Right to Strike. The state labor authorities routinely deny workers the right to strike by declaring their strikes illegal or non-existent in the eyes of the law on the basis of technicalities. In reality, these decisions are purely political. When workers in the communication and transportation fields strike, they may be subject to military seizure of their workplaces. Public employees' and bank employees' rights are also restricted. In clear violation of international labor rights standards, they may only join one state-party controlled union: FSTSE for public employees and the National Bank Employees Union in the case of bank workers. The Boards of Conciliation and Arbitration do not protect workers' rights; rather, they ensure the state-party's ongoing political control of the unions.

10) Labor Boards Deny Workers' Rights. While employers and union officials are generally able to prevent workers from organizing, sometimes workers succeed in taking control of their unions or forcing their union representatives to respond to their demands for higher wages, better benefits, or improved working conditions. When unions threaten employers with a strike, it is common for the Boards of Conciliation and Arbitration to use technical violations of the law or to fabricate violations in order to declare a strike "non-existent."

11) Union Democracy is Virtually Nonexistent. Workers who must belong to the official labor unions are routinely denied the right to democratically control their organizations by deciding policy or electing their own leaders. Many, perhaps a majority, of the "official" unions do not hold regular meetings. Officers of the "official" unions usually are appointed and are beholden to the ruling party for their posts. When rank and file workers succeed in democratically electing their officers, the Boards of Conciliation and Arbitration and the Secretary of Labor, with rare exceptions, refuse to recognize these officials. In addition, dissident workers who engage in democratic activities can be expelled from the union by an exclusion clause, which also allows the employer to fire them.

12) Unions and Employers Collude to Fire Workers. Mexican unions frequently collude with Mexican employers and multinational corporations to deny workers their basic rights. It is common for the union to ask the employer to fire workers who raise demands for union democracy and for unions to expel members who make demands upon employers. Workers expelled from a union are also fired by their employer, since union membership is a condition of employment. When individual firings fail to deter workers from asserting their rights, employers and union officials use mass firings of hundreds or even thousands of workers. The collusive relationship between employers and union officials is not only accepted but also generally supported, even encouraged, by the state Boards of Conciliation and Arbitration and by the Secretary of Labor.

13) Unions and Employers Collude on "Protection Contracts." Many, perhaps a majority, of "official" unions offer "protection contracts" to employers who can then claim that their employees are represented by a union. The affected workers are often unaware that representation or a contract exists. In many cases, these contracts contain clauses which allow standards below the minimum guaranteed to workers under the Federal Labor Law.

14) Violence is Perpetrated against Workers. Violent repression of workers is rife in Mexican labor relations. When individual or mass firings fail to deter workers who seek to assert their rights, employers and union officials have also threatened, beaten, kidnapped, or even murdered labor activists. The thugs who engage in these attacks are frequently officers or employees of the "official" (PRI, CT, CTM) labor unions. Those responsible for the violence are seldom brought to justice. They seem to enjoy impunity because of the protection given by the "official" labor movement, the ruling party, and the state.

15) Massive Police and Military Force is Used against Workers and Unions. The government repeatedly and continually uses massive police and military force to keep workers and unions under the control of the PRI. During the railroad workers' strike of 1959, the Mexican government used the army to suppress the workers, killing at least two, injuring scores, and firing over 9,000. During the electrical workers' movement of 1976, the state used the army to occupy workplaces while large numbers of workers were fired. Throughout the 1970s and 1980s, the state repeatedly used police or military seizures of the workplace against the state telephone company's reform movements, job actions, or strikes by the telephone workers. On January 10, 1989, President Salinas launched a massive police assault on the petroleum workers union in Ciudad Madero. Dozens of leaders of the union were arrested on charges of illegal possession of arms. On August 21, 1989, the army took over the Cananea copper plant to prevent Mine and Metal Workers Union members from protesting the state sale of the company. The repeated use of the police and the military against workers and labor unions acts to deter them from exercising their rights.

16) Police and Courts are Used to Harass Worker Activists. A recent development in Mexican labor relations is the role of the authorities in fabricating charges against union officials or members who organize strikes or union reform movements. The police and the courts have trumped up charges against strike leaders and imprisoned them for weeks or until the movement or strike is defeated, the charges dropped, and the activist released from jail. In some cases, the courts have convicted the activists and sentenced them on the false charges.

17) Political Figures Interfere in Labor Relations. Not only do the labor authorities, the Boards of Conciliation and Arbitration, the Secretary of Labor, and labor courts fail to function to defend workers' rights, but frequently other government departments or officials with no legal standing become involved in labor conflicts. Mayors, state governors, officials of the Federal District, and, perhaps most commonly, officials of the Secretary of the Interior intervene in labor disputes. These interventions are not good-will attempts at mediation, but political interference by state officials to manipulate the conflicts to their own ends, as demonstrated in the Modelo brewery workers' dispute. The constant intervention of PRI officials in union activities indicates that unions are dominated and stifled by the state and that labor authorities cannot act outside of state control.

18) Entire Unions are Eliminated when they Oppose State-Party Policy. When unions adopt a policy independent of the state-party, they are often eliminated, as in the case of the Tepepan Fish Workers Union and the Uramex Nuclear Workers Union. When these unions opposed privatization, their employer was reorganized and their union was eliminated.

19) *Maquiladora* Workers Receive Low Wages and are Granted No Workers' Rights. The predicament of workers in the *maquiladoras* is of particular concern as these in-bond or twin plants are Mexico's chosen development model. There are 1,909 *maquiladoras* employing 226,483 women and 145,297 men. Levels of labor union organization in the *maquiladoras* vary from one city or state to another: in the state of Tamaulipas the level is nearly 100 percent, while in the cities of Ciudad Juárez, Chihuahua or Tijuana, Baja California Norte, the levels are closer to 30 percent. Virtually all of the organized *maquiladora* workers are in the "official," PRI-affiliated labor unions (CTM, CROC, or CROM). In most cases these unions offer employers "protection contracts" which do not meet the labor standards mandated in the Federal Labor Law. Unions cooperate with management to keep wages low, typically between $25 and $30 per 44-hour week, though including bonuses and benefits, pay may rise to $60 per week in some areas. However, because wages are so low and the cost of living high, worker turnover at many *maquiladoras* is between 15 and 20 percent per month, preventing many workers from collecting bonuses or benefits. During the 1980s, employer and union control over workers became even more authoritarian. This has had a deleterious effect on labor rights in non-*maquiladora* industries and unions, particularly in the auto and auto parts industries, to which the *maquiladoras* are closely related.

20) Is the Situation Improving? The Salinas Administration portrays itself as "reforming," "modernizing," or "freeing" the labor movement. All evidence, however, points to the contrary. Like his predecessors, Salinas has used massive police and military force against both the petroleum workers union and the miners of Cananea. The Salinas Administration's move to privatize state-owned industry has resulted in the disbanding of many labor unions, including that of the fishing industry—one of the most autonomous and democratic unions within the CTM. The Salinas Administration used a combination of job-blackmail and brute power in order to bring the electrical workers union and the telephone workers union back under the control of the PRI. The government's increasing control over the previously independent SME is a particularly inauspicious development in a country where the main challenge to labor union rights is state-party control of the unions. While Salinas began his administration by verbally attacking the CT/CTM labor bureaucracy, he has found it necessary to rely on the CT for votes in hotly contested elections. Consequently, the bonds between the CT federations and the state-party are still strong, and the Secretary of Labor and the Boards of Conciliation and Arbitration still support the "official" unions against independent unions and attempts by workers to democratize existing unions.

Mexican and transnational employers are attempting to improve productivity and profitability by introducing new technologies and systems for controlling workers, disrupting the traditional control of the plants by the "official" unions and erasing the meager gains those unions have made. The combination of new technologies, new forms of control, and low wages has led to increasing dissatisfaction and, in some cases, to worker militancy, reform movements, and strikes. This has been met by increased employer and union violence to suppress the workers with the toleration, encouragement, or participation of the state; examples abound, including the Ford plant in Cuautitlán, the Modelo brewery, the Tornel rubber plant, Aeronaves de Mexico, and many others. All evidence indicates that workers in Mexico are not better off than they were pre-modernization, but have lost much of their ability to exercise fundamental labor rights over the last two decades, a condition that shows no sign of improving over the coming years.

Notes

Introduction

1. See Ray Marshall, *Unheard Voices: Labor and Economic Policy in a Competitive World* (New York: Basic Books, 1987).
2. John Sewell and Stuart Tucker, eds., *Growth, Exports and Jobs in a Changing World Economy: Agenda 1988* (Washington, D.C.: Overseas Development Council, 1988).
3. Ray Marshall, "The Shifting Structure of Global Employment," in Sewell and Tucker, *Growth, Exports and Jobs*.
4. See Steve Chernovitz, "The Influence of International Labour Standards on the World Trading Regime," *International Labour Review*, September-October 1987.
5. See Gus Edgren, "Fair Labour Standards and Trade Liberalization," *International Labour Review*, September-October 1979.
6. Willy Brandt, *et al.*, *North-South: A Programme for Survival, Report of the Independent Commission on International Development Issues* (Cambridge, MA.: MIT Press, 1980), p. 288.
7. For a good discussion, see John Cavanagh, *et al.*, *Trade's Hidden Costs—Worker Rights in a Changing World Economy* (Washington, D.C.: International Labor Rights Education and Research Fund, 1988).

Chapter 1

1. Antonio Tenorio Adame, "La Soberania, el Mercado y la Mano de Obra," in Víctor M. Bernal Sahagún, *La integración comercial de México a Estados Unidos y Canadá: Alternativa destino?* (México, D.F.: Universidad Nacional Autónoma de México and Siglo Veintiuno Editores, 1990), p. 230.
2. Author's interview with Rosalbina Garavito, Mexico City, January 1991.
3. Arturo Fuentes and Raimundo Arroio, "El poder adquisitivo del salario, productividad y posición competitiva de México," *Investigación Económica*, 178, October-December 1986, p. 272ff, cited in Raúl Trejo Delarbre, *Crónica del sindicalismo en México, 1976-1988* (México, D.F.: Universidad Nacional Autónoma de México and Siglo Veintiuno Editores, 1990), p. 30.
4. Trejo Delarbre, *Crónica*, p. 30.
5. Author's interview with Rosalbina Garavito, Mexico City, January 1991.
6. Asa Cristina Laurell and Margarita Márquez, *El desgaste obrero en México: Proceso de producción y salud* (México, D.F.: Ediciones Era, 1983, 1985.), pp. 93-94.
7. *Ibid.*, p. 97.
8. In April 1991, the Salinas and Bush administrations initiated a Memo of Understanding (MOU) to exchange technical information on workplace hazards, in the wake of criticism in the United States about the potential impact on U.S. standards of competition with Mexico based on such loose enforcement. This MOU was almost identical in content to one

signed in 1979 by the Carter Administration with the Mexican government, which was abrogated by the Reagan Administration in 1981.

9. Author's interview with Dr. Sherry Baron, Mexico City, March 1986.

10. Asa Christina Laurell and Mariano Noriega, *La salud en la fábrica: Estudio sobre la industria siderúrgica en México* (México, D.F.: Ediciones Era, 1989), p.195.

11. *Ibid.*, p. 188.

12. *Ibid.*, p. 184.

13. *Ibid.*, p. 184.

14. *Ibid.*, p. 185.

15. *Ibid.*, p. 187.

16. Library of Congress, Congressional Research Services—Language Services, Statement of Elizabeth Macías presented on April 22, 1991, translated by Deanna Hammond.

17. Adolfo Gilly, *Nuestra caída en la modernidad* (Tequisquiapan, Qro.: Joan Boldo y Climent, Editores, 1988), p. 75.

18. For a general discussion of women and labor in Mexico, see José A. Alonso, "Mujer y Trabajo en México," in Asa Cristina Laurell, *et al.*, *Condiciones de Trabajo*, Vol. II of *El Obrero Mexicano* (México, D.F.: Siglo Veintiuno Editores, 1984). Written in the 1980s, it is based on 1970s statistics and is now somewhat out of date.

19. Author's interview with Patricia Mercado, Mexico City, January 28, 1991. All of the following quotations from Mercado come from that interview.

20. Author's interview with Lilia Reyes, Monterrey, January 15, 1991.

21. Author's interview with telephone worker Rosario Ortiz, Mexico City, December 18, 1990.

22. Author's interviews with several female workers, union officials, and lawyers.

23. Matt Moffett, "Working Children: Underage Laborers Fill Mexican Factories, Stir U.S. Trade Debate," *Wall Street Journal*, April 8, 1991, p. 1.

24. Author's interview with Matt Moffett, Mexico bureau of the *Wall Street Journal*, Mexico City, January 28, 1991; and author's interview with Antonio Velázquez, a FAT (Frente Auténtico del Trabajo) labor organizer in the state of Guanajuato, January 1991.

25. Héctor Santos Azuela, "El Trabajo de Menores," in *Estudios de derecho sindical y del trabajo* (México, D.F.: Universidad Nacional Autónoma de México, 1987) pp. 251-271.

26. Moffett, "Working Children."

27. *Mexico: Torture with Impunity* (New York: Amnesty International, 1991), back cover.

28. Ellen L. Lutz, *Unceasing Abuses: Human Rights in Mexico One Year After the Introduction of Reform* (New York: Americas Watch, 1991); and *Primer informe semestral*, June-December 1990, Comisión Nacional de Derechos Humanos.

29. Amnesty International, *Torture with Impunity*, p. 5.

30. *Ibid.*, pp. 8-9.

31. *Ibid.*, p. 8.

32. Daniel Gerdts, *et al.*, *Paper Protection: Human Rights Violation and the Mexican Criminal Justice System* (Minneapolis: Minnesota Lawyers International Human Rights Committee, 1990), p. 1.

33. *Ibid.*, p. 14.

34. *Ibid.*, p. 30.

35. Amnesty International, *Torture with Impunity*; and Gerdts, *et al.*, *Paper Protection*.

36. Trejo Delarbre, *Crónica,* p. 19.
37. *Ibid.,* p. 400.
38. Author's interview with Héctor de la Cueva Díaz, Mexico City, December 14, 1990.
39. Author's interview with Jesús Sergio Acosta Ortiz, Mexico City, January 1991.
40. Author's interview with Telésforo Nava Vázquez, Mexico City, December 18, 1990.
41. Author's interview with José Manuel Loyo Aguirre, Mexico City, January 1991.
42. Author's interview with Raúl Escobar, Mexico City, December 17, 1990.

Chapter 2

1. Some of the standard works on the Mexican political system include: Frank Brandenburg, *The Making of Modern Mexico* (Englewood Cliffs, N.J.: Prentice-Hall, Inc., 1964); Brandenburg often uses the word "authoritarian" to characterize the system. L. Vincent Padgett, *The Mexican Political System* (Boston: Houghton Mifflin Company, 1966); Padgett gives an uncritical functional description of the state and the PRI. Pablo González Casanova, *La democracia en México* (Mexico: Era, 1965, 1985); Casanova also describes an authoritarian and undemocratic system. Juan Felipe Leal, in his books *La burguesía y el estado mexicano* (México, D.F.: Ediciones El Caballito, 1977) and *México, estado, burocracia y sindicatos* (Mexico, D.F., Ediciones El Caballito, 1980); Leal gives a description of the Mexican state as "corporativist." Manuel Aguilar Mora's two-volume *El bonapartismo mexicano* (México, D.F.: Juan Pablos Editor, 1982), as the name indicates, gives the "Bonapartist" description of the Mexican state. Daniel Cosío Villegas's *El sistema político mexicano* (México, D.F.: Cuadernos de Joaquín Mortiz, 1972, 1978), calls it an "impure democracy" based on "presidentialism" and a "dominant government party." He discusses "presidentialism" in his book *La sucesión presidencial* (México, D.F.: Cuadernos de Joaquín Mortiz, 1975).
2. On the subject of the relationship between the PRI and the CT and on the organization of the CT and the confederations, see César Zazueta and Ricardo de la Peña, *La estructura del Congreso del Trabajo: Estado, trabajo y capital en México: Un acercamiento al tema* (México, D.F.: Centro Nacional de Información y Estadisticas del Trabajo and Fondo de Cultura Económica, 1984) and Juan Felipe Leal, *et al., Organización y sindicalismo,* Vol. III of *El Obrero Mexicano* (México, D.F.: Siglo Veintiuno Editores, 1985).
3. Manuel Ponce, "Fin al corporativismo en el PRI, acuerdan Colosio y lideres de sectores," *El Universal,* December 12, 1990, p. 3.
4. José Urena and Andrea Becerril, "Insta Colosio a la CTM a probar su fuerza territorial," *La Jornada,* January 6, 1991, p. 1.
5. Author's interview with Manuel García Espinoza, Monterrey, Nuevo Leon, January 15, 1991. See also Abraham Nuncio, *El Grupo Monterrey* (México, D.F.: Editorial Nueva Imagen, 1982).
6. Throughout this section I have relied heavily on Graciela Bensusan, "Construcción y Desarrollo del Derecho Laboral en Mexico," in Graciela Bensusan, *et al., El derecho laboral,* Vol. IV of *El Obrero Mexicano* (México, D.F.: Siglo Veintiuno Editores, 1985).
7. Bensusan, *El derecho laboral,* p. 56.

8. Héctor Sántos Azuela, "La Libertad Sindical En México," in Graciela Bensusan and Carlos García, eds., *Modernidad y legislación laboral* (México, D.F.: Casa Abierta al Tiempo and Friedrich Ebert Stiftung, 1989), p. 39.

9. Bensusan, *El derecho laboral*, p. 58.

10. *Ibid.*, p. 58.

11. *Ibid.*, p. 60.

12. Amy H. Goldin, "Collective Bargaining in Mexico: Stifled by the Lack of Democracy in Trade Unions," *Comparative Labor Law Journal*, Vol 11: 182, 1990, p. 211.

13. Graciela Bensusan, "Restricciones a los Derechos Sindicales," in *Restricciones a Los Derechos Colectivos de los Trabajadores*, Centro Internacional para los Derechos Sindicales Conference, TS, Mexico, March 1990.

14. Sántos Azuela, "La Libertad…," p. 42.

15. Alfonso Bouzas Ortiz, "El Futuro de la Contratación Colectiva," in Bensusan and García, *Modernidad y legislación laboral*, p. 100.

16. Bensusan, *El derecho laboral*, pp. 41-42.

17. *Ibid.*, p. 62.

18. Jorge Durand, *Los obreros de Río Grande* (Zamora, Michoacán: El Colegio de Michoacán, 1986), p. 217.

19. Andrea Becerril discusses the STMMRM contract in a two-part series on the Miners and Metal Workers Union which appeared in *La Jornada* on September 14 and 15, 1989. This reference is from the second article, Andrea Becerril, "Centralistas y represivos, los estatutos de los mineros," September 15, 1989, p. 13.

20. Bensusan, *El derecho laboral*, p. 70.

21. Bouzas Ortiz, "El Futuro…," p. 100.

22. Bensusan, *El derecho laboral*, p. 27. Also see the example in note 33.

23. Arturo Alcalde, "La Legislación Laboral Burocrática: Una Regulación de Excepción," Encuentro Iberoamericano del Derecho del Trabajo, Puebla, Pue., 14 al 16 de Noviembre de 1990, TS, pp. 19-20.

24. *Ibid.*, p. 17.

25. For an account of the use of government seizure of the workplace against the telephone workers, see Rodolfo Rojas Zea, ed., *Tres huelgas de telefonistas* (Mexico: Editorial Uno, S.A., 1980).

26. "La requisa es anticonstitucional," an advertisement placed by STUNAM and SITUAN in *Unomasuno*, April 27, 1979, cited in Rojas Zea, *Tres huelgas*, p. 33.

27. Arturo Alcalde, "El Contrato Colectivo de Trabajo: Técnica de su Negociación," in Bensuan, *El derecho laboral*, p. 128.

28. Alcalde, "La Legislación Laboral…," p. 3.

29. Manuel Fuentes, "Contratos Colectivos y Contratos de Protección," in *Restricciones a Los Derechos Colectivos de los Trabajadores*, p. 10.

30. Interview with Ernesto Salcido Villareal, Mexico City, January 10, 1991.

31. Bensusan, "Restricciones a los Derechos Sindicales," p. 5.

32. Fuentes, "Contratos Colectivos…," p. 10.

33. Interview with Ernesto Salcido Villareal, Mexico, January 10, 1991.

34. Fuentes, "Contratos Colectivos…," p. 11.

35. Ana María Conesa Ruiz, "Los Tribunales de Trabajo en México: Ficción y realidad de una legislación laboral ineficaz," in Bensusan and Garcia, *Modernidad y legislación laboral*, p. 128.

36. Author's interview with Manuel Fuentes, Mexico City, December 12, 1990.

37. Author's interview with Manuel García Espinoza, Monterrey, January 15, 1991.

38. Author's interview with Antonio Velázquez Loza, member of the national coordinating committee of the Frente Auténtico del Trabajo (FAT), January 1991. He discussed the existence of such illegal shops in Leon and Irapuato, Guanajuato. See also Dan LaBotz, *The Crisis of Mexican Labor* (New York: Praeger, 1988), pp. 167-176, dealing with the garment industry in Mexico City.
39. Graciela Bensusan, "Libertad Sindical: Cambio Real o Aparente en el Escenario Laboral,"in Bensusan and García, *Modernidad y legislación laboral*, p. 35.
40. Alcalde, "La Legislación Laboral...," p. 23.

Chapter 3

1. There are many books dealing with the Magón brothers, the PLM, and the unions. See for example, Salvador Hernández Padilla, *El Magonismo: Historia de una Pasión Libertaria: 1900-1922* (México, D.F.: Era, 1984).
2. *Pacto celebrado entre la Revolución Constitucionalista y la Casa del Obrero Mundial* (México, D.F.: Archivo General de la Nación, Centro de Estudios Históricos del Movimiento Obrero Mexicano, 1979.)
3. Barry Carr, *El movimiento obrero y la política en México: 1910-1919* (México, D.F.: Era, 1976), pp. 85-86.
4. The basic source for this period is Rosendo Salazar and José G. Escobedo, *Las pugnas de la gleba* (México, D.F.: Editorial Avante, 1923). The standard English-language history of this period is Marjorie Ruth Clark's *Organized Labor in Mexico* (Chapel Hill: The University of North Carolina Press, 1934). More recent histories include Barry Carr, *El movimiento obrero y la política en México*; Ramon Eduardo Ruiz, *La revolución mexicana y el movimiento obrero: 1911-1923* (México, D.F.: Era, 1978); and Rocío Guadarrama, *Los sindicatos y la política en México: la CROM (1918-1928)* (México, D.F.: Era, 1981).
5. For information on Cárdenas, Lombardo, and the labor movement, see Arturo Anguiano, *El estado y la política obrera del cardenismo* (México, D.F.: Era, 1975, 1978); Arnaldo Cordova, *La política de masas del cardenismo* (México, D.F.: Era, 1974, 1976); Jorge Basurto, *Cárdenas y el poder sindical* (México, D.F.: Era, 1983).
6. Mario Gill, *Los ferrocarrileros* (México, D.F.: Editorial Extemporaneos, 1971).
7. For a general rundown on developments in this period, see Víctor M. Durand Ponte, et al., *Las derrotas obreras: 1946-1952* (México, D.F.: Universidad Nacional Autónoma de México, 1984); Jorge Basurto, *Del avilacamachismo al alemanismo, 1942-1952*, Vol. XI of *La clase obrera en la historia de México* (México, D.F.: Siglo Veintiuno, 1984).
8. Basurto, *Del avilacamachismo...*, p. 254.
9. For an account of the Nueva Rosita strike, see Mario Gill, ed., *La huelga de Nueva Rosita* (México, D.F.: MAPRI, 1959.)
10. The story of the 1958-59 railroad workers strike is told in Antonio Alonso, *El movimiento ferrocarrilero en México: 1958-59* (México, D.F.: Era, 1979); Max Ortega, *Estado y movimiento ferrocarrilero: 1958-1959* (México, D.F.: Ediciones Quinto Sol, 1988). See also *Cuadernos del CIHMO*, No. 1, which contains interviews with participants in the strike.
11. The story of Rafael Galván, STERM, and the TD movement is told in "Homenaje a Rafael Galván," *Solidaridad*, Número Extraordinario, September 27, 1980; Sindicato de los Trabajadores Electricistas de la Repub-

lica Mexicana (STERM), *Insurgencia obrera y nacionalismo revolucionario* (México, D.F.: Ediciones El Caballito, 1973); Silvia Gómez Tagle, *La insurgencia y democracia en los sindicatos electricistas* (México, D.F.: El Colegio de Mexico, 1980); Arnaldo Cordova, *La política de masas y el futuro de la izquierda en México* (México, D.F.: Era, 1979).

Case Study: Steel Industry

1. For this account of the modernization of the steel industry I have relied on Raúl Trejo Delarbre, *Crónica del sindicalismo en México, 1976-1988* (México, D.F.: Siglo Veintiuno Editores and the Universidad Nacional Autónoma de México, 1990), pp. 161-85. It should be noted that Delarbre is not a radical critic of the Mexican system, but a critical supporter of the corporate state *(corporativismo)* who believes that the PRI must reorganize its relationship to the unions and create a *neo-corporativismo.* Nevertheless, he gives an accurate account of the profound problems with Mexican labor relations and their negative implications for labor rights.

2. On the authoritarian character of the union, see Andrea Becerril's two-part series in *La Jornada,* September 14 and 15, 1989.

3. Two accounts of the history of the steel mills are found in Abraham Nuncio, "Crónica de una Quiebra Anunciada," *Excelsior,* May 16, 1986, p. 5A; and Arthur Golden, "Closing of Steel Mill in Mexico Sets Off Economic Donnybrook," *San Diego Union,* June 22, 1986, p. I-1.

4. In the mid-1970s, an opposition group took power in Local 67, and in 1977 struck for six weeks for higher wages. By 1978 supporters of Gómez Sada had once again taken control of the union. When members of the opposition demanded a secret ballot election be held at the plant gate, they found themselves facing criminal charges. At a Local 67 union meeting held on April 21, 1982, gunmen and police arrested several workers: Evaristo Hernández Varo, who was wounded by gunshot, José Lorenzo Hernández, Ismael Betancourt, René Elizondo, Ricardo Cantu, Francisco de la Roca, and Ignacio Chávez. The workers were beaten and tortured (including threats with live rattlesnakes), and forced to sign bogus confessions to planning murder and the use of explosives against union officials. The treatment of these dissident steel workers became a major issue of the day and a group of Mexico City intellectuals published a statement supporting them in the Mexico City newspapers. See *Unomasuno,* May 7, 1982. This is cited in Delarbre, *Crónica,* p. 166.

5. José Neme, "Mítin de 6 mil Metalurgistas en Monterrey: Piden Trabajo," *Excelsior,* May 13, 1986.

6. "Presionarán 7 mil Mineros Contra el Cierre de Fundidora," *Excelsior,* May 26, 1986.

7. Sara Lovera, "Virtual paralización de la plant uno de Altos Hornos de México," *La Jornada,* Sept. 10, 1986; Sara Lovera, "Confirmo Gómez Sada que dejaron de funcionar tres altos hornos," *La Jornada,* Sept. 18, 1986; Sara Lovera, "Comisión de diputados visitarán hoy AHMSA," *La Jornada,* October 8, 1986; Sara Lovera, "Exigen obreros informes a AHMSA sobre la reconversión industrial," *La Jornada,* October 9, 1986.

8. Andrea Becerril, "En el STMMRM, 50 mil trabajadores menos desde 1982," *La Jornada,* September 14, 1989, p. 7.

9. Author's interview with Father Pedro Pantoja, Monclova, Coahuila, January 16, 1991.

10. *Ibid.*

Chapter 4

1. For this account of the Nuclear Workers Union strike, I have relied on two sources: Raúl Trejo Delarbre, *Crónica del sindicalismo en México (1976-1988)* (México, D.F.: Siglo Veintiuno Editores and the Universidad Nacional Autónoma de México, 1990) and Antonio Gershenson, *México: Sindicalismo y poder: la experiencia nuclear* (México, D.F.: Ediciones El Caballito, 1987).

2. Trejo Delarbre, *Crónica*, p. 208.

3. *Ibid.*, p. 211.

4. Gershenson, *México: Sindicalismo y poder*, p. 97.

5. Trejo Delarbre, *Crónica*, p. 214.

6. The sources for this section are primarily two interviews. Most importantly, with Manuel García Urrutia, a former leader of the Tepepan union and of the National Union of the Fishing Industry, as well as a member of the National Coordinating Committee of the FAT, interviewed on January 30, 1991 in Mexico City. I also interviewed Juan Francisco Muñiz, a former member of the Tepepan union, on January 19, 1991 in Chihuahua, Mexico. I also relied on a brief discussion of the history of the company and the union in "Proyecto de Comercialización de Productos Pesqueros, Cooperativa Tepepan," TS, October 1990; and on Leopoldo Ramírez, "Algunos Aspectos de Dominación y Desarticulación de la Actividad Pesquera y la Sociedad: Prioridades y Acciones," Elaborado por: Los Sindicatos de la Secretaria de Pesca, SUTSP y Refrigeradora Tepepan, S.A. de C.V., STERT (Mexico City, *circa* 1985).

7. Author's interview with Manuel García Urrutia, Mexico City, January 30, 1991.

8. Alberto Barranco Chavarría, "Aeroméxico: ¿otro pacto?" *La Jornada*, April 18, 1988, p. 29. See also Sara Lovera and Víctor Cardoso, "Liquidarán al 90% de los Trabajadores de Aeroméxico," *La Jornada*, April 27, 1988, p. 1.

9. Andrea Becerril and Víctor Cardoso, "Desde agosto, el gobierno dejó de aportar recursos a Aeroméxico," *La Jornada*, April 17, 1988, p. 1.

10. Raúl Trejo Delarbre, "Aeroméxico: El estado se puso en huelga," *La Jornada*, April 19, 1988, p. 5.

11. Antonio Gershenson, "Aeroméxico: ¿quiénes ganan?" *La Jornada*, April 24, 1988, p. 5.

12. Andrea Becerril, "Aeroméxio [sic], emplazada a huelga por violar la relación laboral," *La Jornada*, March 30, 1988, p. 7; Jaime Durán, "Fue Emplazada a Huelga Aeroméxico," *Excelsior*, March 30, 1988, p. 5.

13. Andrea Becerril, "Apoyo incondicional del CT a trabajadores de Aeroméxico," *La Jornada*, March 31, 1988, p. 7.

14. Rubén Vizcaino, "Dos Mil Empleados Afectados por la Cancelación de Vuelos," *Excelsior*, April 3, 1988, p. E-1.

15. "Aeroméxico, Impedida Legalmente Para Vender 13 de sus Aviones: Montalvo G.," *Excelsior*, April 5, 1988, p. 13; Jorge López F., "Emplazan a Huelga los Sindicatos de Aeroméxico, Para el 12: Rene Arce," *Excelsior*, April 5, 1988, p. 5.

16. Jaime Contreras S., "Vota el Sindicato de Aeroméxico por ir a la Huelga," *Excelsior*, April 12, 1988, p. E-5.

17. "Se retiró 'temporalmente' de la Bolsa la Cia. Mexicana de Aviación," *La Jornada*, April 12, 1988, p. 29.

18. José Neme Salum, "A Listo la DGA Personal de Confianza Ante la Posible Huelga en Aeroméxico," *Excelsior*, April 12, 1988, p. 45.

19. "Aeroméxico—A los usuarios de nuestras rutas: A la opinión pública," *La Jornada*, April 13, 1988, p. 11.
20. "C. Miguel de la Madrid Hurtado...," *La Jornada*, April 13, 1988, p. 6.
21. Andrea Becerril and Víctor Cardoso, "Comenzó la huelga en Aeroméxico; el gobierno no decretó la requisa," *La Jornada*, April 13, 1988, p. 1; Jaime Durán, "Huelga en Aeroméxico; La empresa demanda la inexistencia: 'No hay base legal'," *Excelsior*, April 13, 1988, p. 1; Humberto Aranda, "En Nada se Violó el Contrato; es un Movimiento Sin Razon," *Excelsior*, April 13, 1988, p. 1.
22. "Llamamiento: Todos a la Defensa de las Empresas Estatales y Nuestra Solidaridad con la Huelga de Aeroméxico," *La Jornada*, April 15, 1988, p. 24.
23. The advertisement placed in the papers by these unions on April 16, 1988 carried the same headline as the April 15 advertisement. "Llamamiento: Todos a la Defensa de las Empresas Estatales y Nuestra Solidaridad con la Huelga de Aeroméxico," *La Jornada*, April 16, 1988, p. 26.
24. Humberto Aranda, "No Hubo Fallo Sobre la Huelga en Aeroméxico," *Excelsior*, April 15, 1988, p. 4.
25. "Lo Mejor es la Quiebra de la Aerolinea, Asegura M. Farias," *Excelsior*, April 16, 1988, p. 21.
26. Víctor Cardoso and Andrea Becerril," "El CT y sindicatos de paraestatales repudían la petición de quiebra," *La Jornada*, April 17, 1988, p. 1.
27. Humberto Aranda, "Continuará la Lucha Sindical en Aeroméxico," *Excelsior*, April 18, 1988, p. 1.
28. Humberto Aranda, "En el Conflicto de Aeroméxico Deben Participar Todas las Partes: Calleja," *Excelsior*, April 4, 1988, p. 44.
29. Humberto Aranda, "Probable Declaración de Inexistencia," *Excelsior*, April 20, 1988, p. 1.
30. Jaime Durán, "Evitemos que Aerolineas de Fuera nos Invaden, Dice ASPA," *Excelsior*, April 20, 1988, p. 1.
31. Humberto Aranda, "Solución a Aeroméxico en Mejores Términos," *Excelsior*, April 21, 1988, p. 1; Andrea Becerril and Víctor Cardoso, "Probable Audiencia de MMH a la representación sindical de Aeroméxico," *La Jornada*, April 21, 1988, p. 7.
32. "Carta Abierta," *La Jornada*, April 20, 1988, p. 24.
33. "Por lo visto..." an ad placed by the unions of nationalized industry, *La Jornada*, April 20, 1988, p. 26; "La quiebra en Aeroméxico es fraudulenta y antipatriótica," an ad placed by La Mesa de Concertación Sindical, *La Jornada*, April 20, 1988, p. 26. Also "Que hablen los huelgistas de Aeroméxico," an ad placed by SITUAM, *La Jornada*, April 21, 1988, p. 18.
34. Andrea Becerril and Víctor Cardoso, "Petición formal para concluir las relaciones laborales," *La Jornada*, April 22, 1988, p. 1.
35. Salvador Martínez García, "Imposible Seguir Otorgando Subsidios," *Excelsior*, April 23, 1988, p. 1.
36. Humberto Aranda, "Se Ampara el Sindicato Contra el Dictamen de Quiebra de Aeroméxico," *Excelsior*, April 23, 1988, p. 17; Andrea Becerril and Víctor Cardoso, "Solicitan amparo contra la demanda de Aeroméxico," *La Jornada*, April 23, 1988, p. 6.
37. Andrea Becerril, "El sindicato de Aeroméxico insiste en la restructuración de la empresa," *La Jornada*, April 24, 1988, p. 3.
38. Sara Lovera and Evangelina Hernández, "Desaparecerán los contratos colectivos en Aeroméxico," *La Jornada*, April 25, 1988, p. 1.
39. Sara Lovera and Evangelina Hernández, "Salvar Aeroméxico como

empresa del Estado, proponen los trabajadores," *La Jornada*, April 26, 1988, p. 3.

40. Lovera and Cardoso, "Liquidarán al 90%...," p. 1; Humberto Aranda, "Se Proyecta Liquidar a Todo el Personal, Dice Ismael Gómez G.," *Excelsior*, April 27, 1988, p. 1; Humberto Aranda, "Decide el Gobierno Instalar un Comité Mixto con ASPA," *Excelsior*, April 3, 1988, p. 4.

41. Rubén Alvarez and Evangelina Hernández, "Aún no cobrán su última quincena los trabajadores de Aeroméxico," *La Jornada*, May 10, 1988, p. 6.

42. José A. Pérez Stuart, "Portafolios," *Excelsior*, April 29, 1988, p. 2F.

43. Andrea Becerril and Víctor Cardoso, "La actual operación de Aeroméxico la llevará al fracaso en 90 días," *La Jornada*, May 11, 1988, p. 5.

44. Evangelina Hernández, "Con 10% de personal de tierra Aeroméxico reinicia actividades," *La Jornada*, May 3, 1988, p. 5.

45. Alvarez and Hernández, "Aún no cobrán..." *La Jornada*, May 10, 1988, p. 6.

46. "Marcha de los trabajadores sindicalizados y de confianza de Aeronaves de México hacia la residencia de Los Pinos," *La Jornada*, May 12, 1988, p. 19. An advertisement placed by Miguel Mejorada Sánchez of the Technicians and Workers Union.

47. Andrea Becerril, "Plantón de sobrecargos frente a la Junta de Conciliación," *La Jornada*, April 14, 1988, p. 9.

48. Humberto Aranda, "Inician el Juicio de Liquidación en Aeroméxico," *Excelsior*, May 21, 1988, p. 5; Andrea Becerril, "La junta es la que debe decidir la liquidación en el caso de Aeroméxico," *La Jornada*, May 21, 1988, p. 9.

49. Andrea Becerril, "Fin a la relación laboral de Aeroméxico con su personal," *La Jornada*, May 28, 1988, p. 5; "Liquidan a 7,500 Empleados de Aeroméxico," *Excelsior*, May 31, 1988, p. 5.

50. Author's interview with Miguel Angel Mejorada Sánchez, Mexico City, December 11, 1990.

Chapter 5

1. Matt Moffett, "Mexico Arrests Powerful Chief Of Oil Union," *Wall Street Journal*, January 11, 1989; "Mexico Arrests Powerful Leader of Oil Workers on Arms Charges," *New York Times*, January 11, 1989. Also see Raúl Trejo Delarbe and Ana L. Galván, *Así Cayó La Quina* (México, D.F.: El Nacional, 1989). This very useful book contains a chronology of events and a collection of hundreds of newspaper articles dealing with the arrest of La Quina.

2. On the early history of the Mexican oil industry, see Dan LaBotz, *Edward L. Doheny: Petroleum, Power and Politics in the United States and Mexico* (New York: Praeger, 1991) and Francisco Colmenares, *Petróleo y lucha de clases en México, 1864-1982* (México, D.F.: Ediciones El Caballito, S.A., 1982).

3. On the early history of petroleum workers' organizing efforts, see Julio Valdivieso Castillo, *Historia del movimiento sindical petrolero en Minatitlán, Veracruz* (México, D.F.: Imprenta Mexicana, 1963).

4. Fabio Barbosa Cano, "El Movimiento Petrolero en 1938-1940," in Javier Aguilar García, ed., *Petroleros* (México, D.F.: G.V. Editores, 1986); Dan La Botz, *Crisis of Mexican Labor* (New York: Praeger, 1988), pp. 78-79.

5. La Botz, *Crisis*, p. 91.

6. See George W. Grayson, *The Politics of Mexican Oil* (Pittsburgh: University of Pittsburgh, 1980), Chapter 4.

7. North American businesspeople also became involved in business arrangements with PEMEX officials. In 1960, George Bush and his associates in the Houston-based Zapata Off-Shore Co. joined with Jorge Díaz Serrano to create Perforaciones Marinas del Golfo, better known as Permargo. All of the records for Permargo from 1960 to 1966, the years that George Bush was involved in the company, were "accidentally" destroyed by the Securities and Exchange Commission in October 1983, just after George Bush became Vice-President of the United States. See Jonathan Kwitny, "The Mexican Connection: A Look at an Old George Bush Business Venture," Barron's, September 19, 1988, pp. 8-9, 28.

8. See La Botz, Crisis, Chapter 8. See also Angelina Alonso and Roberto López, El Sindicato de Trabajadores Petroleros y sus relaciones con PEMEX y el estado, 1970-1985 (México, D.F.: El Colegio de México, 1986) and Grayson, The Politics.

9. Later, two of La Quina's associates said that two of La Quina's bodyguards, Mauro Estrada and Ramón Valadés, confessed to the murder of Torres Pancarda. Then, shortly after La Quina was arrested, Ramón Valadés, who was allegedly a drug dealer, confessed to having murdered Torres Pancarda under instructions from La Quina. See Delarbre and Galván, Así Cayó, p. 27.

10. On the oil boom, see Herberto Castillo and Rogelio Naranjo, Cuando el petróleo se acaba (México, D.F.: Ediciones Oceano, S.A., 1985); Manuel Buendia, Los petroleros (México, D.F.: Ediciones Oceanao y Fundación Manuel Buendia, 1985); and Grayson, The Politics. Díaz Serrano was jailed in 1983, convicted in 1987, and eventually served five years in prison for defrauding the government of $34 million. See Dan Williams, "Ex-Pemex Chief Gets 10 Years for Fraud," Los Angeles Times, May 8, 1987, p. 8.

11. Alonso and López, El Sindicato, p. 252, Table 43.

12. Grayson, The Politics, p. 91.

13. Joseph B. Treaster, "Mexican Union Chief Is King To the Oil Workers at Home," New York Times, January 15, 1989, p.1.

14. This document is discussed in Antonio Gershenson, México: Sindicalismo y poder: La experiencia nuclear (México, D.F.: Ediciones El Caballito, 1987), p. 55.

15. Joseph B. Treaster, "Arrest of Oil Union Chief in Mexico Sets Off Strike," New York Times, January 12, 1989.

16. Interview with petroleum workers, Mexico City, December 1990 and January 1991.

17. Delarbre and Galván, Así Cayó, pp. 23-4.

18. Ibid., p. 25.

19. Ibid., p. 31.

20. Ibid., p. 32.

21. Matt Moffett, "Mexico Labor Strongman Is Arraigned, But Unions' Protests So Far Are Muted," Wall Street Journal, January 13, 1989; Joseph B. Treaster, "Strikes Wane At Mexico Oil Sites; Union Leader Faces New Charges," New York Times, January 13, 1989.

22. Delarbre and Galván, Así Cayó, p. 28.

23. Ibid., p. 28.

24. "STPRM," El Nacional, January 23, 1989, cited in Delarbre and Galván, Así Cayó, p. 246.

25. Interview with petroleum worker, Mexico City, December 1990.

26. Ibid.

27. Ibid.

28. Ibid.

29. *Ibid.*
30. *Ibid.*
31. *Ibid.*
32. Alan Robinson and Anna Szterenfeld, "Mexico Set for Weakening in Labor Influence After Showdown With Oil Workers," *Business Latin America,* January 23, 1989, pp. 18-19.
33. Matt Moffett, "Mexico Arrests Powerful Chief of Oil Union," *Wall Street Journal,* January 11, 1989.
34. Louis Uchitelle, "Pemex Adopts a Corporate Tone," *New York Times,* August 17, 1990.
35. For Greene's role in Mexico, see C.L. Sonnichsen, *Colonel Greene and the Copper Skyrocket* (Tucson: University of Arizona Press, 1974).
36. Fernando Talavera, *et al.*, *La resistencia obrera en Sicartsa y Cananea* (Taller de Indicadores Económicos, Facultad de Economía, Universidad Nacional Autónoma de México), pp. 12-13.
37. Ramón Alfonso Sallard, "24 millones 500 mil dls. ha perdido Cananea en 35 días," *La Jornada,* September 24, 1989, p. 1.
38. "Comunicobre, boletín informativo de la Compañía Minera de Cananea," January 21, 1989, cited in A. Sepulveda and F. Santacruz, "Es un 'Atentado al Sindicalismo'," *Excelsior,* August 22, 1989, p. 1.
39. H. Aranda and F. Santacruz, "Declaran en Quiebra a la Compañía Minera de Cananea," *Excelsior,* August 21, 1989, p. 1.
40. Anibal Ramírez, "Reajustar a 343 obreros, propone Minera de Cananea," *La Jornada,* August 8, 1989, p. 15.
41. Evangelina Hernández, "De un plumazo pretenden deshacer 52 años de lucha," *La Jornada,* August 18, 1988, p. 8.
42. Luis Alberto Pérez Aceves, Director of Cananea, later denied these charges. See Renato Dávalos, "Concluirá la Indemnización en 2 o 3 Semanas: Pérez A.," *Excelsior,* August 23, 1989, p. 1.
43. A. Sepulveda and F. Santacruz, "Es un 'Atentado al Sindicalismo'," *Excelsior,* August 22, 1989, p. 1.
44. Humberto Aranda, "Nos Entregan Cananea en 15 Días o la Ocupamos: Obreros," *Excelsior,* August 8, 1989, p. 1.
45. "Cananea: Un Golpe a la Constitución, a la Historia y al Pueblo," *La Jornada,* August 22, 1989, p. 16.
46. Humberto Aranda, "El Ejercito no Tocará a Trabajadores de Cananea: Gómez Sada," *Excelsior,* August 23, 1989, p. 1.
47. Andrea Becerril, "Impide Gómez Sada el Apoyo del CT a Obreros de Cananea," *La Jornada,* September 7, 1989, p. 7.
48. Renato Dávalos, "Concluirá la Indemnización en 2 o 3 Semanas: Pérez A," *Excelsior,* August 23, 1989, p. l.
49. Carlos Fernández-Vega, "'Unica opción viable', la quiebra de Cananea: Nafinsa," *La Jornada,* August 24, 1989, p. 1; "Cananea no es parestatal: Secofeg [sic]," *La Jornada,* August 24, 1989, p. 25.
50. "Demanda Colosio la reapertura de Cananea," *La Jornada,* August 25, 1989, p. 1.
51. José Ureña, "No habrá marcha atrás en Cananea, advierte Salinas," *La Jornada,* August 26, 1989, p. 1.
52. A. Sepulveda and F. Santacruz, "Cananea Abrirá Antes de 2 Meses: Liera," *Excelsior,* August 28, 1989, p. 1.
53. "Acto en Defensa de Cananea: Cuna de la Revolución," advertisement, *La Jornada,* September 1, 1989, p. 1.
54. A. Sepulveda and F. Santacruz, "Liquidaciones Voluntarias, Proponen los Trabajadores," *Excelsior,* August 30, 1989, p. 1.

55. Andrea Becerril, "Rechaza el sindicato nacional el monto de las indemnizaciones para mineros de Cananea," *La Jornada*, September 13, 1989, p. 1.
56. "25% de acciones a mineros despedidos, propone Farell," *La Jornada*, August 31, 1989, p. 1.
57. Andrea Becerril, "Se reservó la junta dictar acuerdo sobre el término de relaciones laborales en Cananea," *La Jornada*, September 1, 1989, p. 1.
58. José Ureña, "El gobierno protegerá los derechos laborales de mineros," *La Jornada*, September 2, 1989, p. 13.
59. Ramón Alfonso Sallard, "Posturas diferentes respecto al conflicto obrero en Cananea," *La Jornada*, September 2, 1989, p. 8.
60. Anibal Ramírez, "Se aceptaría la liquidación masiva en Cananea según el contrato colectivo, afirma Bustamante," *La Jornada*, September 4, 1989, p. 1.
61. "Al Presidente de la Republica Carlos Salinas de Gortari, Al Pueblo de México," *La Jornada*, September 8, 1989, p. 26. Placed by Oscar Sainz Cota, president of the strike committee.
62. Anibal Ramírez, "Inmediata recontratación de 2 mil 500 obreros ofreció la compañía," *La Jornada*, September 12, 1989, p. 1.
63. "La JFCA resolvío la terminación de las relaciones laborales," *La Jornada*, September 12, 1989, p. 1; "A Los Trabajadores de la Compañía Minera de Cananea," advertisement, *La Jornada*, September 12, 1989.
64. Triunfo Elizalde, "Los trabajadores aceptaran la copropiedad, confia Finasa," *La Jornada*, September 13, 1989, p. 1.
65. Ramón Alfonso Sallard, "Desconfianza ante las proposiciones oficiales," *La Jornada*, September 13, 1989, p.1.
66. Andrea Becerril, "Rechaza el sindicato nacional el monto de las indemnizaciones para mineros de Cananea," *La Jornada*, September 13, 1989, p. 1.
67. Francisco Santacruz, "Ningún Trabajador de Cananea Aceptará su Liquidación: Saenz," *Excelsior*, September 14, 1989, p. 29.
68. Ramón Alfonso Sallard, "Frente común en la minera entre los sindicalizados y de confianza," *La Jornada*, September 14, 1989, p. 6.
69. Francisco Santacruz, "Bloquean los Mineros la Carretera a Cananea," *Excelsior*, September 15, 1989, p. 4.
70. "Carta Abierta a la Opinión Pública," *La Jornada*, September 15, 1989, p. 24.
71. Humberto Aranda, "Reanudar Labores en Cananea Ofrece Finasa," *Excelsior*, September 26, 1989, p. 1.
72. Humberto Aranda, "Rechazan los Obreros Condiciones Propuestas Para Abrir Cananea," *Excelsior*, September 28, 1989, p. 4; and a four-part series by Ramón Alfonso Sallard, "Rechazaran trabajadores la propuesta de Finasa, I," *La Jornada*, September 30, 1989, p. 1; "El contrato de Finasa deja en la *indefensión* a los mineros, II," *La Jornada*, October 1, 1989, p. 12; "Finasa ha desoido la oferta de hacer copropietarios a obreros, III," *La Jornada*, October 2, 1989, p. 14; and "Tienen silicosis, casi todos los obreros de Minera de Cananea, IV," *La Jornada*, October 3, 1989, p. 12.
73. Anibal Ramírez, "Presentarán mineros una contrapropuesta de CCT," *La Jornada*, October 2, 1989, p. 13.
74. Anibal Ramírez, "Se comprometió el sindicato de la quiebra a reabrir Cananea," *La Jornada*, October 3, 1989, p. 13.
75. Francisco Santacruz, "Trabajadores de Minera Cananea se Oponen a Tomar las Instalaciones," *Excelsior*, October 3, 1989, p. 1E.
76. Triunfo Elizalde, "Cananea podría ser reabierta en 48 horas: Finasa," *La*

Jornada, October 5, 1989, p. 8.

77. Ramón Alfonso Sallard, "Demandan que Minera de Cananea sea de sus obreros," *La Jornada,* October 9, 1989, p. 13; "Al Pueblo de México...Declaración de Hermosillo," advertisement, *La Jornada,* October 15, 1989, p. 17.

78. Jacinto Noe Hernández, "Trabajadores de Cananea Aceptan en Principio Reanudar las Labores," *La Jornada,* October 17, 1989, p. 1.

79. Jacinto Noe Hernández, "Se Respetarán los Derechos de los Trabajadores en Cananea: Saenz C.," *Excelsior,* October 18, 1989, p. 4.

80. Humberto Aranda and Francisco Santacruz, "Aceptan Reanudar Labores en Cananea," *Excelsior,* October 20, 1989, p. 1.

81. Martínez García, "Cananea y su Sindicato no Desaparecen; Tendrán Nuevas Metas de Productividad y Justicia Para los Trabajadores," *Excelsior,* October 26, 1989, p. 1.

82. Francisco Santacruz, "En Tres Semanas Minera Cananea Trabajará a Plentitud," *Excelsior,* November 2, 1989, p. 1E.

83. Ramón Alfonso Sallard, "A 18 días del acuerdo, la Minera de Cananea reinició sus labores," *La Jornada,* November 8, 1989, p. 10; F. Santa Cruz, "Con 710 Trabajadores Menos Reabrió Minera Cananea," *Excelsior,* November 9, 1989, p. E-1.

84. "Jorge Larrea Intenta Eliminar el Contrato Colectivo, Dicen Trabajadores de Cananea," *El Financiero,* January 28, 1991, p. 29; "No permitirá la Minera Cananea Modificaciones al Contrato Colectivo," *El Financiero,* February 1, 1991.

85. On this period of the telephone workers union, see Rodolfo Rojas Zea, ed., *Tres huelgas de telefonistas* (México, D.F.: Editorial Uno, S.A., 1980).

86. Raúl Trejo Delarbre, *Crónica del sindicalismo en México, 1976-1988* (México, D.F.: Siglo Veintiuno Editores and the Universidad Nacional Autónoma de México, 1990), p. 328. I rely largely on the section of this book titled "Trabajadores Telefonistas," pp. 326-337.

87. Salvador Corro, "Teléfonos lleva su campaña antisindical hasta los golpes a trabajadores," *Proceso,* number 428, January 14, 1985, pp. 6 ff, cited in Trejo Delarbre, *Crónica,* p. 335.

88. Statement by Gloria Peinado, a TELMEX secretary, quoted in Corro, "Teléfonos lleva…," cited in Trejo Delarbre, *Crónica,* p. 335.

89. Emilio Lomas, "Venden Teléfonos de México al grupo Carso, encabezado por Carlos Slim," *La Jornada,* December 10, 1990; Jesús Rivera Valero, "Garantiza el Control de la Firma por Parte de Mexicanos," *Excelsior,* December 10, 1990; Sara Lovera, "Los trabajadores, corresponsables de la modernización de Telmex," *La Jornada,* December 18, 1990; Sara Lovera, "Hernández Juárez: empleo seguro para 5 mil operadoras," *La Jornada,* December 21, 1990.

90. The name of the organization was originally to have been Federación de Sindicatos de las Empresas Paraestatales (Federation of Unions of the State Companies). However, since the government began selling off the state companies, the name had to be changed to Federación de Sindicatos de Empresas de Bienes y Servicios (Federation of Unions of Goods and Services).

91. Author's interviews with Rosalbina Garavito, manager of *El Cotidiano,* Mexico City, December 17, 1990, and with Telésforo Nava Vázquez, professor at the Metropolitan Autonomous University (UAM).

Chapter 6

1. Carlos López E., *En La Modelo Un Modelo de Huelga* (México, D.F.: Centro de Asesoría Sindical Valentín Campa, May, 1990), pp. 11-15.
2. Fernando Talavera Aldaña, *et al.*, *Las Huelgas de los Cerveceros Mexicanos: La Modelo, Testimonio de abril de 1990; Distribuidora Moctezuma, Testimonio de 1987* (Taller de Indicadores Económicos, Facultad de Economía, Universidad Nacional Autónoma de México), p. 8.
3. For the demands, see Carlos López, *En La Modelo*, p. 14. For health and safety problems, see Talavera Aldaña, *et al.*, *Las Huelgas*, pp. 11-12, 24. See also Sara Lovera, "Por mejores condiciones de trabajo, la huelga en Modelo," *La Jornada*, February 26, 1990, p. 13.
4. Andrea Becerril, "La JFCA declaró inexistente la huelga en la Modelo," *La Jornada*, February 17, p. 15.
5. The *plantón* (encampment) in front of a struck plant is a traditional form of Mexican labor protest, much like the picketline in the United States.
6. Sara Lovera, "Exigió la JFCA la entrega de las instalaciones de Cervecería Modelo," *La Jornada*, February 2, 1990, p. 1.
7. Sara Lovera, "Nuestro movimiento es laboral, no político, dicen obreros de la Modelo," *La Jornada*, February 23, 1990, p. 11.
8. Sara Lovera, "Por mejores condiciones de trabajo, la huelga en Modelo," *La Jornada*, February 26, 1990, p. 13.
9. Sara Lovera, "Rompe la relación laboral con sus obreros la Cervecería Modelo," *La Jornada*, February 24, 1990, p. 44.
10. Andrea Becerril and Julio Denegri, "Trabajadores de la Modelo, en libertad de elegir un nuevo comité," *La Jornada*, February 26, 1990, p. 13.
11. Sara Lovera, "Fidel: la CTM ayudaría a trabajadores de la Modelo," *La Jornada*, February 27, 1990, p. 11.
12. Andrea Becerril, "Resolución legal favorable a empleados de la Modelo," *La Jornada*, March 3, 1991, p. 3.
13. Miguel Angel Granados Chapa, "Plaza Dominical," *La Jornada*, March 4, 1990, p. 1.
14. Andrea Becerril, "Requieren mil millones de pesos obreros de la Modelo," *La Jornada*, March 4, 1990, p. 11. See also "Sindicato de Trabajadores de la Cervercería Modelo, S.A. ...Apelamos a la Solidaridad del Pueblo de México," *La Jornada*, March 4, 1990, p. 16; and "Llamado Sindical a La Solidaridad," *La Jornada*, March 4, 1990, p. 2.
15. Sara Lovera, "Ofrece la CTM intervención incondicionada en la Modelo," *La Jornada*, March 6, 1990, p. 11.
16. For accounts of the eviction of the workers from in front of the plant, see Carlos López E., *En La Modelo*, p. 33; and Talavera Aldaña, *Las Huelgas*, p. 21.
17. Carlos López E., *En La Modelo*, p. 47. A somewhat different list of the eight points can be found in Talavera Aldaña, *Las Huelgas*, p. 22.
18. Andrea Becerril, "Rechazan los obreros de la Modelo el regreso a labores 'por listas'," *La Jornada*, April 3, 1990, p. 3.
19. Humberto Aranda, "Reanuda Parcialmente sus Labores la Modelo," *Excelsior*, April 5, 1990, p. 1.
20. COR, like the CTM, is an "official" labor organization affiliated with the CT, though at this time COR was supporting both the Modelo and Ford workers.
21. Andrea Becerril, "O todos o ninguno, consigna de los trabajadores de Modelo," *La Jornada*, April 6, 1990, p. 6.

22. Andrea Becerril, "Esta semana, fecha límite para que regresen los trabajadores de Modelo," *La Jornada*, April 6, 1990, p. 3.
23. Andrea Becerril and Clara G. García, "Fue detenido un asesor de trabajadores de la Modelo," *La Jornada*, April 7, 1990, p. 11.
24. Juan Ochoa Vidal, "Garantías por Escrito o no hay Arreglo: Obreros de la Modelo," *Excelsior*, April 8, 1990, p. 5; Andrea Becerril, "Reanudar las pláticas en la Modelo, piden los obreros," *La Jornada*, April 8, 1990, p. 5; Andrea Becerril, "Resuelven continuar su huelga los trabajadores de la Modelo," *La Jornada*, April 11, 1990, p. 12.
25. Andrea Becerril, "Cervecerías de EU financiaron a huelgistas, acusa la CTM," *La Jornada*, April 11, 1990, p. 11.
26. Andrea Becerril, "Señalan irregularidades que cometío la juez Cervantes," *La Jornada*, April 14, 1990, p. 5.
27. Andrea Becerril, "Queman obreros de Modelo a Fidel, la juez, Farell y Sánchez Navarro," *La Jornada*, April 15, 1991, p. 3.
28. Andrea Becerril, "Personal de emergencia de Modelo decidío no regresar a laborar," *La Jornada*, April 16, 1990, p. 3.
29. Humberto Aranda, "Bloquearon Huelgistas de la Modelo el Acceso a la Planta Durante 2 Hrs.," *Excelsior*, April 18, 1990, p. 49; Andrea Becerril, "Trabjadores ocuparán la Modelo si no hay solución," *La Jornada*, April 18, 1990, p. 11.
30. Andrea Becerril, "Se buscará hoy una solución negociada para La Modelo," *La Jornada*, April 19, 1990, p. 11; Andrea Becerril, "Posible arreglo conciliatorio en la Modelo, en breve: DDF," *La Jornada*, April 20, 1990, p. 10; Andrea Becerril, "Se espera una pronta respuesta favorable: Reglín," *La Jornada*, April 21, 1990, p. 9.
31. Andrea Becerril, "Solución inmediata en la Modelo, demandan organizaciones obreras," *La Jornada*, April 22, 1990, p. 13.
32. Andrea Becerril, "Mañana podría haber solución al conflicto en la Modelo: Reglín," *La Jornada*, April 23, 1990, p. 7.
33. Andrea Becerril, "Regresán a trabajar los obreros de la Modelo," *La Jornada*, April 25, 1990, p. 1; Humberto Aranda, "Concluyó el Conflicto en la Modelo; Reglín Será Liquidado," *Excelsior*, April 25, 1990, p. 4.
34. Andrea Becerril, "Aún no hay fecha segura para reiniciar labores en la Modelo," *La Jornada*, April 26, 1990, p. 9.
35. "Casi 2,000 Obreros de la Modelo no han Sido Recontratados," *Excelsior*, April 29, 1990, p. 5.
36. Andrea Becerril, "Recibieron su liquidación los dirigentes de la Modelo," *La Jornada*, May 19, 1990, p. 9; Sara Lovera, "Se despidió de los obreros de Modelo el comité ejecutivo," *La Jornada*, May 21, 1990, p. 7. See the final evaluation of the strike published by the Modelo workers union, headed by German Reglín, "Los setenta días que cambiaron la vida sindical de México," *Excelsior*, May 21, 1990, p. 46.
37. Author's interview with Rogelio Hernández Medina, member of the Representative Commission of the Tornel workers, Mexico City, January 1991.
38. Fernando Talavera Aldaña, *et al.*, *Tornel: Un Eslabón Mas de la Lucha Obrera: 1989-1990* (versión preliminar) (Taller de Indicadores Económicos, Facultad de Economía, Universidad Nacional Autónoma de México), p. 3.
39. *Ibid.*, pp. 3-5.
40. *Charro* refers to state-controlled union bureaucrats who have often been imposed by force and contrary to the will of the rank and file workers.
41. Talavera Aldaña, *Tornel*, pp. 5-6.

42. Author's interview with Rogelio Hernández Medina, Mexico City, January 1991.
43. Andrea Becerril, "En diciembre del 89 se pudo haber resuelto el caso de Tornel," *La Jornada*, August 26, 1990, p. 13.
44. "Secuestran a 5 Obreros de Hulera Tornel," *Excelsior*, May 4, 1990, p. 4; Andrea Becerril, "Inútil, la pugna por contratos colectivos: Farell," *La Jornada*, May 4, 1990, p. 19.
45. "Cesan a 25 trabajadores de Tornel por los problemas intersindicales," *El Universal*, June 22, 1990, p. 5.
46. Talavera Aldaña, *Tornel*, pp. 14-15.
47. The legal charges were filed in complaint numbers ACI/511/9008 and ACI/507/990. Humberto Aranda, "Zafarrancho Para Evitar un Recuento de Trabajadores Entre CTM y CROC," *Excelsior*, August 5, 1990, p. 5; Andrea Becerril and Judith Calderon, "Suspendieron el recuento en Tornel por 'falta de garantías'," *La Jornada*, August 5, 1990, p. 3.
48. Andrea Becerril and Judith Calderon, "Forman parte de un grupo de choque," *La Jornada*, August 11, 1990, p. 3.
49. Clara Guadalupe García, "Afirma Pino de la Rosa que estaba en favor del recuento en Tornel," *La Jornada*, August 23, 1990, p. 3.
50. Anibal Ramírez, "Pacto de no agresión entre obreros de la empresa Tornel," *La Jornada*, August 7, 1990, p. 15.
51. Andrea Becerril, "Despiden en Tornel a otros cinco trabajadores," *La Jornada*, August 8, 1990, p. 3.
52. Anibal Ramírez, "Interesa la empresa un pronto arreglo en Tornel," *La Jornada*, August 9, 1990, p. 3; Andrea Becerril, "En Tornel 'los Agredidos fuimos nosotros,' dice Fidel Velázquez," *La Jornada*, August 10, 1990, p. 3.
53. Andrea Becerril and Judith Calderon, "Impiden ingresar a su trabajo a cerca de 500 obreros de Tornel," *La Jornada*, August 11, 1990, p. 3.
54. Andrea Becerril, "Instalan los obreros de Tornel un plantón frente a la JFCA," *La Jornada*, August 17, 1990, p.3.
55. Anibal Ramírez, "La JFAC dió *carpetazo* al conflicto labor de Tornel," *La Jornada*, August 22, 1990, p. 11.
56. "Al C. Lic. Carlos Salinas de Gortari, Presidente de la República Mexicana," *La Jornada*, August 31, 1990, p. 12.
57. Andrea Becerril, "Fijó la JFCA nueva fecha para el recuento en la Hulera Tornel," *La Jornada*, November 16, 1990, p. 17; Andrea Becerril, "Descarta Perez Tovar que se prepare una agresión en Tornel," *La Jornada*, November 17, 1990, p. 15; Anibal Ramírez, "Piden los obreros a Salinas impedir un fraude en Tornel," *La Jornada*, November 18, 1990, p. 17; Andrea Becerril, "Hoy se realizara el recuento entre trabajadores de Tornel," *La Jornada*, November 22, 1990, p. 12.
58. "Deciden Retornar a la CTM los Trabajadores de 'Tornel'," *Excelsior*, November 23, 1990, p. E-3; "Los obreros de Tornel no participaron en el recuento," *La Jornada*, November 23, 1990, p. 17.
59. "Recurrirán Empleados Despedidos de la Tornel a Organismos de los DH," *Excelsior*, November 28, 1990, p. 17.
60. For general background, see Paulina Fernández, "Ford-CTM," *La Jornada*, January 10, 1990, p. 9.
61. Author's interview with Raúl Escobar, Mexico City, December 17, 1990.
62. *Ibid.*
63. Author interview with Manuel Fuentes, attorney for the Ford workers, Mexico City, December 12, 1990.
64. Andrea Becerril and Anibal Ramírez, "Trabajadores de Ford exigen referendum sobre Uriarte," *La Jornada*, January 7, 1990, p. 7.

65. Author's interviews with Raúl Escobar and Manuel Fuentes, Mexico City, December 1990.
66. Author's interview with Matt Witt, Mexico City, December 1990.
67. Author's interview with Raúl Escobar, Mexico City, December 1990.
68. Six workers were severely injured in this attack: Jesús Mendoza, Armando Vargas, Eduardo Olvera, Andrés Camargo, Demetrio Hernández, and Antonio Durán. Two others were also hospitalized: José Luis Carranza Cano and Luis Valencia. See Andrea Becerril, "Salvaguardar sus derechos, piden los obreros de Ford a la JFCA," *La Jornada*, January 10, 1990, p. 3.
69. Interview with Manuel Fuentes, Mexico City, December 1990.
70. Luciano Tapia and Eduardo A. Hacho, "Uriarte, Acusado de Agresor," *Excelsior*, January 10, 1990, p. 5.
71. Humberto Aranda, "Inicia Negociaciones la Ford con la CTM," *Excelsior*, January 10, 1990, p. 5.
72. Becerril, "Salvaguardar sus derechos..."
73. Wallace de la Mancha, "Wallace de la Mancha no participó en la agresión a trabajadores de la Ford," [letter to editor], *La Jornada*, January 10, 1990, p. 2; Andrea Becerril, "Prueben que participe en lo de la Ford: De la Mancha," *La Jornada*, January 11, 1990, p. 9.
74. Becerril, "Salvaguardar sus derechos..."
75. Andrea Becerril, "Demandó Ford la terminación de la relación laboral en Cuautitlán," *La Jornada*, January 11, 1990, p. 40.
76. "Aviso, Ford Motor Company," *Excelsior*, January 11, 1990, p. 32.
77. Ricardo Alemán, "Complicidad de la CTM y la empresa Ford in la agresión," *La Jornada*, January 11, 1990, p. 8.
78. Manuel Ino, "Convoca Fidel Velázquez a Obreros de la Ford Para el Lunes," *Excelsior*, January 12, 1990, p. 2.
79. Miguel Angel Rivera, "Ofreció a obreros de Ford solución a sus demandas," *La Jornada*, January 13, 1990, p. 1.
80. Andrea Becerril, "El trabajador asesinado fue velado en la planta," *La Jornada*, January 12, 1990, p. 44.
81. Eduardo A. Hacho, "Foro de Solidaridad Para Obreros de la FMC," *Excelsior*, January 14, 1990, p. E-1.
82. Luciano Tapia, "Dan su Apoyo Hermosillo y Chihuahua a los de la Ford," *Excelsior*, January 15, 1990, p. 4.
83. Sara Lovera, "Fueron a la sede de la CTM los trabajadores de Ford," *La Jornada*, January 16, 1990, p. 12.
84. Andrea Becerril, "Fueron liberados bajo fianza los golpeadores en la Ford," *La Jornada*, January 18, 1990, p. 90.
85. *Ibid.*
86. Héctor Adorno Ruíz, "Acción Penal Contra Wallace de la Mancha," *Excelsior*, January 19, 1990, p. 5.
87. Rodolfo Wong, "Acusan de Amenazas a Héctor Uriarte M.," *Excelsior*, January 21, 1990, p. 5.
88. Anibal Ramírez, "Garantías, reinstalaciones y nuevo comité exigen obreros de Ford para reanudar labores," *La Jornada*, January 23, 1990, p. 1.
89. Anibal Ramírez, "Piden aprehender a Uriarte, presunto autor intelectual del ataque a los trabajadores," *La Jornada*, January 23, 1990, p. 1.
90. Andrea Becerril, "La CTM responde por Uriarte, afirma Calleja," *La Jornada*, January 24, 1990, p. 15.
91. Servando Pineda Jaimes, "No Saldrá de la CTM el Sindicato de Ford," *Excelsior*, January 28, 1990, p. 5.

92. Manuel Lino Ramos, "Secuestraron a 2 Trabajadores," *Excelsior*, January 28, 1991.
93. Anibal Ramírez, "Obreros de Ford en Cuautitlán no reanudaran labores," *La Jornada*, January 29, 1990, p. 7.
94. "Circular A Los Trabajadores Miembros de la Sección Cuautitlán...," *La Jornada*, January 31, 1990, p. 24.
95. Miguel Barba Cárdenas, "A Través del Sindicato de Ford, Demandas de Aumento," *Excelsior*, February 4, 1990, p. 5.
96. Humberto Aranda and Luciano Tapia, "Rescindío la Ford Contratos de Trabajo a 2,200 de sus Trabajadores en Cuautitlán," *Excelsior*, February 2, 1990, p. 5.
97. Humberto Aranda, "Demanda la COR la Detención del Contrato Colectivo de la Ford con sus Trabjadores," *Excelsior*, February 7, 1990, p. 41.
98. Andrea Becerril, "Envió Ford a sus trabajadores cientos de avisos de rescisión," *La Jornada*, February 7, 1990, p. 12.
99. Andrea Becerril, "Rescisión de contrato a 2 mil 300 obreros, anuncia Ford," *La Jornada*, February 8, 1990, p. 40; Humberto Aranda and Luciano Tapia, "Rescindió la Ford Contratos de Trabajo a 2,200 de sus Trabajadores en Cuautitlán," *Excelsior*, February 8, 1990, p. 5.
100. Anibal Ramírez, "El de la Ford es un conflicto 'intersindical'," *La Jornada*, February 10, 1990, p. 13.
101. See Andrea Becerril and Luis Alberto Rodríguez, "Dió marcha atras la Ford en el cese de trabajadores," *La Jornada*, February 9, 1990, p. 16; Sara Lovera, "Entorpece la Ford el proceso de reincorporación: obreros," *La Jornada*, February 16, 1990, p. 13.
102. Sara Lovera, "Solo 162 obreros reanudaron labores en Ford Cuautitlán," *La Jornada*, February 13, 1990, p. 5.
103. Sara Lovera, "Parcial reanudación de labores en la planta Ford Cuautitlán," *La Jornada*, February 15, 1990, p. 8.
104. Lovera, "Entorpece la Ford...; " Eduardo A. Hacho, "A la Ford de Cuautitlán han Regresado ya 2,500 Trabajadores: Carlos Bandala," *Excelsior*, February 16, 1990, p. 15; Eduardo A. Hacho, "Suspende Ford Cuautitlán la Reinstalación de Trabajadores," *Excelsior*, Febarury 17, 1990, p. E-1.
105. Andrea Becerril, "Parcialidad de la Junta en el caso de la Ford: Manuel Fuentes," *La Jornada*, February 17, 1990, p. 15.
106. Humberto Aranda and Luciano Tapia, "Cita Farell a las Partes en el Conflicto de Ford," *Excelsior*, February 22, 1990, p. 5.
107. Andrea Becerril, "Fin del conflicto labor en la Ford de Cuautitlán," *La Jornada*, March 2, 1990, p. 17.
108. Sara Lovera, "La casa matriz de Ford hace una auditoria en Cuautitlán," *La Jornada*, March 13, 1990, p. 13. This article also reported that Ford was going to conduct an investigation of alleged malfeasance by local management at the Cuautitlán plant, a charge which the company denied, without denying the other allegations in the article, in a letter to *La Jornada* published in the March 17, 1990 edition on page 1.
109. Andrea Becerril, "Impide la policía realizar la falta colectiva en Cuautitlán," *La Jornada*, April 20, 1990, p. 11.
110. Humberto Aranda, "Insisten Trabajadores de la Ford en Incorporarse a la COR," *Excelsior*, March 20, 1990, p. 5.
111. Evangelina Hernández, "Trabajadores de Ford abandonaron la CTM," *La Jornada*, April 24, 1990, p. 3.
112. Author's interview with Manuel Fuentes, Mexico City, December 12, 1990.

113. *Ibid.*
114. The complete report from the Committee of Independent Observers, including a letter to Jaime Serra Puche from Farell detailing his conversation with Ford about "the necessary work" that must be done in compliance with the CTM staff in charge of "controlling the workers" to ensure that the workers would not win the election and leave the CTM, is available from the International Labor Rights Education and Research Fund.
115. Author's interview with Raúl Escobar, Mexico City, December 17, 1990.
116. Author's interview with Rogelio Hernández Medina, Mexico City, January 1991.

Chapter 7

1. Author's interview with Jorge Carrillo Viveros at the Colegio de la Frontera Norte (COLEF), Tijuana Campus, January 25, 1991.
2. I have used the summary of the report found in Triunfo Elizalde, "Salió del país más de 75% del gasto de las maquiladoras de exportación," *La Jornada,* December 29, 1990, p. 11.
3. Jorge Carrillo V., "Transformaciones en la industria maquiladora de exportación," in Bernardo González-Arechiga and Rocío Barajas Escamilla, eds., *Las maquiladoras: Ajuste estructural y desarrollo regional* (Tijuana, B.C.: El Colegio de la Frontera Norte and Fundación Friedrich Ebert, 1989), p. 45. 4. Carrillo V., "Transformaciones en la industria..." p. 49.
5. Diane Lindquist, "Maquiladoras Draw Pilgrimage of Youth," *San Diego Union,* May 28, 1989, p. 1.
6. Rebeca Lizarraga R., "Crecera 17% la industria maquiladora en 91 en relación con el año pasado, estima la Secofi," *El Financiero,* January 7, 1991.
7. Jorge Carrillo V., *Conflictos laborales en la industria maquiladora* (Tijuana, B.C.: Centro de Estudios Fronterizos del Norte, 1985), p. 17.
8. Elivia Gutiérrez, "La Industria Maquiladora Redujó su Ritmo de Crecimiento en 1990," *El Financiero,* January 2, 1991, p. 6A.
9. Author's interview with factory manager in Ciudad Juárez, January 1991. See also Carrillo, *Conflictos laborales,* p. 21.
10. María Patricia Fernández-Kelly, *For We Are Sold, I and My People: Women and Industry in Mexico's Frontier* (Albany: State University of New York Press, 1983), p. 68.
11. Rafael Moure-Eraso, "Back to the Future: Sweatshop Conditions on the Mexico-U.S. Border: Community and Occupational Health Impact of Maquiladora Activity in the Mexico/United States Border" (University of Lowell Work Environment Program, April 11, 1991), pp. i-ii.
12. Robert Sánchez, "Contaminación de la Industria Fronteriza: Riesgos Para la Salud y el Medio Ambiente," in González-Arechiga and Barajas Escamilla, eds., *Las maquiladoras,* pp. 155-169.
13. *Ibid.,* p. 165.
14. Moure-Eraso, *et al.,* "Back to the Future," p. 8.
15. Leslie Kochan, *The Maquiladoras and Toxics: The Hidden Costs of Production South of The Border* (Washington, D.C.: ALF-CIO), 1989.
16. The information on unionism in the *maquiladoras* in this section is generally taken from a number of different reports written by Jorge Carrillo Viveros of COLEF. In addition to his academic work, he is a recognized expert on *maquiladora* unionism.

17. Jorge Carrillo Viveros, "Dos décadas de sindicalismo en la industria maquiladora de exportación: Examen de Tijuana, Ciudad Juárez y Matamoros" (México, D.F.: Facultad de Ciencias Políticas y Sociales. Universidad Nacional Autónoma de México, 1989), p. 176.
18. Diane Lindquist, "Unions lag in Mexico industrial rush," *San Diego Union*, May 29, 1989.
19. L.D.F. & SECOFIN staff, *Los Dos Laredos: Industrial Fact Book—Laredo, Texas and Nuevo Laredo, Mexico* (Laredo: Laredo Development Foundation, n.d.).
20. Author's interview with Jorge Carrillo, Tijuana, Mexico, January 25, 1991.
21. José Negrete Mata, *Integración y Industrialización Fronterizas: La Ciudad Industrial Nueva Tijuana* (Tijuana: El Colegio de la Frontera Norte, 1988), pp. 15, 39-40.
22. Author's interview with Jorge Carrillo, Tijuana, Mexico, January 25, 1991.
23. Diane Lindquist, "Baja's 'White Unions' Shadowy Force," *San Diego Union*, May 30, 1989, p. A-1.
24. Jorge Carrillo and Alberto Hernández. *Mujeres fronterizas en la industria maquiladora* (México, D.F.: Secretaria de Educación Pública and Centro de Estudios Fronterizos del Norte de México, 1985), pp. 90-100.
25. Author's interview with Gustavo de la Rosa Hickerson at his law firm, Despacho Obrero, Ciudad Juárez, Chihuahua, January 22, 1991. All of de la Rosa's quotations come from this interview.
26. *Ibid.*
27. Carrillo and Hernández, *Mujeres fronterizas*, p. 146.
28. *Ibid.*, p. 129.
29. *Ibid.*, p. 130.
30. A full-page advertisement denouncing the health and safety conditions was published in the Ciudad Juárez newspapers on June 18, 1982. See Sandra Arenal, *Sangre joven: Las maquiladoras por dentro* (México, D.F.: Editorial Nuestro Tiempo, S.A., 1986), pp. 51-93.
31. Carrillo and Hernández, *Mujeres fronterizas*, p. 137.
32. Author's interview with Teresa Almada of the Organización Popular Independiente. All of Almada's quotations are taken from the same.
33. Author's interview with Xochitl Romero Ortiz at SEDEPAC offices in Mexico City, December 13, 1990. All Romero's quotes taken from same.
34. The 1986 incident in the Zenith plant in Reynosa was reported in *The Monitor* on April 25, 1986. The 1990 incident at the Deltronics plant in Matamoros was reported in both *The Brownsville Herald* and *El Bravo*. See Moure-Eraso, *et al.*, "Back to the Future," pp. 10-11, 12, 48.
35. Moure-Eraso, *et al.*, "Back to the Future," p. 31.
36. Sindicato Autónomo de Trabajadores de Dickies de Piedras Negras, "Condiciones Laborales de la Industria Maquiladora en el Estado de Coahuila y Propuestas para Tratar de Mejorarlas," presented at the SEDEPAC *maquiladora* conference, 1990.
37. The events recounted here have been reconstructed from a timely series of Chihuahua newspaper articles, and from interviews with workers who were involved.
38. Zapata's career is described in a long letter to the editor from Francisco Muñiz P. of the Frente Auténtico del Trabajo (FAT) which was published in the *Diario de Chihuahua*, January 11, 1991.
39. "Con gritos y golpes obreras de Almbrados lograron la destitución del dirigente estatal," *Norte*, December 2, 1990.
40. "Empleados de Maquila Protesta Porque Fueron Despedidos sin Justificación," *El Heraldo de Chihuahua*, January 3, 1991.

41. Enrique Ramírez, "Acusan a Zapata de haber manipulado asamblea sindical en una maquiladora," *Norte,* January 3, 1991; Luis Froylon Castaneda, "Conflicto laboral en una maquiladora," *Vanguardia,* January 4, 1991.

42. "Se Quejan Supuestos Líderes Sindicales de Despido de una Maquiladora; la CTM Asegura que no son Directivos Legales," *Diario de Chihuahua,* January 4, 1991.

43. "Acusa el FAT a Doroteo Zapata de Violar los Derechos de Trabajadores," *El Heraldo de Chihuahua,* January 10, 1991.

44. "En Alambrados y Circuitos plant II, Acusan a CTM de causar clima tenso en planta maquiladora," *Vanguardia,* January 10, 1991.

45. Enrique Ramírez García, "Por 'órdenes de arriba' despiden a ganadores sindicales de una maquiladora," *Norte,* January 10, 1991, p. A-1.

46. "Quedó Resuelto el Conflicto Interno en Alambrados," *El Heraldo de Chihuahua,* January 13, 1991, p. 2B; "Por 'rara maniobra' gana planilla de oposición a CTM en la maquiladora Alambrados y Circuitos," *Norte,* January 13, 1991.

47. Carrillo, "Dos décadas...," p. 173.

48. *Ibid.,* p. 178.

49. *Ibid.,* p. 182. See also Jorge Carrillo V. and Miguel Angel Ramírez, "Maquiladoras en la frontera norte: Opinión sobre los sindicatos," (Typescript).

50. Carrillo, "Dos décadas...," p. 181.

51. Moure-Eraso *et al., Back to the Future,* p. i.

Glossary of Acronyms

ASARCO	American Smelting and Refining Company
BIP	Mexican Border Industrialization Program
CBI	Caribbean Basin Initiative
CDHAC	Miguel A. Pro Suarez Center for Human Rights A.C.
CFE	Federal Electrical Commission
CGOCM	General Confederation of Workers and Peasants of Mexico
CGT	General Confederation of Workers
CILAS	Center for Labor Investigation and Union Consultation
CNC	National Confederation of Cooperatives, *also* National Peasant Confederation
CNOP	National Confederation of Popular Organizations
COLEF	Colegio de la Frontera Norte
COR	Revolutionary Workers Confederation
CROC	Revolutionary Confederation of Workers and Peasants
CROM	Regional Confederation of Mexican Workers
CT	Congress of Labor
CTC	Confederation of Workers and Campesinos
CTM	Confederation of Mexican Workers
FAT	Authentic Labor Front
FESEBES	Federation of Unions of Goods and Services
FNAP	National Front of Popular Action
FNASA	National Federation of Autonomous Union Associations
FNSI	National Federation of Independent Unions
FSTSE	Federation of Unions of Workers at the Service of the State
GATT	General Agreement on Tariffs and Trade
GSP	Generalized System of Preferences
ILO	International Labor Organization
IMSS	Mexican Institute of Social Security

INEGI	Mexican National Institute of Statistics, Geography, and Information
INFONAVIT	Government workers' housing program
ININ	National Institute of Nuclear Investigations
IWW	Industrial Workers of the World
LFT	Federal Labor Law of 1931
MAS	Women in Labor Union Action
MSF	Railroad Workers Union Movement
OPI	Independent Peoples Organization
OPIC	Overseas Private Investment Corporation
PAN	National Action Party
PARM	Authentic Party of the Mexican Revolution
PCM	Mexican Communist Party
PEMEX	Petróleos Mexicanos
PL	Labor Party
PLM	Mexican Liberal Party
PMS	Mexican Socialist Party
PNR	National Revolutionary Party
PPS	Popular Socialist Party
PRD	Party of the Democratic Revolution
PRI	Institutional Revolutionary Party
PRT	Revolutionary Workers Party
PSUM	Unified Socialist Party of Mexico
SEDEPAC	Service, Development, and Peace
SME	Electrical Workers Union
SNTE	Teachers Union
STERT	Tepepan Refrigeration Workers and Employees Union
STFRM	Railroad Workers Union
STMMRM	Miners and Metal Workers Union
STPRM	Petroleum Workers Union
STRM	Telephone Workers Union
SUTIN	Nuclear Workers Union
TD	Democratic Tendency
TELMEX	Teléfonos de México
URAMEX	Mexican Uranium Company

Index

215

220

About the Author

Dan La Botz is a member of the History Department at the University of Cincinnati, and the author of several books, including *Edward L. Doheny: Petroleum, Power and Politics in the United States and Mexico*, and *A Troublemaker's Handbook: How to Fight Back Where You Work—and Win*. La Botz worked as a truck driver in the 1970s, and later as an organizer for AFSCME, the Los Angeles Jobs With Peace Campaign, AFT Local 1990, and the Justice and Peace Office of the Catholic Diocese of Covington, Kentucky. He lives in Cincinnati with his wife, Dr. Sherry Baron, and their children, Traven and Reed, for whom they hope to create a better working world.

About the ILRERF

The International Labor Rights Education and Research Fund (ILRERF) is a non-profit organization that represents human rights, labor, religious, consumer, academic, and business groups dedicated to assuring that workers in all countries labor under reasonable conditions, and that workers are free to associate, organize and bargain collectively. Founded in 1986, the ILRERF is committed to environmentally sound development, especially development that promotes broad-based economic growth and an equitable distribution of wealth, and to U.S. trade, investment, and aid policies that further these goals.

Other books in the ILRERF series include: *Global Village vs. Global Pillage: A One-World Strategy for Labor* (Jeremy Brecher and Tim Costello, 1991), *South Korea—Dissent Within the Economic Miracle* (George E. Ogle, 1990), and *Labor Rights in Haiti* (Lance Compa, 1989). To receive more information on the ILRERF, subscribe to Worker Rights News, or order books please contact:

The International Labor Rights
Education and Research Fund
Box 74, 100 Maryland Avenue, N.E.
Washington, D.C. 20002
Tel. 202-544-7198, Fax 202-543-5999
Email (PeaceNet): laborrights

About South End Press

South End Press is a nonprofit, collectively run book publisher with over 175 titles in print. Since our founding in 1977, we have tried to meet the needs of readers who are exploring, or are already committed to, the politics of radical social change.

Our goal is to publish books that encourage critical thinking and constructive action on the key political, cultural, social, economic, and ecological issues shaping life in the United States and in the world. In this way, we hope to give expression to a wide diversity of democratic social movements and to provide an alternative to the products of corporate publishing.

Other titles of interest from South End Press: *Storm Signals: Structural Adjustment and Development Alternatives in the Caribbean* by Kathy McAfee; *The U.S. Invasion of Panama: Operation JUST CAUSE* by the Independent Commission of Inquiry on the U.S. Invasion of Panama; *Labor Law Handbook* by Michael Yates; and *Strike!* by Jeremy Brecher.

Through the Institute for Social and Cultural Change, South End Press works with other political media projects—*Z Magazine*; Speak Out!, a speakers bureau; the Publishers Support Project; and the New Liberation News Service—to expand access to information and critical analysis. If you would like a free catalog of South End Press books or information about our membership program—which offers two free books and a 40% discount on all titles for one year—please write to us at South End Press, 116 Saint Botolph Street, Boston, MA 02115.